DEUS TRINITAS

Deus Trinitas

THE DOCTRINE OF THE TRIUNE GOD

David Coffey

New York   Oxford
Oxford University Press
1999

Oxford University Press

Oxford   New York
Athens   Auckland   Bangkok   Bogotá   Buenos Aires   Calcutta
Cape Town   Chennai   Dar es Salaam   Delhi   Florence   Hong Kong   Istanbul
Karachi   Kuala Lumpur   Madrid   Melbourne   Mexico City   Mumbai
Nairobi   Paris   São Paulo   Singapore   Taipei   Tokyo   Toronto   Warsaw

and associated companies in
Berlin   Ibadan

Published by Oxford University Press, Inc.
198 Madison Avenue, New York, New York 10016

Oxford is a registered trademark of Oxford University Press

Library of Congress Cataloging-in-Publication Data
Coffey, David.
Deus Trinitas : the doctrine of the triune God / David Coffey.
p.   cm.
Includes bibliographical references and index.
ISBN 0-19-512472-3
1. Trinity.   I. Title.
BT111.2.C62   1999
231'.044—dc21   98-28134

Scripture quotations are from the Revised Standard Version of the Bible, copyright 1946, 1952, and 1971
by the Division of Christian Education of the National Council of the Churches of Christ in the USA,
and from the New Revised Standard Version of the Bible, copyright 1989 by the Division of Christian Education of
the National Council of the Churches of Christ in the USA. Used by permission.
Some changes to these quotations have been made for reasons of theological precision.

1 3 5 7 9 8 6 4 2

Printed in the United States of America
on acid-free paper

Domine deus une, deus trinitas, quaecumque dixi
in his libris de tuo agnoscant et tui;
si qua de meo, et tu ignosce et tui.
Amen.

O Lord one God, Trinity God, whatever of Thine
I have said in this book, may Thine acknowledge;
whatever of mine, do Thou and Thine forgive.
Amen.

Concluding sentence of
St. Augustine's *De trinitate*

Acknowledgments

This book is dedicated to Father Edward J. Kilmartin, S.J., who died on 16 June 1994, in Boston. Professor at the Pontifical Oriental Institute in Rome, and recipient of the 1978 John Courtney Murray Award of the Catholic Theological Society of America for distinguished achievement in theology, he had built up over a long career an outstanding reputation in the fields of liturgy, sacramental theology, and ecumensim. Not surprisingly, his entire scholarly project was characterized by a strong trinitarian consciousness. This contributed to making his work a model of authentic Catholic theology. He was revered by his peers and the younger theologians whom he helped educate. He certainly played an important part in my life. He visited Australia in 1970, staying as a guest at my college. At that point I was just beginning to think out my ideas on Christology, grace, and the Trinity. One day I took him on a long walk and tried out these ideas on him, asking if he thought they were worth working up into books or articles. His encouragement was immediate and enthusiastic. It was this above all that moved me to take the step into serious theological writing. Later, when my publications began to appear (some of them in Australia and therefore not readily accessible in North America), he more than anyone else and with undiminished enthusiasm propagated them in the United States and continued to do so right up to the time of his death. After our 1970 meeting I never saw him again, and we corresponded only rarely. But he knew how important he had been in my life and how grateful I was to him. There is none to whom I would rather dedicate this present book.

Finally, I wish to extend a word of thanks to people who have helped me significantly in the execution of this project, first to His Eminence Cardinal Edward Clancy, Archbishop of Sydney, who has encouraged and supported me over many years; to Rev. Anthony Kelly, CSsR, of the Yarra Theological Union, Melbourne, who provided invaluable help in the early stages of the manuscript; to Dr. David Dockrill of the University of Newcastle, N.S.W., who organized a symposium based on the manuscript; in the United States, to Father Kilian McDonnell, O.S.B., of the Institute for Ecumenical and Cultural Research, Collegeville, Minnesota, for his constant encouragement; to colleagues at Marquette University, Milwaukee, Drs. Ralph G. del Colle, Bradford E. Hinze, and Lyle D. Dabney, and my assistants, James Wakefield and Timothy Johnson, all of whom read the manuscript and helped in important ways; and finally to graduate student Kristin Schaupp, who helped with the index.

Contents

DEUS TRINITAS

Introduction

Like many of my generation, in my undergraduate studies I took a course on the Trinity that left me puzzled as to what conceivable relevance this topic could have for the rest of theology (apart, perhaps, from that of the Incarnation) or for the challenge of the Christian life. With hindsight it is not difficult to see that this was because the tract on the Trinity was separated from that on the One God and because it focused exclusively on the immanent Trinity (the Godhead considered "in itself," apart from the economy of salvation). This situation, repeated all over the world, led in the sixties to the quiet dropping of the Trinity as a topic of study in theological curricula almost everywhere. Only now is the trend being reversed. This change is not just a matter of fad or fashion. It is occurring because of a growing perception and appreciation of the fact that salvation itself, the very gift of the spiritual life, has a trinitarian (and also ecclesial) structure, that is, it is God (the Father's) salvation mediated to the Church by Jesus Christ in the power of the Holy Spirit. We cannot understand salvation, spirituality, Christian living in the world without understanding at least something of the Trinity.

My own progress toward the Trinity took place in the context of giving courses on Christology and grace over many years in the Catholic Institute of Sydney. In particular it was the challenge of the grace course that drove me back to the theology of the Trinity, especially as the Western theological tradition, unlike the Eastern, was so lacking in trinitarian awareness. It was Karl Rahner's theology of uncreated grace that provided for me the link between the theology of grace and the theology of the Trinity. My work on grace, leading into the Trinity, came to expression in a book followed by a series of journal articles. I am pleased to note that this labor of years has now been ably reported and documented by Ralph Del Colle in his recent book *Christ and the Spirit*.[1] The present book, devoted explicitly to the Trinity, seems to me to be a suitable sort of climax to this segment of my theological endeavor. It is not intended, however, as a textbook; it does not purport to be comprehensive. I see it merely as an opportunity to say some things that I consider worth saying about the Trinity.

Where earlier writing concentrated on the immanent Trinity to the neglect of the economic Trinity, the present trend is in the opposite direction. While the emphasis on the economic Trinity is a positive gain (in that it broadens trinitarian theology to make it include almost the whole of systematic theology, and links it firmly to salvation, thereby demonstrating its relevance), some of the more recent writing shows a lack of balance in that it evinces a dismissive or reductive attitude toward the immanent Trinity, which, after all, was a major concern of the Church Fathers and the early councils. This attitude reveals itself in a tendency either to dissolve the immanent Trinity into the economic Trinity altogether or to be agnostic about the existence of the immanent Trinity. In this book I am at pains to avoid this trap in either of its forms. While I share with other theologians a desire to emphasize the economic Trinity, I still want to uphold the immanent Trinity as an important, indeed essential, element of trinitarian theology. My project in this regard is carried out with the help of Bernard Lonergan's theory of knowledge (and not so much his trinitarian theology). The reader must decide whether this effort has been successful.

One respect in which I have not been very traditional is my stance on the "psychological analogy" of Western, particularly Catholic, trinitarian theology, whereby the processions of the Son and the Holy Spirit from the Father are understood in terms of the divine knowledge and love, respectively. Eastern theology is similarly critical on this matter. I note with satisfaction that Rahner's theology has been said to be rather "Eastern" in this regard, but, I have to admit, I pay even less attention to the psychological analogy than he does. It is not that it is wrong or without value. I concede that exploring on the basis of the "image of God" the correspondence of the human to the divine spirit as revealed in the doctrine of the Trinity can provide a powerful stimulus to Christian life authentically grounded in and ordered to God. It can also explain various things about the Trinity, for example, why there are three, and only three, persons. But I see it, in all its forms (including the Lonerganian), to be no more than an *illustration* of the Trinity and therefore to lack the status of a theology properly so called. This is because in my view it does not have sufficient scriptural warrant and because methodologically its starting point is not the appropriate one, namely the New Testament statements about Jesus and the Spirit as emissaries of the Father. Though the psychological analogy goes back to St. Augustine, blame for the turn taken by Western Catholic theology in this regard can hardly be laid at his door. Of the fifteen books of the *De trinitate*, the first seven are devoted to the mystery of the Trinity in itself, particularly to its scriptural revelation in terms of the missions of the Son and the Holy Spirit, while the question of the image of God in human beings is reserved for the last half of the work, from book 8 to the end.

There exists today a significant trend, among both Catholics and Protestants, to read off the theology of the Trinity from the life and death of Jesus as, first, recipient and then sender of the Spirit upon the Church. With this movement, which is an exercise of ascending, synoptic Christology, I align myself wholeheartedly. My own efforts in this regard have resulted in a model of the Trinity in which the Holy Spirit is seen as the objectivization of the mutual love of the Father and the Son. This was in fact an already established Western, indeed Augustinian, conception, with some resonance (admittedly slight) even in Eastern theology. The thinker most closely associated with it and who in some sense mediated it to later reflection was the twelfth-century theologian Richard of St. Victor, who argued from the nature of love that, given the existence of God, there must be three divine persons existing in mutual relations of love.[2] But Richard did not concern himself with the origins of the Son and the Holy Spirit from the Father; nor did he in this matter take the economy of salvation into account. Therefore, even apart from the rationalism and anthropomorphism of which it is often accused, his theory does not rank as a trinitarian "model" in the sense in which I am using the term here, as explaining both the origins of the Son and the Holy Spirit and the manner of operation of the Trinity in the economy. I believe that I am the first to use the mutual love theory as a trinitarian model in this sense.

I worked out my version of it in my early writings, and my subsequent work, culminating in this book, has been aimed at its consolidation and development. At first I called it the "bestowal" model, in that it has the Holy Spirit as bestowed by the Father and the Son on each other, but later I preferred to call it the "return" model. The latter name brings out the desired contrast with the traditional model (whether in its Western or Eastern form), in which the Son (together with the Spirit) proceeds from the Father, a formulation determined by descending, Johannine Christology and which I call the "procession" model. It also encompasses the entire process by which Jesus, having been sent forth from the Father, returns to him through his life and death in the power of the Holy Spirit. By this statement I have already indicated a further important feature of the model, its comprehensive aspect: in its developed form it includes the sending forth in the sweep of the larger movement of return.

In consequence of this I have a suggestion to make about the ecumenical problem of Filioquism (the Western view, that the Holy Spirit proceeds from the Father and the Son) as against Monopatrism (the Eastern view, that the Holy Spirit proceeds from the Father *alone*). The Filioque itself can accommodate Monopatrism, that is, inasmuch as the Son himself proceeds from the Father, but only provided that Monopatrism not exclude a secondary role for the Son, that is, if its key statement be interpreted in the sense that "the Holy Spirit proceeds *ultimately* from the Father alone." But the very silence of Monopatrism on the role of the Son, coupled with its use of "alone," reveals that it is extremely one-sided (as also, of course, is the Filioque). The similar silence of the original formula of the Nicene-Constantinopolitan Creed, that the Holy Spirit "proceeds from the Father," also reveals it as one-sided, but not extreme. Hence, while a good case can be made for the restoration of the original formula in the West, a more balanced statement would be that "the Holy Spirit proceeds from the Father and receives from the Son." Solidly grounded in Scripture and tradition, this compromise should be acceptable to both sides. But I emphasize that only the mutual love theory can identify exactly what the Holy Spirit receives from the Son: the quality of being the Son's love for the Father. This is the case argued in this book. Incidentally, it does not seem to me a significant problem that Filioquism and Monopatrism have both been dogmatized in their respective ecclesiastical traditions.

Two problems I have encountered in writing this book and that should be mentioned here are those of nonsexist language and the related issue of the names of the divine persons. Preserving the traditional names, Father, Son, and Holy Spirit, should not automatically be interpreted as endorsing a patriarchal and oppressive vision of Christianity. Indeed, it should do the opposite, provided the significance of the names be properly understood. However, the very names Father and Son indicate that the only appropriate pronominal forms for them, personal and posses- sive, are "he" and "his" respectively. For God and the Holy Spirit I feel obliged in some desperation in the present state of development (or undevelopment) of the English language to settle for the same forms, "he" and "his." I say in desperation because there are at present no acceptable alternatives. To say "she" and "her" in these cases seems to me to be tendentious, as these forms lack a background, which "he" and "his," for all their present unsuitability, do not, and also because, given their lack of background, they explicitly identify God as sexual, which "he" and "his," given their actual background, do not. Nor do I favor alternating masculine and feminine forms, as I find this practice confusing. In the case of the word "God" I forbear simply to repeat this word along with "Godself," as some theologians do, even several times in the same sentence, as this solution seems to me a linguistic barbarism. And as the persons of the Trinity are determinate, the solution mentioned in the next paragraph for indeterminate persons is not an option.

As for indeterminate person in the singular (what we mean when we can say "he or she"), the problem has been much reduced by the possibility of using "they" and "their" as singulars. This usage is attested by the Oxford English Dictionary for the period between the early fifteenth and the late nineteenth centuries. Even though there has been a gap of a century up to the present, there appears to be no convincing reason against reviving the usage, particularly as there is now pressing need for it. I have used it in the book, and I notice that a good number of other people are also using it. It is often said that English rejects artificially concocted solutions to linguistic problems. Here is a solution that far from being artificial has a solid history behind it within the language itself. I was first alerted to it as a possibility by an article by Casey Miller and Kate Smith.[3]

The greatest outstanding unsolved problem in this domain is to find a nonsexist word for the inclusive sense of "man," like *Mensch* in German. It is a great pity (and theology suffers thereby) that there is now no acceptable way of saying in English what, for example, was formerly meant by the statement "God became man." (Nei- ther "God became a human being" nor "God became human" has this precise mean- ing.) I have nothing to suggest here, as anything I might suggest would fall under the condemnation of artificiality. This means that there is quite a lot that could formerly be said in theology that can no longer be said (at least at present), a situation crying out for remedy.

This book has not engaged with feminist issues, important though they be in themselves. But it should be realized that as used by Jesus the term "Father" is metaphorical, not literal, though it remains privileged in that it was his favored mode of address of God in prayer. Also, despite the (on other grounds) recommended use of masculine pronouns, all actual gender characterizations, male as well as female, should be excluded in regard to the Holy Spirit. A suggestion made again recently by G. Clarke Chapman is that we should call the second person of the immanent Trinity Word instead of Son.[4] However, little would be gained by this, because Word is metaphorical (in the economic as well as the immanent Trinity), secondary, and *not* privileged.[5] "Son," like "Father," is analogical in the immanent Trinity, in the sense that there is a positive analogy between the way the second person proceeds from the first and the way something is generated in the world.[6] But the analogy does not extend to the gender of these words. If literalness means correspondence in all essential respects, they therefore cannot be said to be literal. The choice of Sophia (Wisdom), a feminine form for the second person of the immanent Trinity, introduced to balance the dominant maleness through a female element, seems an understandable but ultimately fruitless exercise.[7] There is no escaping "Son" in the economic Trinity, because of its frequency and importance in the New Testament and because of its ultimate reference to Jesus' maleness, which, Mark 12.25 and parallels notwithstanding, is not abolished by the Resurrection. It remains to say that in what he meant by addressing God as Father, in his values and attitudes, and in his demeanor toward others, women and men, Jesus showed himself far from patriarchal in any way, a most unusual phenomenon for his time. There is no reason, therefore, that Jesus' divine Sonship, the sole literal male reference in the immanent or economic Trinity, should be allowed to become a liability for the women's movement in the Church.[8] Indeed, in the light of Jesus' shining example, it could be turned into an asset. In this book the whole thrust has been, in the interests of soteriology, to grasp and present anew the entire range of biblical data concerning Father, Son, and Holy Spirit in the light of the most thorough and advanced theology of the immanent Trinity available. While this effort does not directly engage the feminist agenda, it is perfectly compatible with it and in the long term can further it.

Adhering to the traditional names, Father, Son, and Holy Spirit, is considered by some as reactionary. In addition to those given above, there are at least two other reasons for holding to these names. The first is that so far the suggested alternatives have turned out to be more problematical than the traditional set. In a general way (apart from two reservations, given later), one can endorse the remarks of John Macquarrie on this subject in his review of Robert Jenson's *The Triune Identity*:

> One is glad to find Professor Jenson defending the traditional phrase, "Father, Son and Holy Spirit," against some of the alternatives one now hears in the United States, such as "Creator, Redeemer and Sanctifier" or "Ground, Logos and Spirit." These up-to-date alternatives may have "desexed" the language but they have also rendered it unfit for liturgical use. As Jenson says, "All such parodies disrupt faith's self-identity at the level of its primal and least reflected historicity" (p. 17). These phrases are not names, so they cannot address. They are reminiscent of the Arians' proposal: "When you pray, say: 'O God Unoriginate . . . '."[9]

The first reservation is that I cannot endorse Macquarrie's gratuitous singling out of the United States or Jenson's tendentious use of the word "parodies." The alternatives mentioned by Macquarrie have to do with the economic Trinity only, and so raise the question as to whether in every instance they are strictly proper to the particular person in question or are appropriations (e.g., "Creator," "Ground"). The more serious reservation, however, is that it is not only by name that people may be addressed; they may be addressed also by title. Strictly speaking, Father, Son, and Holy Spirit are not names either.

In this quotation, Jenson has provided the best reason for retaining the traditional names (the word here being used not in the strict sense), and it is my own second reason alluded to in the previous paragraph. I now give it in my own words.

Christianity is a historical religion, centered more on a person, Jesus Christ, and the reality that he accomplished, salvation, than on a set of doctrines (though these are important too). Though they had a background in Jewish religion, the names "Father" and "Son" as we have them arose out of the historical consciousness of Jesus himself (the first directly, the second indirectly); and, though "Holy Spirit" also came from Judaism, it, as denoting the Spirit of Christ and the eschatological Spirit of God, received new content and meaning as a result of Jesus' Resurrection. This accounts for the fact that the privileged position of "Father," "Son," and "Holy Spirit" is already firmly established in the New Testament. *Whatever* is historical will be culturally conditioned and therefore subject to limitations, which, as time goes on, become increasingly evident in the light of changing and raised consciousness. If we simply eliminate such limitations (which, be it remembered, also have a very positive, revelatory side) we run a real danger of disengaging Christianity from its historical roots and subtly changing it from the person-centered religion that it is to a mere philosophy of life, or, worse still, an ideology. It is better, therefore, to accept the historical limitations (as part of the "scandal" of the Incarnation), at the same time trying to minimize them as far as possible. Further, though "Father," "Son," and "Holy Spirit" have a privileged status, they are not exclusive. The liturgy itself, though recognizing this status, does not hesitate to address the divine persons by other names and titles on occasion. In principle, therefore, there is no problem about calling the divine persons by other names, provided they are appropriate. The one thing, however, to be avoided is that the privileged position of "Father," "Son," and "Holy Spirit" be thereby jeopardized.

1

Setting the Scene

The Second Vatican Council taught that the God of Christians is identical with the God of the Jews and the God of Muslims.[1] Commenting on this statement of the council, Aloys Grillmeier writes that what unites Judaism, Christianity, and Islam is "belief in the one Creator, the God of mercy and the Judge" and "the fact that they share the revelation made to Abraham."[2] These three great religions agree, then, both on the unicity and the essential nature of God and on the all-important fact that he seeks out human beings, revealing himself to them progressively through history. Despite these significant points of agreement, however, each religion is unique in its own way. Specifically for Christianity, distinctiveness must rest on the claim it makes for the person of Christ. The most important feature of the claimed uniqueness of Christ can be expressed in two ways, the first of which is functional and directly biblical, and the second ontological and only having its roots in the New Testament. The first is that Christ has been granted by God his own prerogative of being "the Savior of the world" (see Jn 4.42); and the second is that he is confessed as divine, as "of one Being with the Father."[3]

These two expressions are not, of course, identical in their designation; they only approximate to each other in their attempts to capture in some way the uniqueness of Christ. The first comes from the biblical world of meaning, which grasped the deepest reality of persons and things in terms of their self-revelation in relational action. So, for example, that God was seen as Savior does not express one of several functions that he, already understood in his being prior to any activity, might subsequently take up; rather, it is the most profound way that the Bible has of saying who and what God is: he reveals himself in this highly significant mode of action. But far from articulating this truth in a way that would leave God objectified, unrelated to those who thus understand him, it does it in a way that expresses simultaneously the relationship to human beings that this concept ("Savior") implies and that from the human side is rightly identified as hope, indeed transcendental hope, the hope that is not fulfilled by any worldly good but can only be fulfilled in and by God. That the New Testament, then, wants to say of the *man* Jesus precisely that he is the Savior of the world, with all that this implies, is highly significant. If God accomplishes his saving work in and through this man, then in *this* perspective of the New Testament (which is not, as we shall see, the only one) there is no longer any ground for distinguishing between him and God.

The second expression says both more and less than this. It is the product, of course, of the Council of Nicaea in 325, and renders the council's famous expression, *homoousion to patri* (DS 125). It says more in that, coming as it does from the Hellenistic world, which was marked by the influence of the different schools of Greek philosophy, it penetrates to a metaphysical level of reality that was scarcely the concern of the biblical writers. But, also, it says less, in that it awaits appropriate expression in action, an expression, moreover, that, humanly speaking, is unpredictable in advance. Nor does it predicate a relationship to other human beings as does the first expression. The result has been that, as theology concerns itself with understanding this action, it is necessarily driven back to the biblical concept of Savior, which it now has to appropriate in terms of the homoousion, finding that it has to produce elaborate theories to do so. This is exactly what happened, for example, in the case of the most influential theology of the Atonement, the satisfaction theory of St. Anselm of Canterbury.[4] But unfortunately, this kind of exercise is, as it were, cut loose from the question of Christ's divinity and gets handled as a separate issue; and the relational content of the term "Savior" becomes almost entirely lost to sight. Only now, with the aid of new philosophical insights, are these defects being identified and remedied by theology.

Without surrendering the fundamental conviction of the unicity of God, then, the New Testament saw God's very divinity as shared in uniquely by the man Jesus, and hence recognized a certain duality introduced into the Godhead. I emphasize the word "uniquely" here, because another thing that the New Testament wants to say is that all who believe in Christ become "participants of the divine nature" (2 Pet 1.4). The New Testament is endlessly at pains to stress the uniqueness of Christ and indeed to present him as the mediator of whatever gifts of grace others possess. It was he who "gave gifts to his people" (Eph 4.8). In the functional perspective of the New Testament this unique status for Christ did not cause the same problem as it did in the ontological perspective of the later Church. Whatever the New Testament says about Christ, no matter how exalted it may be, is said of him as a man, as a human being. His essential humanity is never pushed beyond legitimate limits by anything it says of him, and so he is never seen as even a possible rival to the one God of Israel, to whom he himself prayed. But when his divinity begins to be conceived ontologically, a whole new batch of problems is generated, which sets the agenda for later theology. These include the following: How can a human being be ontologically divine? and, how can there be multiplicity within the unity of the one God? questions respectively for Christology and the theology of the Trinity.

Matters, however, do not rest there. In the New Testament itself this duality in the one God is expanded, by the addition of the Holy Spirit, to a trinity. The Hebrew and Greek words, *ruah* and *pneuma*, respectively, which underlie the word "spirit" as just used, are most accurately rendered in this context by "power," though their basic concrete designations are "breath" and "wind." As for the word "holy," it refers primarily to God in his separateness and hence in his inaccessibility and "awe-inspiring transcendence,"[5] and only by extension to what is brought into his domain. "The Holy Spirit" is thus "the Spirit of God," the power of God.[6] It is therefore not difficult to see how "the Holy Spirit" is to be understood at times impersonally, simply as God's power, and at other times personally, as God himself, inasmuch as in the functional perspective of the Bible God can hardly be grasped otherwise than in his dynamism, that is, in the exercise of his power. In this latter approach, though, there is no suggestion that the Holy Spirit is a divine person distinct from Yahweh, the God of Israel; rather, he is Yahweh himself apprehended in his action.

Maintaining this approach, we see that the same basic structure applies in the matter of the relation of Christ and the Holy Spirit. It is a point well made by James D. G. Dunn that as a result of the Resurrection Jesus is transferred to the sphere of the Spirit where he continues to act in relation to his community on earth, doing so in and by this Spirit, which assumes his personality.[7] As with Yahweh and the Holy Spirit in the Old Testament, so with Christ and the Spirit in the New; it cannot be said that the Holy Spirit precisely as Spirit of Christ (or "spirit of Jesus") is conceived as distinct from Christ. Rather, he is the spiritual medium and power, hitherto associated exclusively with God (Yahweh, and then the Father), in which the personal presence and activity of Christ are experienced by his community. Here, then, the personality acknowledged to the Spirit is that of Christ. However, the process thus begun continues in the New Testament itself. The eventual attribution to the Holy Spirit of distinct personal activities and receptivities such as, for example, teaching, thinking, and being "grieved," as well as the use, in regard to him, of the personal pronoun "he" (*ekeinos*), suggests the dawning of an apprehension of an identity for him distinct from that either of the Father or of Christ. But even so, and uniquely, no distinct personality is awarded him. The *content* of the experience of Holy Spirit remains either the Father or Christ; and inasmuch as the Father is transcendent and hence ineffable, in practical terms this content must simply be said to be Christ. After the Resurrection, then, the Holy Spirit has a personality, but it is the personality of Christ. To facilitate the grasping of this point, it may be helpful to distinguish between personality, which is a psychological reality, and personhood, which is ontological, though in all cases apart from the Holy Spirit they correspond. That they do not in this case stems, as we shall see later in this study, from the unique relations of the persons in the Trinity. To say that in the New Testament the Holy Spirit is credited with personality is not yet to say that he is credited with personhood. But, as we saw, even with a dawning sense of personhood the New Testament's convictions about the personality of the Spirit as that of Christ remained unchanged.

At the First Council of Constantinople in 381 for the first time in official teaching the distinction was made between *ousia* (substance) on the one hand and *hupostasis* (hypostasis or subsistent reality) and *prosopon* (person) on the other: Father, Son, and Holy Spirit possessed a common substance in three hypostases or persons.[8] This meant that the personhood of the Holy Spirit was now established in the teaching of the Church. This development occurred as the climax of a theological process that worked itself out in the context of the philosophical culture of Hellenism. But the process had begun already in the New Testament, through the dialectic of identity and difference, or unity and distinction, found there among the members of the Trinity, Father, Son, and Holy Spirit. With Christ the movement was from distinction to unity; that is to say, it was obvious at the outset that the man Jesus was other than God, but as the faith of his disciples in him grew, he was perceived more and more as being one with God, this perception attaining its climax in the Resurrection, though this unity was never conceived as abolishing his otherness. With the Holy Spirit the movement was in the opposite direction. At first the Spirit was simply identified with God, and then, as we saw, with Christ; but, because he was seen as bestowed on Jesus by God so as to become the special possession of Jesus and the principle of the unique divine sonship in which Jesus stood over against God (the Father),[9] he (the Holy Spirit) came gradually to be distinguished from the Father; and because he was eventually seen as sent by Christ upon the Church, he came to be distinguished in some measure also from Christ. Again, though, this otherness was never considered to abolish his fundamental unity with God and with Christ. This dialectic never has been, and never will be, overcome. All that happened at Constantinople was that it was given clearer expression in a new cultural context. The New Testament does not teach that the Holy Spirit is a person; indeed the concept of person was not available to it; but the seeds of the doctrine are there, as I have indicated.

This New Testament doctrine of the Trinity, as we may call it, is not something given to the first Christian communities in the first instance in words. It is given in the event of Christ as experienced in the power of his Resurrection. The words are found only later, to give appropriate expression to this transcendental experience of salvation. Thus, the ultimate (eschatological) salvation that comes from God and that consists, as we would say today, in his very self-communication, actually came to them in the person of Jesus, not, however from Jesus as he was remembered in the "flesh" (*sarx*), but rather from the same Jesus as he exists and acts now, in the "spirit" (*pneuma*). Therefore, for them the concept of God that they had inherited from Judaism had to be expanded to include both Jesus (confessed now as "the Christ") and the Holy Spirit. Baptism, the rite of entry into the community of salvation, was performed not just in the name of God, but "in the name of Jesus Christ" (Acts 2.38), or, to put it more comprehensively, "in the name of the Father and of the Son and of the Holy Spirit" (Mt 28.19).

It will be clear from what has been said that this New Testament doctrine of the Trinity is functional rather than ontological in character. An important point to make at the outset is that the New Testament maintains this functional perspective throughout—without exception. As this is by no means obvious, even to many exegetes and theologians of the Trinity, it needs to be argued rather than simply asserted. This, therefore, is the task to which I now turn.

Functional Theology of the New Testament

In my view, nowhere in the New Testament, not even in the Prologue of the Fourth Gospel, is the concept of a metaphysical (or ontological) incarnation attained.[10] By this term is meant the assumption unto himself of a human nature, by a divine being (or person), who in himself is in no way human, so that thenceforward it can truly be said that God has become human (without, naturally, ceasing thereby to be divine). It can be argued, of course, that a certain concept of incarnation is inculcated in verse 14 of the Prologue of John, "And the Word became flesh and lived among us." To "become flesh" is to undergo an incarnation: this is the literal meaning of the word. But the question is: What does John mean by the expression "to become flesh"? It is my contention that it has been all too readily assumed to be an exact synonym for "to become human." The major argument is that in the Bible in general and in the Fourth Gospel in particular "flesh" is to be understood in terms of its relationship to its antonym, "spirit," and that this consideration supplies the clue to the meaning of verse 14. (Unfortunately, English does not have a noun form to express "becoming human" in distinction to "becoming flesh" [incarnation], as, for example, does German with its word *Menschwerdung*.)

If "spirit" means "power," "flesh" means "weakness." If, in this context, "spirit" denotes precisely God in his power, his dynamism, his incorruptibility, "flesh" denotes humankind in its contrast to God, in its weakness, its vulnerability to decay and to sin, and particularly its predestination to death. John says that the Word became "flesh" rather than "human" because he thought of the Word as already and always a human, the divine, preexistent man who had lived with God from eternity in the sphere of the Spirit but who at a certain point exchanged this mode of existence for that of mortal men and women, the sphere of the flesh. This is the force of the concluding words quoted from verse 14, "and lived among us." This approach represents a development of a suggestion made by Pierre Benoit in a 1970 article titled "Préexistence et Incarnation."[11] There he wrote, on the Johannine preexistence texts, "He (Jesus) is the same before, during and after his coming, changing his condition, putting aside his glory and then taking it up again, but identical with himself in his profound being."[12]

The other main argument is based on the figure of the Son of Man in John's gospel. It is this figure that dominates in the body of the gospel. Here John's scheme is the Son of Man's descent from heaven and his eventual reascent there on completion of his earthly mission, the principal texts being John 3.13 and 6.62. Though the Prologue has no echo (or pre-echo) of a Son of Man Christology, it has a similar fundamental scheme (minus the reascent): the preexistence of the heavenly man, and his descent to earth in which he identified with the human lot in every respect but sin. It is clear that from start to finish the Johannine Son of Man is a human being, though one endowed with divine qualities.[13] Now if we can expect correspondence rather than contradiction between the body of the Gospel and the Prologue, it is reasonable to conclude that the Logos of the Prologue too is the preexistent man Jesus. By way of confirmation of this, the wording of the profession of faith in 1 John 4.2, "Jesus Christ has come in the flesh," suggests interpretation along the same lines.

Even if this argument is not found to be cogent, if we bear in mind the indisputable fact that in biblical theology "to become flesh" does not necessarily mean "to become human" we must admit that there is no reason to claim that John 1.14 is saying anything more than does Colossians 2.9 when it says that "in him (Christ) the fullness of deity dwells bodily," that is, in the human figure of Jesus the very Word or Wisdom of God is embodied. It is clear that this does not demand to be understood in the sense of a metaphysical incarnation.

I have concentrated on the Fourth Gospel and particularly its Prologue because recent studies have narrowed down New Testament teaching of an actual preexistence of Christ to this gospel, and its teaching of a metaphysical incarnation to verse

14 of the Prologue. Dunn writes in the conclusion of his *Christology in the Making* that "only in the post-Pauline period did a clear understanding of Christ as having pre-existed with God before his ministry on earth emerge, and only in the Fourth Gospel can we speak of a doctrine of the incarnation."[14] The same author had written of John 1.14, "Here we have an explicit statement of incarnation, the first, and indeed only such statement in the NT."[15] Elsewhere he describes this statement as "deliberately metaphysical,"[16] and he chides Maurice Wiles for saying that "incarnation, in its full and proper sense, is not something directly presented in scripture."[17] But if even John 1.14 does not present a metaphysical doctrine of incarnation, as argued in the previous pages, then Wiles is right after all, and we have to look to the development of doctrine in the early Church and the teachings of the councils for the acquisition of this particular teaching. This sort of procedure should cause no problem in Catholic theology with its ready acknowledgment of tradition combined with Scripture to constitute the source of divine revelation.[18] If the Prologue was originally a Philonic Logos hymn taken over by the evangelist from the Hellenistic synagogue of Alexandria and modified to fit his gospel's picture of a preexistent and incarnate Savior, as Robert Hamerton-Kelly argues,[19] it is not surprising that early Church Fathers such as Justin Martyr, who shared the same Middle-Platonist background, should begin to interpret it in the sense of a metaphysical incarnation.[20] Nor, if such was the case, should this development be dismissed as some sort of deviation from the path of truth. Later I shall show that the functional incarnation of the Prologue demanded the metaphysical incarnation of later Church teaching as part of the process of interpretation (hermeneusis) of doctrine in the transition from functional to ontological thought categories.[21] But for the present it is sufficient to have shown that there is no concept of metaphysical incarnation in the New Testament itself.

The Biblical, the Immanent, and the Economic Trinity

If the New Testament contains no concept of metaphysical incarnation, this means that there can be no doctrine of what is called "the immanent Trinity" in it either. This expression denotes the Trinity "remaining within" itself, the Trinity considered in itself and therefore not in relation to the divine plan of salvation, the *oikonomia*. Obviously, the alternative to this will be to consider the Trinity precisely as involved in this plan, through the redemptive mission of the Son in the person of Jesus Christ and its continuation through the mission of the Holy Spirit in the Church and in the hearts of individual persons, the ultimate agent of both missions being the Father. From this point of view the Trinity is called "the economic Trinity" (from oikonomia). A disadvantage of this terminology is that it may give the impression that there are two trinities, but obviously this cannot be so. It merely indicates the two perspectives in which the Trinity can be conceived.

It will be helpful at this point to consider the relationship between the immanent and the economic Trinity. Karl Rahner has proposed as an axiom the statement that "the 'economic' Trinity is the 'immanent' Trinity and the 'immanent' Trinity is the 'economic' Trinity."[22] While this is a clear assertion of the unicity of the Trinity and of the ability of each perspective to throw light on the other, it does not tell us which perspective is the more fundamental, nor does it throw light on the order of our knowledge of the Trinity. For the sake of clarity let us recognize immediately that there are two orders in question here. The first is the epistemological order, the order of knowledge, of discovery; and the second is the ontological order, the order of being, of givenness. These do not necessarily coincide; it is possible that the one be the reverse of the other, and indeed such is the case in the matter of the Trinity.

Let us take the epistemological order first. The doctrine of the Trinity is a revealed truth, one that can be known only from divine revelation. It belongs to the category of truths the revelation of which is said by the First Vatican Council to be "absolutely necessary" if they are to be known at all.[23] True, there were adumbrations of the Trinity in non-Christian philosophy, specifically in Neoplatonism, and this source inspired as seminal a thinker on the nature of God as St. Augustine, not just before his conversion but throughout his life.[24] But such ideas of the one God unfolding from basic unity into a certain multiplicity by no means coincide with the Christian doctrine; at best they provide a horizon against which it can be set and that can be exploited in the service of its intellectual exposition. The doctrine of the Trinity stands revealed, implicitly, as we said above, in the event of Christ experienced in the saving power of his Resurrection, which is the constitutive event of the Christian religion. More explicit statements than this even in the New Testament itself, such as Matthew 28.19, are only intellectual derivations from this basic event. Yet, as we stated earlier, the New Testament doctrine of the Trinity, even at its most sophisticated, in the Fourth Gospel, remains on the functional plane and does not penetrate to the level of the immanent Trinity.

The transition to ontological explanatory categories took place when the Johannine Prologue began to be interpreted according to the philosophy of Middle Platonism, as exemplified in Justin Martyr. Here the Logos (the Word) was no longer simply identified with the man Jesus, the preexistent Son of Man of the body of the Gospel; rather, it was a preexistent divine being (whose exact status remained to be determined) who first became human at the moment of the Incarnation, which was now understood in metaphysical terms. This was no mistake. To borrow, and apply in a more dynamic sense, a phrase of Jacques Maritain to indicate the logical analysis, concealed from the actual thinker, of a particular act of reason,[25] an "immanent dialectic" was at work in this process of transition, supplied by the demand that the functional divinity of Christ taught by the New Testament be interpreted as an ontological reality in the new philosophical context of thought. Otherwise, the message of the gospels could not be preserved. Spelled out, the dialectic may be set forth as follows. An ontological divinity for Christ requires the simultaneous distinction and unity in him of a human and a divine element. The human element, being finite, must have an absolute beginning, which must be identified as its creation (ex nihilo) at the moment of conception. The divine element, being infinite, must be not just preexistent but eternal, and, because of its identification with Christ the Son of God, must at the same time be distinguished from God the Father and therefore be a distinct divine person, *and* be the actual person of Christ. The human element, because it enters into unity of person with this person, cannot itself be characterized as person, though it is fully human. It is therefore called a human "nature." These constituents of the dialectic crystallized into explicit formulation over a century and a quarter, at the first four ecumenical councils, Nicaea, Constantinople I, Ephesus, and Chalcedon.

What we have here is not just a transition from biblical to ontological categories; it is a transition from the biblical doctrine of the Trinity to the doctrine of the immanent Trinity. The methodology is correct. Regarding this methodology, Walter Kasper has written approvingly of what Piet Schoonenberg had to say:

> He (Schoonenberg) starts out from the principle which has guided my own reflections up to now: "Our whole thinking moves from reality towards God and can never move in the opposite direction. . . . In no respect do we conclude from the Trinity to Christ and to the Spirit given to us, but always the other way round."[26]

But this principle, formulated by Schoonenberg and endorsed by Kasper, is, on my view, only half correct. It is correct in that it approves the transition from the biblical Trinity (as I shall henceforth call the biblical doctrine) to the immanent Trinity and disapproves any transition from the immanent to the biblical Trinity in the sense of the generation of new fundamental data. But it is incorrect in that it takes no account of the necessity of a return from the immanent Trinity to the biblical data to acquire the doctrine of the economic Trinity. The latter is not simply identical with the biblical Trinity. The doctrine of the biblical Trinity, as outlined above, has as its distinguishing feature a purely functional character. The economic Trinity, on the other hand, is the integration of the immanent Trinity with the biblical data, and this entails a return, a move in the direction disallowed by Schoonenberg and Kasper. Thus the Son in the economic Trinity is the eternal Logos become man, or human, in the Jesus of Nazareth of the gospels, a figure not identical, in description at least, with the Son of either the biblical or the immanent Trinity. And something similar can be said of the Holy Spirit and the Father as well.

These reflections throw light on exactly what the study of the Trinity should be. It is not just the biblical doctrine, for while that is its indispensable starting point, it is *only* the starting point. If we remained there, we would be opting for a biblical fundamentalism. Nor is it just the doctrine of the immanent Trinity, as it has often been assumed to be, for that on its own is unconnected with the mystery of salvation. No wonder that an exclusive concentration on the immanent Trinity has brought the theology of the Trinity into disrepute among Catholics and Protestants alike, and has often led to its being dropped altogether from the theological curriculum. The proper study of the Trinity is the study of the economic Trinity, which of course presupposes both the biblical and the immanent Trinity. With this enlightened return to the biblical data the inquiring mind comes to rest. There is nothing more for it to do. But the point at which it rests is the point of intersection between God in his gracious activity and the world of men and women. This provides the raw material of both theology and spirituality, and its relevance requires no further demonstration.

The Epistemological and the Ontological Order

The Epistemological Order

The epistemological order postulated here—biblical Trinity, immanent Trinity, economic Trinity—is justified by a reflection from the work of Bernard Lonergan. In *Insight* he writes:

Experiencing is only the first level of knowing; it presents the matter to be known. Understanding is only the second level of knowing; it defines the matter to be known. Knowing reaches a complete increment only with judgment, only when the experienced has been thought and the merely thought has been affirmed. But the increment of knowing is always completed in the same fashion. Experience is a kaleidoscopic flow. Objects of thought are as varied as the inventiveness of human intelligence. But the contribution of judgment to our knowing is ever a mere "Yes" or "No," a mere "is" or "is not." Experience is for inquiring into being. Intelligence is for thinking out being. But by judgment being is known, and in judgment what is known is known as being. Hence knowing is knowing being, yet the known is never mere being, just as judgment is never a mere "Yes" apart from any question that "Yes" answers.[27]

When we consider this triple-layered structure of knowing in relation to our knowledge of the Trinity, we see that the biblical data, what we have called the biblical Trinity, are the "matter to be known," inasmuch as they are the primary data of revelation. The immanent Trinity is our understanding of these data in the world of our own intellectual culture, which has been formed, at least initially, by the ontological categories of Hellenism. Finally, the doctrine of the economic Trinity is our affirmation that *this* is the case. It is the judgment by which we return from our reflective understanding to the real spiritual world brought to its perfection in the Christ event, and this not just as revealed and experienced but as understood and affirmed. This analysis is not invalidated by the fact that what I have called primary data has already been through the process just described and represents the *judgment* of the biblical writers: as far as *we* are concerned, it remains primary data.

In this connection let me comment on a footnote in Anthony Kelly's *The Trinity of Love*. Kelly writes:

It seems to me that any distinction between ontological and functional Christology or Trinitarianism, as well as any distinction between the "immanent" and the "economic" is utterly foreign to Johannine theology. The later theological use of such distinctions have [sic] a limited role and, perhaps, a very provisional one against the day of a critical Christian realism able to distinguish between data, understanding, and judgment.[28]

I have already given my reasons for finding the first sentence of this statement inadequate to the reality it addresses. But the second sentence was what first alerted me to a correlation between the threefold doctrine of the Trinity and Lonergan's epistemological structure, and for this I am grateful to Kelly, though it seems to me that the "critical Christian realism" to which he looks forward, far from abolishing the distinctions between "immanent" and "economic" and "functional" and "ontological," will preserve them, integrating them into its overall achievement, in something like the way I have indicated.[29]

Of course the actual situation is considerably more complex than has appeared so far. Our experience, understanding, and judgment involve us in a process. First, when we understand the biblical data in terms of the immanent Trinity, this understanding, that is, the immanent Trinity, is no more than an abstraction. When we return, by the third step, to the data, we find we have to make *two* affirmations of actual reality, the first, that is, of the immanent Trinity, which because of the divine transcendence must exist in its own right,[30] and the second of the economic Trinity, that is, of this same Trinity, but now as involved in the divine plan of salvation through the missions of the Son and of the Holy Spirit.

Second, this reflection reveals to us that at the level of understanding we have actually understood *more* than the Trinity alone. We have needed to understand simultaneously (by which is not meant "instantaneously") something of philosophical and theological anthropology, so that we can combine our understanding of the divine Son with that of a single human nature in order to acquire some understanding, however deficient, of a possible "incarnation," *and* combine our understanding of the Holy Spirit with that of a plurality of human persons in order to understand, though again in a deficient way, the life of grace as it might be lived on both a communal level (that of a possible "church") and an individual level. This means that even at the second step, abstraction, we grasp the Trinity as both immanent *and* economic. This in turn means that the economic Trinity that we affirm by the third step includes affirmations about humanity as possessed by Christ and by ourselves both as members of the Church and as individuals.

Third and finally, the three-stepped process just outlined is not something that is ever accomplished once and for all. The data of the first step consist of more than just the biblical doctrine of the Trinity. They include all that our culture, tradition, education, and religious experience bring to bear on our apprehension of the biblical doctrine, however much we try to exclude them in order to focus solely on the Bible. This consideration in itself, not to mention the communal and personal biases to which we are subject, imposes a certain selectivity on our choice of biblical data: some we shall see as important and therefore emphasize, others we shall by comparison neglect or overlook altogether. As a result, our understanding, correct though it may be as far as it goes, will of necessity be inadequate. And our affirmations, again correct as they may be, will amount only to a partial knowledge of the economic Trinity. But our contribution will add to a store of knowledge that will in turn contribute to the experience (the data) and the understanding of those who follow us, and so, with occasional setbacks as wrong or fruitless courses are chosen, our communal knowledge of the Trinity will increase into the future in a never-ending cycle, through both simple advancement and dialectic.

These complications need not detain us unduly. The theology of the Trinity can be considered either inclusively, as the whole of theology (as we have been doing), or exclusively, as a branch that discards all that belongs specifically to Christology or to the theology of the Church or of grace. In the latter alternative all that it would retain from these other branches would be their relationships to each other. Realistically, this is the more appropriate alternative to choose. At the second level, therefore, all understanding that is not necessary for the theology of the immanent Trinity should be bracketed out as belonging elsewhere. We can be content with attempting to advance the theology of the Trinity by restricting our attention to the New Testament data (realizing that this attention will be both sophisticated and selective) and to their metaphysical understanding in terms of the immanent Trinity, so that we can complete the process by returning to the biblical data and there affirming the Trinity as both immanent and economic, in the latter case restricting ourselves to the relations discovered between Christ, the Church and graced individuals, in an effort guided throughout by the motif of salvation. But our affirmation of the immanent Trinity should not be seen as an end in itself. Taking its point of departure from the biblical data, it is meant in turn to serve our knowledge of the economic Trinity. We affirm its existence, therefore, for two interconnected reasons and these alone. The primary one is that the divine transcendence obliges us thereto; and the secondary one is that the immanent Trinity is what "drives" the economic Trinity: without the immanent Trinity the economic Trinity would not exist. Hence at the end of our reflection we return to what I said at the beginning, that the epistemological structure, biblical Trinity—immanent Trinity—economic Trinity, is sound, corresponding as it does to the three steps of Lonergan's analysis of knowing. This structure is not only epistemological; it is also methodological, and as such will determine in general the form and order of procedure in this book.

It is appropriate to offer at this point a comment on this aspect of the trinitarian theology of Karl Barth. Ever anxious to safeguard the divine transcendence, Barth insisted on God's untrammeled freedom, not only in regard to the world but also within the Trinity itself.[31] Timothy Bradshaw sums up Barth's trinitarian understanding of freedom thus:

> The freely *self-determining* character of God is a crucially important conclusion for this study of Barth's doctrine of the Trinity. God *in se* is the God who is *determined*, the *forma servi*, and the *free God*, the mysterious, sovereign Father. God transcends his dual nature because he is the Spirit, never abolishing the Father-Son source but being its Lord.[32]

For Barth the relationship between God and the world was irreversible, from God to the world, rather than vice versa.[33] Hence Barth stood opposed in principle to any kind of ascending Christology or theology generally.[34] Of course, he recognized that it was only in Christ that the immanent Trinity was revealed. Indeed he did more than recognize this; arguably, he erected it into the main feature of his trinitarian theology. But for him this meant that this revelation was given in the New Testament itself, according to a very traditional understanding of John 1.14. And on our part the acceptance of this revelation required no intellectual inference from the humanity of Christ, but only an "acknowledgment" of its presence, i.e. through the "miracle" of faith.[35]

Two of the key points made here by Barth merit concurrence, the centrality of Christ in the revelation of the Trinity and a certain priority of the immanent over the economic Trinity. But in the elaboration of these points Barth makes a number of assertions with which I disagree or at least can no longer agree. Thus his appeal to a revelation that is divine in a sense precluding all human contribution is supported only by an outmoded exegesis, for example, in regard to John 1.14. While I agree that the immanent Trinity stands revealed in the Mystery of Christ, this is an acquisition of the reflection of the patristic Church on the New Testament, rather than of the New Testament alone. The "acknowledgment" of which Barth speaks must be at the same time an intellectual inference (without prejudice to the fact that it is also faith), and hence must represent a spiritual and intellectual ascent from the world to God, a fact that more than justifies the recent trend to ascending Christology among Catholic as well as Protestant theologians (including some prominent disciples of Barth). This leads me to my second point. Undoubtedly there is an ontological priority of the immanent over the economic Trinity. And even in the epistemological order there has to be a return from the sphere of God to the data supplied in the world. But, as I have shown from Lonergan, this return is necessarily preceded by an ascent from these data to the sphere of God. A distinction between the ontological and the epistemological orders would have greatly helped Barth in his dilemma here.

Finally, the divine transcendence is ill served by the freedom that Barth asserts for God within his own being, for contrary to Barth's intention it actually compromises that transcendence by introducing contingency into the Godhead: the Father who freely determines himself might just as freely have decided not to do so. And in being thus contingently generated, the Son in turn is compromised in his own divinity. Barth would not be pleased to find himself compared to Arius, but the comparison is not unreasonable. More reliable as a guide is the statement of the fifth-century confession, the *Fides Damasi*, "Pater Filium genuit non voluntate, nec necessitate, sed natura" (The Father generated the Son not by his will [i.e., freely, contingently], nor by necessity [i.e., as determined from outside], but by nature [because it was his natural property to do so]).[36] This is so because *whatever* happens within the immanent Trinity does so not contingently but according to the necessity of the divine nature. This, however, does not compromise the freedom of God in regard to the world. As the creation itself is by no means necessary, neither is any action of God in the world of which creation is the presupposition—at least it is not necessary in the ultimate sense (I do not deny, for example, that there is a certain consequent necessity that God fulfill the promises that he has freely made).

The method I have acquired with the help of Lonergan's epistemology raises the question about the legitimacy of theologies of the Trinity based on concepts belonging to the immanent Trinity. A case in point is Leonardo Boff's *Trinity and Society*.[37] This book attempts the laudable task of presenting the Trinity in the light of liberation theology. In so doing, it adopts as central the concept of *perichoresis*, the interpenetration of the three divine persons of the immanent Trinity, seeing this as the model for liberation in human society. Boff maintains that this concept provides "impulses to liberation."[38] This may be true, but, if so, it is hardly true in a very effective way, seeing that we have no experience of the interaction among the persons of the immanent Trinity. The desired impulses come more strongly from the New Testament, and in a more sophisticated form from the doctrine of the economic Trinity, from the teaching that all human beings are created equal before God and are destined to be his children in Christ, and therefore brothers and sisters of each other, in the power of the Holy Spirit. Our statements about the immanent Trinity may be formally correct, and therefore do correspond, albeit in a highly inadequate way, to the reality of God, but for us they lack the experiential content that is necessary as a basis for a theology, granted that today any theology seeking acceptance must be able to evince pastoral relevance. Experiential content is acquired by completing the three-stepped process outlined above, by returning to the biblical data and from there developing a theology in dialogue with the tradition and with the contributions and questions of the present age.

I cannot leave this subject without addressing a problem that has arisen in recent years in regard to the epistemology of the Trinity. I refer to a line of questioning, on epistemological grounds, that has led to agnosticism concerning the immanent Trinity. I can conveniently carry out this task in reference to an article by Roger Haight, "The Point of Trinitarian Theology."[39] With many others now writing on the Trinity, including me, Haight is convinced that what "drives" the theology of the Trinity is the doctrine of salvation. He writes, "The doctrine of the Trinity emerges out of the experience of salvation through Jesus and in God's spirit."[40] It is because God's salvation comes to us from the Father, through the risen Christ acting in the power of the Spirit that is both the Father's and his own, that God is experienced and confessed by Christians as Father, Son, and Holy Spirit.

Where Haight departs from the traditional view is that he regards this perspective as obliging the theologian to an agnostic position on the subject of the immanent Trinity. Of our faith-encounter with God "in Jesus and the Spirit" he says that "this encounter does not *necessarily* yield really distinct differentiations within God that can be named."[41] He recognizes that "one can certainly speculate," but immediately goes on to say that "one will never be able to define such differentiations in any final way."[42] But, on the other hand, "neither does the theologian have the grounds to deny such differentiation in God."[43]

In the face of the tradition such agnosticism needs to be justified both dogmatically and theologically. Haight attempts both tasks. At the dogmatic level, he advances two "insights" on the basis of which he interprets the Nicene homoousion in the purely economic sense that "no less than God was present and active in the life of Jesus."[44] The first of these insights is that, whereas the New Testament presents a plurality of Christologies, Nicaea absolutizes just one of them, the Johannine, and in a manner detrimental to the others, tending to undermine or negate them.[45] The second is that the positive sense of a conciliar decree whose primary thrust is negative, that is, the condemnation of heresy (in this case Arianism), should be regulated and limited by its negative sense.[46]

Neither of these insights, however, merits acceptance. With regard to the first, we recognize with Haight the existence of a plurality of Christologies in the New Testament. Methodologically, these reduce to two, the descending Christology typical of John and the ascending Christology typical of the synoptics. As I have shown in earlier writings and intend to show again in this book, these in turn imply differing models of the biblical Trinity, which I call respectively the mission model and the return model. To these there correspond in the immanent Trinity the procession model (of Nicaea and First Constantinople) and (again) the return model. True, the Nicene Christology was unbalanced in that it depended on John and not at all on the synoptics, but of itself it did nothing to undermine or negate the latter tradition. By means of the return model, I hope to give this tradition, however belatedly, a voice, and one that relativizes but ultimately harmonizes with, and takes its place as complementary to, that of the Johannine tradition. To establish all this is one of the principal aims of this book.

As regards his second insight, I can agree that the negative sense of a conciliar decree is an important guide to its positive sense, but if the form of the teaching is positive, as in Nicaea, the positive sense has to be paramount. This is essential for the possibility of development of doctrine. It is quite clear from the text of the Symbol of Nicaea and its accompanying canon that positively it speaks of the eternal and divine status of the Logos.[47] Haight himself recognizes this, but relegates such content to the formulation's "imaginative framework," so that its true meaning may emerge as the rejection of subordinationism.[48] But it is a faulty and reductionist hermeneutics that identifies the meaning of a text with its underlying intention (however helpful it may be to know this) rather than with what it actually says. Admittedly, what an ancient text says can often be problematical for a modern understanding and so will require reinterpretation, but this is a different matter from jettisoning its actual statement altogether in favor of its intention. Haight's second insight is therefore also incorrect. Hence his interpretation of Nicaea, based as it is on these two insights, is left without foundation.

Coming now to Haight's theological justification of his position, we note that he does not think it *impossible* for there to be differentiation within the being of God. His problem is only about our sure knowledge of it on the basis of the economy. But why is this a problem for him? In a footnote he quotes St. Gregory of Nyssa in witness to the Eastern apophatic tradition,[49] but the same Gregory was not so apophatic as to be in any doubt about the differentiation of the divine being into Father, Son, and Holy Spirit. Nor was, or is, any other Eastern writer. And the Latin tradition, for its part, is avowedly cataphatic. Why, then, is Haight so skeptical?

Haight lays emphasis on "the absolute mystery and incomprehensibility of God," a phrase he employs twice.[50] Presumably, by "mystery" he means transcendence and he is using "incomprehensibility" in the Eastern sense of absolute unknowability. In the tradition deriving from Paul, "mystery," despite the fact that it has to do with transcendence, does not denote or connote such unknowability; rather it indicates the object of divine *revelation* and points to the fact that what was previously unknown because hidden in God has become known through revelation (see Rom 16.25–27; 1 Cor 15.51–52). The immanent Trinity belongs to this category. Unknowable by reason alone, it is knowable on the basis of revelation. Not that it is revealed directly: it is revealed indirectly, in Christ and the Spirit. And as for incomprehensibility, in the Western tradition divine incomprehensibility does not mean absolute unknowability; it means simply that God cannot be known *fully* by the human intellect, that his reality cannot be exhausted by human knowledge. It is only in this sense that he is rendered incomprehensible by his transcendence. This is the case even in the beatific vision. All the more is it the case in this life, where God cannot be known directly, but only by negation and by analogy with the objects of our direct knowledge, the beings that constitute our world. These limitations apply not only to our "natural" knowledge of God but also to our knowledge of him from revelation. Haight's appeal to God's absolute mystery and incomprehensibility, therefore, does not of itself constitute an argument for agnosticism concerning the immanent Trinity, even if, as we saw, divine incomprehensibility be taken in its Eastern, apophatic sense. (We leave aside, as highly unlikely, the possibility that Haight's skepticism is ultimately philosophical, arising from a Kantian view of the knowability of being as such.)

Haight does argue, in a footnote, against Rahner's defense of the immanent Trinity:

> Rahner consistently argues that if there were no real self-differentiation in God, then what one experienced in Jesus and the Spirit would not be a real *self*-communication of God. But the force of this argument or assertion is not clear. There is no logical connection that demands a correlation of an internal differentiation within God and

God's actual self-communication to human existence. If God were conceived as single, simple, spiritual, personal, and sovereignly free subject, this characterization of God could of itself account for God's *self*-communication to Jesus and each human being.[51]

This would be true only if on the basis of revelation God's self-communication to Jesus had to be recognized as exactly the same as that made to each human being; but we know on the same basis (a point Rahner takes for granted) that in a differentiated sense they are different. While each is the self-communication of God (and in that sense the same), what is received by the humanity of Jesus is the divine "Word" (as Rahner says in this context)[52] and what is received by us is the Spirit (and in that sense different). And while Jesus actually *is* the divine Word, we only *have* the Holy Spirit. Thus the two modes of self-communication differ radically from each other. As I shall show in chapter 3, even from the donative (as distinct from the receptive) perspective of the divine self-communication, the two are, in the differentiated sense, different: the first, as the communication of the Son, is the self-communication of the Father alone, and the second, as the communication of the Holy Spirit, is the self-communication of the Father and the Son.

While I carry the matter beyond Rahner (by attending to the donative as well as to the receptive aspect of the divine self-communication), I recognize that he states correctly the nub of the argument when he says, "The mediations of God among us [i.e., in Word and Spirit] are no created intermediaries or world powers."[53] But perhaps this statement needs a little "unpacking." It means, presumably, that on the basis of the economy we know that the Word and the Spirit, despite being profoundly the same as each other and the Father (in their divinity), are just as profoundly different (as persons). But, if there is no differentiation in the divine being itself, the difference of Word and Spirit (each, be it remembered, being a *self*-communication of God) that we experience in the economy would have to be a difference of nondivine realities only, in which case the Word and the Spirit could only be created intermediaries or world powers. But we know with the certainty of faith that this is not the case. Therefore the difference of Father, Word, and Spirit must be given in the being of God itself, that is, in the immanent Trinity.

An important point not mentioned by Haight is that the process of hermeneusis and development in the first centuries of the Christian era, occasioned as it was by christological, pneumatological, and trinitarian controversies, demanded that the functional theology of the New Testament be reformulated in ontological terms. The new level of discussion required that on the basis of the biblical data ontological statements be made about the very being of God. There was, and is, no problem about this provided such statements remain within the bounds of a suitable modesty prescribed by the twofold and philosophically legitimate method of negation and analogical affirmation, and do not presume to speak about the being of God as though it were a direct object of knowledge. Haight is correct when he says, "There simply are no data on the inner life of God upon which comparisons and differentiations can be made,"[54] provided "data" be understood here as direct data. But this does not justify his agnosticism, which is thus shown up as deficient methodologically as well as epistemologically.

A significant thesis for the formation of Haight's position is the following: "Although the doctrine of the Trinity is derivative, it tends to become an objectified premise of theology."[55] Let us deal first with the subordinate statement, that the doctrine is derivative. First, it is claimed to be derivative historically, in that, "not found in the New Testament," it "developed over a long period of time through reflection and debate."[56] But we have seen that there is a vitally important sense in which it *is* found in the New Testament, a sense in which it must be admitted to be primitive and functional as distinct from sophisticated and ontological, which it became later through reflection and debate. But this sense is important for us, because according to the Lonerganian epistemological scheme which I have invoked it provides the basis, the data, for the acquisition of the doctrine of both the economic and the immanent Trinity as affirmed in later official teaching.

Further, the doctrine of the Trinity is asserted to be derivative "existentially and logically as well," in that "it depends on a prior datum, the experience of salvation in Jesus," along with "explicit views on the nature of salvation, and beyond that certain specific christological theories."[57] We should not question this assertion; indeed already in this chapter I have said similar things. But I would want to add that *every* dogma of the Christian and Catholic faith is derivative in this sense, and has to be. In this respect there is nothing unusual about the doctrine of the Trinity, except perhaps that, being closer to the experience of salvation, "the foundation of the Christian faith," than most other dogmas, it stands higher than them in the "hierarchy of truths" of which Vatican II speaks.[58]

The upshot of this is that there is no problem with the Trinity's being "an objectified premise of theology." In the Lonerganian scheme just referred to, the doctrine of the immanent Trinity does this in two ways. First, affirmed as existing in its own right, it declares and safeguards the transcendence of God and his knowability and experiential accessibility to believers in their spiritual lives. And second, it provides the intellectual framework and reference for the confession of the economic Trinity in the relatively sophisticated form that is necessary for educated and reflective Christians today.

The Ontological Order

Having considered the epistemological order, let us turn now to the ontological order. What is given logically first in this order is the immanent Trinity, God as he exists in himself, Father, Son, and Holy Spirit. Since God's gracious involvement with the world of his creation becomes recognizably trinitarian only in the Incarnation (however understood), this, therefore, must be said to be given logically second. There is no point here in distinguishing the biblical from the economic Trinity, as in this context these terms only indicate different stages of the intellectual appropriation of God's involvement once it has become clearly trinitarian. However, these statements themselves need to be put into perspective. We have no access to the ontological order except through the epistemological order, which therefore must be recognized as primary and fundamental. As Lonergan has observed, "[W]hile objectivity reaches what is independent of the concrete existing subject, objectivity itself is not reached by what is independent of the concrete existing subject. On the contrary, objectivity is reached through the self-transcendence of the concrete existing subject."[59] Statements about the ontological order, therefore, serve only to balance and relativize statements about the epistemological order. We can never succeed in getting outside our human perspective on reality, including divine reality. We cannot simply put ourselves in the place of God and see things as he does.

A question that arises in the consideration of the ontological order is: In the immanent Trinity, which is logically prior, the unity of the divine nature or the fact that there are three divine persons? (It is of course understood that there can be no question here of any temporal priority.) It is widely accepted that the Eastern tradition adopted as primary the New Testament distinctions of Father, Son and Spirit, and then rediscovered the divine unity in the homoousion as understood by St. Athanasius, in the identity of each person with the divine being, though this view is now challenged as an unwarranted generalization imported uncritically from the nineteenth-century theologian Théodore de Régnon.[60] In any case, for St. Augustine in the West God's unity was paramount on philosophical grounds. In his understanding, the one God unfolded into diversity through knowledge and love of himself. But also, be it noted, the Augustinian view followed the order of revelation: the God first revealed as one in the Old Testament was finally revealed as threefold in the New. My own view is that these considerations do not settle the matter. *Faith* acknowledges in God a dialectical tension between the unity of being and the diversity of persons that does not allow an absolute priority of either member of the dialectic over the other, while *theology*, for the sake of rationality, has to choose one or the other as a starting-point. Certainly, because of its dependence on the psychological model Western Catholic theology has traditionally awarded priority to the unity over the trinity of God, but with the fading of this model the alternative emphasis becomes possible. My own preference, as will become clear when I expound the two complementary models of the Trinity, is to begin with the "Western" order and end with the "Eastern."

Another question that should be addressed in considering the ontological order is the Eastern Orthodox distinction of the "essence" and the "uncreated energies" of God,[61] which I take up again in chapter 5. This distinction is found in the Cappadocian Fathers and was developed from that source in the fourteenth century by St. Gregory Palamas, archbishop of Thessalonica, to help resolve a contemporary controversy over the nature of the divine transcendence. In this form it became part of the official teaching of the Orthodox Church, but in the West reactions have varied: most simply ignore it, some condemn it, and a few (myself included) extend it a qualified approval. It is based on the conviction that God as he is in himself (his essence) is not to be equated without qualification with God as he relates to us (his operations, or energies). In this way it protects the divine transcendence. Palamas himself was not precise as to the nature of the distinction, but nowhere did he go so far as to say that it was "real," as he is often interpreted in the West (a readier condemnation thus being secured). On the other hand, there would be no point in insisting on a distinction that was simply logical. A distinction apparently mediating between these two positions is not unknown to Western scholasticism, namely, Scotus's "formal" distinction, his *distinctio formalis a parte rei*, the distinction between different but inseparable formalities of the one object, used by him principally to distinguish between the divine attributes. Western defenders of Palamas invoke this distinction not only to interpret his position to the West but to present it there in a favorable light, as both orthodox and coherent. Palamas himself would probably have been baffled by this Western defense! It should be pointed out that in itself a formal distinction is not really a mid-position between a real and a logical distinction, but a logical distinction "with a foundation in reality." If in the unique case of God it is thought necessary to situate the distinction between his essence and his energies in this mid-position and for that reason call it a formal distinction, then it must be borne in mind that this distinction in God is a unique kind of distinction and is called formal only because that is the category that appears closest to it.[62] I return to Scotus's distinction in chapter 5.

God's Relation to the World

The problem of how to relate God to the world without compromising his transcendence is perhaps the most fundamental question in all theology. A more sympathetic response to Palamas should follow once it is realized that any attempted solution will present difficulties. How can any theologian claim to systematize in categories of rational thought a relation one term of which is the ultimate mystery itself? Here recourse to mystery is not a cheap evasion, as so often it can be, but is of the essence of the matter under discussion. St. Thomas Aquinas's own solution is no exception to what has been said. He taught a "mixed" relation between God and the world, a relation that was real on the side of the world but only logical on the side of God.[63] In this way he hoped to preserve God from being affected by the world, thus saving his infinity and perfection.[64] To me it seems that the term "mixed relation" is acceptable and that the relation from the world to God is real, but that the weakness in the position lies in calling the relation of God to the world "logical," as though that is the only acceptable alternative to "real." On the other side, the weakness of Palamism as a *system*, is, as Rowan Williams points out, that it depends on a metaphysics that is simply an "ontologizing" of Aristotle's logic, driven by the regulative idea of participation.[65] The result is "a system not of terms but of real relations":[66] "An *ousia*-statement simply tells you what *sort* of thing you are dealing with; it does not refer to a mysterious core of essentiality to which qualities are added. But this is really what Palamas is implying."[67] Though Thomas Weinandy does not draw the conclusion himself, his eloquent words in defense of St. Thomas argue for a relation that cannot be called real only because it is so much *more* than what we mean by "real," not less (as is a logical relation).[68] But we cannot give it an exact name, because it lies beyond the scope of our experience, whence all our names come; it belongs to God alone and therefore, in keeping with his transcendence, has to remain nameless, unless it be named "super-real." Palamism and Thomism, each coming out of its own context (Neoplatonism and Aristotelianism, respectively), are trying to do the same thing, but neither does it perfectly: each tries to protect the transcendence of God while allowing creatures to be really related to him. This book, coming as it does out of the Western tradition, will make only a limited use of Palamas's distinction, but its sympathy for his attempt will, I hope, be evident.

An unfortunate corollary of Palamism, found in both Palamas and his modern followers, is the denial of a necessary correspondence between the economic and the immanent Trinity. Vladimir Lossky, for example, writes, "For Orthodox thought, the energies signify an exterior manifestation of the Trinity which cannot be interiorized, introduced, as it were, within the divine being, as its natural determination."[69] And again:

> [T]he Eastern Church has criticized western theology for confounding the exterior aspect of God's manifesting activity in the world (an activity in which the Holy Spirit, as a consubstantial Person sent by the Father and the Son, reveals the Son), and the interior aspect of the Trinity, in which the Person of the Holy Spirit proceeds from the Father alone, without having any relation of origin with the Son.[70]

Western theology, however, cannot accept this criticism. In the first place, it does not "confound" the exterior and the interior aspect of the Trinity; it merely claims a necessary correspondence between the two, here denied by Lossky. Second, though Lossky would find plenty of Western company in this particular misapprehension,[71] a correct methodology of trinitarian theology does not proceed from the economic to the immanent Trinity as asserted above, but rather in the opposite direction, as I have been at pains to point out. This is why there has to be a correspondence between the two. Lossky's view is based on an outdated biblical scholarship that would recognize at least some New Testament texts as speaking directly of the immanent Trinity. We have already ruled out this possibility in the case of the Son, second person of the Trinity, of whom the New Testament knows no metaphysical incarnation. It is to be ruled out also in the case of the Holy Spirit, despite John 15.26, which alone in the New Testament says that the Holy Spirit "proceeds from the Father." On this text Raymond Brown writes:

> This description made its way into the 4th-century creeds to describe the eternal procession of the Third Person of the Trinity from the Father. Many of the Greek Fathers thought that John was referring to eternal procession. . . . However, even though the tense of the verb is present, the coming forth is in parallelism with the "I shall send" in the next line and refers to the mission of the Paraclete/Spirit to men. . . . The writer is not speculating about the interior life of God; he is concerned with the disciples in the world.[72]

With the underpinning of Lossky's view thus removed by biblical criticism, it becomes impossible for him to say anything of the immanent Trinity at all, even that it exists, for any such statement would pertain to the essence of God, of which, according to him, we know nothing, since it is, in his words, "inaccessible, unknowable and incommunicable."[73] But we do claim knowledge of the immanent Trinity, on the basis, as argued, of the New Testament revelation; and it is this knowledge that allows us, in turn, to speak of the economic Trinity. Nevertheless, something of value for us can be salvaged from Lossky's view that Rahner's assertion of the absolute identity of the immanent and the economic Trinity needs to be toned down. The first half of his statement, that "the 'economic' Trinity is the 'immanent' Trinity," we can admit, but not the second half, that "the 'immanent' Trinity is the 'economic' Trinity." To give an analogy, while it is true that all humans are bipeds, it is not true that all bipeds are human beings. The immanent Trinity cannot be limited to an exact equation with the economic Trinity, for the economic Trinity is just *one* possible limitation of the immanent Trinity. The immanent Trinity must be more than the limited access that we have to it from the biblical revelation allows us to grasp. This is not to question the validity of our knowledge of the immanent Trinity; it remains true, but it is inadequate to the reality. A healthy Eastern apophaticism is a needed corrective to Western rationalism here.

Some Key Trinitarian Terms

Before drawing this chapter to a conclusion, I need to comment briefly on certain key terms belonging to the theology of the immanent Trinity, "generation," "procession," and "spiration." In the East, "procession" is used only in the specific sense of the coming forth of the Holy Spirit from the Father. The coming forth of the Son is taught to be by generation, but the "procession" of the Holy Spirit cannot be explained beyond the negative statement that it is *not* generation. It remains essentially mysterious (which is not to say that the generation of the Son is not also mysterious). In the West, "procession" is used in a generic sense to denote the coming forth of one divine person from another or from the other two. Therefore there are said to be two processions in the Trinity, that of the Son from the Father and that of the Holy Spirit "from the Father and the Son" (the Filioque). The *mode* of each procession is then specified by the use of two further words, that of the Son being said to be by way of generation (as in the East) and that of the Holy Spirit to be by way of "spiration" (being "breathed forth"). The origin of the latter concept can be traced back to the Cappadocian Fathers. St. Basil had said that the Holy Spirit proceeds from the Father "not by generation like the Son, but as Breath (*Pneuma*) of his mouth,"[74] an idea further refined by St. Gregory of Nyssa through his insight that, just as human breath accompanies human words, so God's hypostatic (personal) Word is accompanied by his hypostatic Breath, the Holy Spirit.[75] However, once the material connotation of actual breath is removed, "spiration" is seen to be just as lacking in positive meaning as "procession." The only effective difference between them is that "spiration" has an active sense, in that it is *the Father* who breathes forth (or "spirates") the Holy Spirit, while "procession" has a passive sense, in that it is *the Holy Spirit* who proceeds. In the West, St. Augustine, assisted by the analogy of the human operations of knowing and loving, came to understand the Holy Spirit as proceeding by way of divine love,[76] a view that has always been resisted in the East. We find the Cappadocian contribution enunciated above expressed by the exact word "spiration" in the statement of the Second Council of Lyons (1274): "We confess faithfully and devoutly that the Holy Spirit proceeds eternally from the Father and the Son, not as from two principles but from one, not by two spirations but by a single spiration."[77] Finally, St. Thomas Aquinas brought these two ideas, spiration and love, together in the *Summa Theologiae*, thus investing spiration with a positive meaning: "From the perspective of the subjects (*supposita*) of the spiration, the Holy Spirit proceeds from the Father and the Son in their plurality, for he proceeds from them as the love uniting the two (*ut amor unitivus duorum*)."[78] Note, however, that in this instance love does not have the same meaning as in Augustine's psychological analogy, where knowledge and love are the two operations of the human (and also the divine) spirit. Here it is an *interpersonal* reality, the proper activity of a person, uniting him or her to other persons.[79] As we shall see in the next chapter, this idea too goes back to St. Augustine.

St. Thomas, basing himself on St. Augustine, explains the difference between the two processions in terms of the difference between the intellect and the will: the first procession, that of the Son, takes place according to the divine intellect, the second, of the Holy Spirit, according to the divine will.[80] For him the distinctive feature of generation is the production of a being with "a likeness in the nature of the same species" to that which produces it, for example, a son coming from his father,[81] and he finds precisely this likeness verified in the word produced by the human intellect in the act of self-knowledge, and hence also in the divine Word produced by God in *his* act of self-knowledge, whence he concludes that the procession of the divine Word is rightly called generation and the Word himself is rightly called God's Son.[82] The procession according to the will, however, results in the production not of a likeness but "of an urge and motion towards something" (*secundum rationem impellentis et moventis in aliquid*), and so "what proceeds in God as love does not proceed as generated or as son, but rather as spirit, that is, as a vital motion and impulse, as when someone is said to be moved or impelled by love to do something,"[83] and in God this is none other than the Holy Spirit. Like the Father and the Son by nature, the Holy Spirit is unlike them as a person. Thus it is never said of him, as it is said of the Son in his humanity, that he is the "image" of the Father (Phil 2.6, Col 1.15, Heb 1.4). This is seen most clearly when the Holy Spirit is conceived as the mutual love of the Father and the Son. Though Father and Son are alike as persons, even in this respect there is an element of unlikeness, insofar, that is, as they are different persons. In their mutual love they reach out to each other in their otherness from each other, that is, in their personal unlikeness-in-likeness. Their mutual love, therefore, is their adaptation to each other precisely in their unlikeness, and if the Holy Spirit is the outcome of this love, then clearly he will be still more unlike them as a person than they are unlike each other, so much so that it would be incorrect to call his manner of production generation at all.

Theologians of the Western, Catholic tradition are generally agreed that St. Thomas's explanation is a brilliant account of the difference between the two divine processions and hence of the difference between the Son and the Holy Spirit, though Lonergan, and his exponents, claim, not entirely without reason, to have transcended the "faculty psychology" implicit in the Thomistic scheme by their own "intentionality analysis." They would therefore hold that the Thomistic theology of the Trinity as outlined above is superseded by seeing God as the paradigmatic "Being-in-Love," in which the Father is "originating love," the Son "judgment of value expressing that love," and the Holy Spirit "originated loving" (all Lonergan's terms). However, it is also claimed that St. Thomas's theology is here not abandoned, but only "transposed" "into a more phenomenologically oriented description."[84] (I shall comment later on Lonergan's view.)

St. Thomas himself, however, cautions that it is not enough to distinguish the processions simply on the basis of the difference between the intellect and the will: it is necessary also to involve the Son in some way in the procession of the Holy Spirit, for, unless the Holy Spirit proceeds from the Son as well as from the Father, "he could in no way be a distinct person from the Son."[85] As a formal statement, this is undoubtedly correct. Leaving aside for the moment the reasons St. Thomas gives for his assertion, we must recognize that such is the divine simplicity, that two divine persons said to proceed from an original divine person, where such processions constitute the relevant *facts* (as distinct from the respectively different explanations or descriptions given those processions in human terms), could not but coincide ontologically so as to become a single person (proceeding from the original person). Hence we conclude that, formally, the primary trinitarian facts should comprise not just the processions of the Son and the Holy Spirit from the Father but also the involvement of the Son (in some way) in the procession of the Holy Spirit. I recognize that I have here argued against the position that obtains in the East, that the primary trinitarian facts are the generation of the Son and the procession of the Holy Spirit, each from the Father. Lossky spoke for the East when he wrote: "These two persons (the Son and the Holy Spirit) are distinguished by the different mode of their origin: the Son is begotten, the Holy Spirit *proceeds* from the Father. This is sufficient to distinguish them."[86]

If "procession" (or "spiration" in its pre-Thomistic sense) means only not-generation, then the coming forth of the Holy Spirit is properly called "procession" (or "spiration"). But that the two processions take place according to the divine intellect (by knowledge) and the divine will (by love), respectively, is something that could be known only if revealed, and revealed it simply has not been. If my views on the Prologue of the Fourth Gospel, argued earlier, are correct, that Jesus is there called the Word of God does not provide a legitimate point of departure for such speculation, as calling a human being a "word" cannot be literal, and indeed can only be metaphorical, speech.[87] Jesus is said to be the Word of God only inasmuch as in his person he embodies divine revelation. Therefore the Thomist-Lonerganian system, to the extent that it rests on Augustine's psychological analogy, must be said to be a rather shaky edifice. Lacking proper grounding in the Bible, it should probably be characterized as philosophico-religious speculation rather than theology strictly so called.[88] At best it is an illustration of something already revealed in other ways. However, though we cannot rely on the statement that the Holy Spirit proceeds by way of the divine love, the same verdict should not be passed on the concept of the Holy Spirit as the interpersonal love of the Father and the Son, which, as I pointed out above, comes out of a completely different scheme. This thesis I undertake to expound positively from the New Testament in the next chapter. But the philosophical principle underlying it can be stated here, and quite simply. If it can properly be said that the Father and the Son are divine persons, then the bond between them can literally, and not just metaphorically, be said to be love, since love, and especially interpersonal love, is the adequate expression in act, of a person. As Peter Carnley has expressed it, "Loving . . . is not just one of a number of attributes a person may be said to possess; a person's loving is the person himself or herself, going out and giving him or herself to another."[89]

It seems that there are just three scriptural texts that relate the Holy Spirit and love in a direct way. As they are not texts that I shall be invoking in the next chapter to establish my thesis of the Holy Spirit as the mutual love of the Father and the Son, I shall attend to them briefly here. Each of them is Pauline, and each has to do with interpersonal love (as distinct from love considered simply as an operation of spirit). The first is Romans 5.5, which reads, "God's love has been poured into our hearts through the Holy Spirit that has been given to us"; the second, Romans 15.30, "I appeal to you, brothers and sisters, by our Lord Jesus Christ and by the love of the Spirit, to join me in earnest prayer to God on my behalf," where the love spoken of must be a fraternal love evoked by the Spirit rather than a love of which the Spirit is the object; and the third, Galatians 5.22, in which fraternal love is significantly listed first in the ninefold "fruit of the Spirit." Each shows the dynamic of interpersonal love at work, inasmuch as the first speaks of God's love for us and the remaining two of our love for others, inspired by his love for us. One sees the point of St. Augustine's frank admission in *De trinitate*: "Scripture has not said that the Holy Spirit is love. Had it done so, it would have done away with no small part of this inquiry."[90] However, as will become clear in the next chapter, it is the Holy Spirit as the bond of love between the Father and his Son Jesus Christ that explains both the Father's love for us (in Christ) and our consequent Christian love for each other.

I have reached a point in my presentation where an important methodological principle may be enunciated. We cannot permit any philosophy, ancient or modern, to presume to present us with trinitarian facts. Because the Trinity is a revealed doctrine, all such facts must be extrapolated by a sound methodology from the Bible, and particularly from the New Testament. Catholic and Orthodox claims that tradition stands with Scripture as a source of divine revelation cannot be allowed to weaken this statement, for, as the Second Vatican Council teaches, Scripture and tradition are not separate sources but rather constitute together a single source.[91] Hence everything in tradition must be grounded in Scripture in some way. Once trinitarian facts are acquired from Scripture through a proper process, be it simple or complex, they can then be shown to be noncontradictory—can be clarified, explained and illustrated—with the help of a sympathetic philosophy. If philosophy be allowed a greater role than the ancillary one here described, then rationalism enters the scene, and the saving doctrine of the Trinity begins to be dissolved, through theologically unanchored speculation, into a kind of psychology or cosmology. We recognize, of course, that this methodological principle has been violated many times in the history of trinitarian theology. It, essentially, is the reason for my dissatisfaction with Lonergan's trinitarian theology. Also, as we shall see in chapter 5, much contemporary Process Theology, in which the Trinity is subordinated to a fundamental cosmological vision, is likewise open to criticism. In this book I hope to avoid such pitfalls by strictly observing the discipline of the principle here enunciated.

This background briefing on some key trinitarian terms highlights the methodological problem with which we are confronted once we take the stand that all statements about the immanent Trinity must be grounded in the biblical doctrine of the Trinity. That the Son must be eternally generated by the Father passes this test with relative ease and is happily accepted on both sides, East and West. But both Western Filioquism and Eastern Monopatrism (the doctrine that the Holy Spirit proceeds "from the Father alone") appear less obviously based, and hence must engage our attention later in the book.

Conclusion

Conscious that my subject is the Christian concept of God, I shall be careful always in this book to take our point of departure from the New Testament. Whatever I have to say about the immanent Trinity must be validated from that source. Over the centuries much has been said, in both East and West, about the immanent Trinity. Some of this remains at the level of theology, about which there is both agreement and disagreement between the two traditions. Other material has attained the status of official teaching. The climax of shared teaching was reached with the doctrine of the First Council of Constantinople on the Holy Spirit.[92] Thereafter the principal development in the West was the dogmatization of the Filioque (literally: "and from the Son"), the doctrine that the Holy Spirit proceeds from the Father and the Son as from one principle and by a single spiration, at the Second Council of Lyons in 1274 and the Council of Florence in 1439.[93] In the East the main developments have been the triumph, since the time of Palamas, of Monopatrism, which was first introduced by Photius in the ninth century in reaction to Western Filioquism; and Palamas's doctrine of the distinction of the divine essence and energies, confirmed by two councils at Constantinople in 1347 and 1351, along with the conclusion drawn from this about the noncorrespondence of the economic and the immanent Trinity. There has never been a serious problem between Catholicism and Protestantism as such about the Trinity; the problem exists between the East and the West, and constitutes the key dogmatic difference between them and indeed the principal ecumenical challenge of the present day. But if the immanent Trinity provides the arena for debate and conflict (which is hardly surprising, since, as I pointed out, it is achieved at the level of understanding) it is not the ultimate goal of my endeavor; that is the economic Trinity, to which I return in an effort to systematize so far as I can the action of God in Christ on the world of men and women, which action is ordered to salvation, indeed salvation at every level, ecological, personal, and communal.

2

From the Biblical to the Immanent Trinity

The Mission-Procession Scheme of the Trinity

The New Testament has a single overall purpose, which is stated succinctly in the "first ending" of the Fourth Gospel: "[T]hese things are written so that you may come to believe that Jesus is the Christ, the Son of God, and that through believing you may have life in his name" (Jn 20.31). In other words, the New Testament is nothing other than witness to Christ, and to him as being "for us and for our salvation," to quote the Nicene Creed. This *pro nobis* ("for us") presentation of Christ has several consequences.[1] One is that the New Testament is less interested in telling us of Jesus' inner life and relationship to the Father than in presenting him objectively as our teacher in his lifetime and as our savior through his death and Resurrection. Many of the questions, therefore, that the modern age, with its interests in psychology and spirituality, wants to address to the New Testament concerning him simply cannot be answered from that source, or at best can be answered only indirectly. Often this will mean that such answers necessarily lack the rigor that is possible for answers about Christ in his objective aspect, and hence it is clear that it would be unreasonable to criticize them on that account.

Another consequence is that the New Testament will regularly present Christ as "sent" by the Father (many times in the Johannine writings, occasionally in the synoptics, once in Paul). This event is the "mission" of the Son by the Father. If Christ brings us the Kingdom of God (to use his own words), or God's salvation (to use the words of New Testament theology), he must be seen as sent by God to this end. This sending, or mission, does not necessarily imply preexistence for Jesus. As we saw in the last chapter, it is only in the Johannine writings that the New Testament penetrates to this concept, and where, therefore, the sending assumes the sense of a commissioning that takes place in another world, heaven, the home and sphere of God, for a work to be carried out in this world. But otherwise in the New Testament this sending is to be understood in the sense in which any religious person conscious of a special vocation might say that they were "sent" by God. It is a commissioning that takes place in this life and in this world, and of which the commissioned person becomes aware through their discernment of God's will.

The salvation brought by Jesus is not terminated with his death but is perpetuated as an offer to all men and women through the power and activity of the Holy Spirit in the Church. Accordingly, Luke and John, whose theologies, being late, stand as relatively sophisticated in the New Testament, see Christ as "sending" the Holy Spirit, in the power of which he acted in his life, from God upon the infant Church and its members (Lk 24.49; Acts 2.33; Jn 15.26; 16.7; 20.22). The Holy Spirit, received in the past directly from God, is now received through the active mediatorship of Christ, principal recipient of the same Spirit in his lifetime. The clearest and most explicit of these texts is the statement of Christ in John 15.26: "When the Paraclete comes . . . , whom I will send to you from the Father, he will testify on my behalf." This does not mean that the Father renounces or lessens his own role as sender, as John makes clear in John 14.26 and Paul in Galatians 4.6; nor does it mean that there are two sendings. There is just the one sending, beginning, probably, on the cross in the Johannine theology (see Jn 19.30),[2] and at Pentecost in the Lucan (see Acts 2.1–4), in which there are two coordinated senders, the Father, the ultimate source, and Christ, the mediator, of the Spirit. The event thus spoken of is the "mission" of the Holy Spirit. The coordination of the Father and the Son is best explained in sacramental terms. That is to say, the visible or at least sense-perceptible sending by Christ (so described because it takes place in a visible or perceptible act of ministry by Christ) is the sacrament of the invisible or nonperceptible sending by the Father (so described because all activity of the Father remains hidden except insofar as revealed in Christ). By "sacrament" here I mean that which reveals and communicates a divine reality, or, to use the traditional terms (which, being rather mechanical, are not entirely satisfactory), the sign that is simultaneously the cause of the divine reality signified. And I may say "cause" here because the sending of the Spirit by Christ is a free human act on his part,[3] though at a deeper level the causality operates the other way round because of the sovereignty of God over all human activity, including that of Christ.

The *pro nobis* presentation of Christ in the New Testament, then, is supported there by an appropriate presentation of the Trinity: the Father sends Christ his Son to be the Savior of the world, and after his death Christ sends the Holy Spirit from the Father to perpetuate his saving presence and work in the Church and in the world. Thus is provided the functional point of departure from which the ontological doctrine of the immanent Trinity (at least in one basic form) is extrapolated in the first four centuries of the Church. Without tracing point by point the actual historical development of this doctrine (which can be had from any good textbook on the Trinity), let me simply articulate the "immanent dialectic" of this New Testament doctrine, as I did in the last chapter in the matter of the divinity of Christ. In so doing, of course, I reject the neo-Palamite denial of a necessary correspondence of the immanent and the economic Trinity, but I do this without apology, convinced, as I said earlier, that, provided I avoid the Western pitfall of rationalism, I follow a sound, indeed the only possible, methodology.

The ontological doctrine of the Trinity is intimately related to the ontological doctrine of the divinity of Christ. Once our "immanent dialectic" has brought us to the point of realizing that a functional divinity of Christ implies a metaphysical Incarnation of the preexistent divine Son, we see that, as this person in his human life depended in every dimension of his being, ontological, psychological, and spiritual, on the Father by whom he was sent, so in the sphere of the Godhead itself he likewise depends on the same Father in his very being. In this sphere, where there is no time but only the eternity of God, there can be no temporal succession, but there can still exist a real (and not just a logical) order, and therefore the dependence associated with the mission necessarily implies in the Godhead the order (or taxis) Father—Son and an eternal "generation" of the Son by the Father, also called, in the West, from the perspective of the Son, his "procession" from the Father. As regards the Holy Spirit, the functional dialectic of identity and difference between him and, respectively, the Father and the Son in the New Testament grounds a similar, ontological dialectic in the immanent Trinity, from which necessarily emerge his ontological divinity, his distinct personhood, and his procession from the Father, as well as the extension of the *taxis* to become Father—Son—Holy Spirit.

The question of what part, if any, is played by the Son in the procession of the Holy Spirit, the most contentious outstanding issue between East and West, cannot be settled so quickly. St. Thomas's *formal* requirement, discussed in the last chapter, that the Holy Spirit proceed from the Father and the Son (in order to be distinct from the Son), itself needs to be grounded in Scripture before it can be accepted. It might be thought that from the fact that Christ sends the Spirit as his own the Filioque can be immediately inferred, but another possibility that would have to be considered is that, having received the Spirit from the Father, Christ has also received the *authority* (and nothing more) to send this Spirit in turn upon the Church. After all, every one of the four gospels stresses the unique authority of Christ. This could be enough in itself to justify calling the Holy Spirit the Spirit of Christ, as well as the Spirit of God. In fact, the Eastern position must be something like this. I defer discussion of it for the present, hoping to shed some new light on it through material to be introduced later.

The Return Scheme of the Trinity

The limited outcome we have achieved with our "immanent dialectic" had as its point of departure the New Testament presentation of Christ as pro nobis. But in addition to this, and completing it, the New Testament has a further, though from the pro nobis perspective secondary, concern, the return of Christ, and of us with him, to the Father, in the power of the Holy Spirit. From a different point of view this concern appears no longer as secondary, but as primary: Christ came forth from the Father only to return to him with us, in the Spirit of the Father. Indeed, as one commentator pointed out, this could be the underlying scheme of the Fourth Gospel with its identification of Jesus with the Word of God, and he pointed to Isaiah 55.10–11 as the likely Old Testament inspiration of this approach: "[A]s the rain and the snow come down from heaven, and do not return there until they have watered the earth, making it bring forth and sprout, giving seed to the sower and bread to the eater, so shall my word be that goes out from my mouth; it shall not return to me empty, but it shall accomplish that which I purpose, and succeed in the thing for which I sent it."[4]

This scheme is seen to be fleshed out in the Gospel by the Incarnation, life, redemptive death, Resurrection, and Ascension of Jesus, Word of God and Son of Man. Paul and John, particularly Paul, see the Spirit, Spirit of Christ, as uniting us with Christ by faith, thereby giving us a share in his divine Sonship and thus in his fellowship with God. In the words of Robert Koch, the effects of the Pauline new creation and the Johannine rebirth in the Spirit are to be identified as "above all, sonship of God [we would add 'daughterhood' as well], the victorious act of faith, burning love for the brethren and the bearing of inspired witness," to which should be prefixed one further effect, the forgiveness of sins.[5]

It is certainly appropriate to speak of our "return" to God. Not only did we come out from God by creation, but we have departed from him by sin, communal and personal. Therefore the work of God's grace, reclaiming us through his Spirit, is to bring about our return to him in our personal and communal history through the overcoming of our alienation from him and the achievement of our fulfillment in him. In this process we note an inversion of the traditional taxis, to which witness is borne in Ephesians 2.18: "[T]hrough him [Christ] both of us [Jews and Gentiles] have access in one Spirit to the Father." The Holy Spirit unites us to Christ and thus to the Father, and so the taxis becomes Holy Spirit—Son—Father. If there were no other operative considerations, we might be tempted to accept Matthias Scheeben's image of a "conductor" (presumably a lightning conductor) to explain this.[6] The idea would be that, just as this kind of conductor is extended from base to tip and electricity flows from the tip back to the base, so God's outreach to us through Christ and the Spirit (taxis: Father—Son—Holy Spirit) makes contact with us through the Spirit and leads us back through Christ to the Father (taxis: Holy Spirit—Son—Father). This image appears to justify our making a simple inversion of the traditional taxis and leaving it at that.

That there are other considerations, however, becomes apparent in the case of Christ. First, there arises the propriety of speaking of a "return" of Christ to the Father, given that he was without sin and so never departed from him in that sense. Admittedly, in this precise sense there can be no question of a return. But John's gospel, modeled as it probably is on Isaiah 55.10–11, has Jesus speak on several occasions in equivalent terms of a return to the Father. The clearest is John 16.28: "I came from the Father and have come into the world; again, I am leaving the world and am going to the Father." Further, the Ascension of Jesus in this gospel is to be understood as a return, as is clear from John 6.62 and 20.17. The achievement of his destiny in the world is in one sense a "return" to the Father by the Son, who in other senses never left him. But second, in the case of Christ the traditional taxis seems to break down altogether, for the synoptic tradition (as distinct from the Johannine) sees the Holy Spirit bestowed directly on Jesus by the Father in an act that brings him (or his humanity, as we must say in the light of later knowledge) into existence as the unique ("beloved") Son of God. Here the taxis is Father—Holy Spirit—Son. There is no way in which this can be explained in terms of an inversion of the traditional taxis. This leads us to question whether in the case of our own return to God we would be correct in following Scheeben by simply inverting the normal taxis. This important element of synoptic theology along with its systematic implications I now present, in two parts.[7]

In the synoptic theology the unique divine Sonship of Jesus is brought about by the bestowal of the Holy Spirit on him by the Father. This is the burden of Mark's account of the baptism of Jesus (Mk 1.9–11). The charge (hardly fair under the circumstances) of Adoptionism that might be leveled against Mark here is precluded by Matthew and Luke, who present this bestowal of the Spirit of Sonship as the founding event of Jesus' life: the act in which God bestows the Spirit is the very act by which he brings Jesus into existence (cf. Mt 1.18–25 and Lk 1.26–38). Modern Christology, like, for example, that of Rahner, takes its cue from biblical Christology and sees Christ's divinity not as something separate or even distinct from his humanity but as its supreme actualization under grace (see note 3 of this chapter). I should simply add that the grace in question, the actualizing power, is the bestowal of the Holy Spirit here spoken of. The uniqueness of Jesus' Sonship is evident in the utter radicality of this bestowal of the Holy Spirit, to which witness is borne also by John in John 3.34 (on the most probable interpretation). The New Testament, especially in Paul and John, speaks of the granting of the Holy Spirit to ordinary believers, but only as a rebirth, on the basis of faith and conversion, and as an *adoption* to divine sonship and daughterhood, all points of sharp contrast with Jesus though contained within the common attribute of sonship/daughterhood. The special Sonship of Jesus comes to expression both negatively and positively, negatively in his absolute sinlessness, and positively in his unswerving fidelity and obedience to the Father throughout life and especially in his death, through which he is appointed Leader and Savior (see Acts 5.31). Here the Sonship treatment resumes the Old Testament theme of the Suffering Servant of God of Isaiah 42.1 to which allusion is made in the baptism accounts as also in the parable of the wicked tenants (Mk 12.1–9 pars.). The servant too is equipped with the Spirit to live his life in dedicated obedience to God. But what distinguishes the Son from the servant is that, while both are loved by God and both serve him in love and obedience, the Son is more loved by God than is the servant, and, whereas the servant serves God in loving obedience, the Son serves him in obedient love.

In this theology the Holy Spirit emerges as the bond of love between the Father and Jesus. The Spirit is the love of the Father for Jesus, poured out on him in a radical and unique way and experienced as such on the part of Jesus. The Spirit, through the answering love it evoked from him, enabled him to live his whole life in dedicated obedience to the Father's will. All this comes to expression in Jesus' consciousness in the manner of his address of God in prayer, *Abba*, "My Father." Here we see at once a sense of unique intimacy and love, but also the supreme authority to which total and lifelong submission is due. Where previously the Spirit has been seen only as God's power, as in the creation, and as his inspiration, as in the prophets (which is really only a higher, i.e., personal, form of power or empowerment), now in the case of Jesus it is revealed as his love. On reflection we see that there is nothing surprising in this identification of the Spirit with God's love, understood, of course, only as interpersonal love, and not, as in the later Western psychological analogy, as the second of the two operations of spiritual being as such. Is not this love just the supreme *personal* expression of the same divine reality which in its lower manifestations is grasped as creative or empowering? (Indeed, this is true not just of divine love but of all love.) If this reality stands *fully* revealed in Jesus, what else can it be but love? And it will at the same time contain the lower manifestations within itself; that is, it will also be creative and empowering.

In the second part of the argument I range beyond the synoptic tradition which has occupied us hitherto. This part has three steps. The first is that, as I have had occasion to mention before, in Paul and John the Spirit becomes the medium through which Christ remains present in the Christian community after his Resurrection. Further, in Luke and John, though not in Paul,[8] Christ along with the Father becomes the sender of the Spirit. Thus, in the theology of John, corroborated in different aspects by Paul and Luke, Christ sends to believers the Spirit by which he remains present and active in their midst. In giving them the Spirit, he gives them his very self. He gives them himself in the Spirit. In this fact stands revealed the utter radicality of Jesus' original appropriation of the Spirit. The synoptic theology presented above told us of the radicality of the Father's bestowal of the Spirit on Jesus, and only hinted at a corresponding radicality on the part of Jesus in receiving the Spirit, but this theology tells us explicitly of this second radicality: the Father makes the Spirit Jesus' very own. And Jesus develops this appropriation through the course of his life by his love and obedience, so that it reaches its climax in his death. I said that we would have to consider, at least as a possibility, that Jesus, having received the Holy Spirit from the Father, receives the authority, and nothing more, to send the Spirit upon the Church. In this hypothesis the Spirit remains external to Jesus, joined to him by only a legal bond. However, the Johannine theology just presented reveals the inadequacy of this hypothesis, for, far from having the Spirit external to Jesus, it has the Spirit enter into his very constitution. So intrinsic does the Spirit become to Jesus that in handing it on he hands on his own self.

The second step (which I intimated in the last chapter) is to recognize that the gift of oneself is exactly what is meant by love, even if the word itself is not used. If Christ gives himself to us in the Spirit, then the Spirit has become Christ's love for us. Just as the Spirit as given by the Father to Jesus was the Father's love for him, so the Spirit given us by Christ is Christ's love for us. In the sacramental structure of the twofold (but one) giving of the Spirit, of which we spoke earlier, the visible gift of love by Christ becomes the sacrament of the invisible gift of love by the Father, in which he loves us in Christ. This is the proximate ground for my statement in the last chapter that for us the content of the experience of the Holy Spirit is either the Father or Christ, or, more properly, simply Christ, and hence that the Spirit despite being a distinct person does not have a distinct personality. But to continue, Christ's love of us, being, as I said earlier, a human, or more properly, "theandric," love, must be recognized as correctly designated as his "love of neighbor." And to Karl Rahner we owe the insight that love of neighbor and love of God are not different loves however closely united, but two distinct but inseparable dimensions of a single love.[9] Rahner establishes this as a thesis of his own transcendental theology, but points out that Scripture already has this insight, though it lacks the theological sophistication (nor in any case is it its business) to present it systematically. In justification of this claim he indicates not just the factual linking of the two loves in Scripture, in Mark and First John, but also the following specific arguments: first,

Matthew and Luke see the combination of the two loves as the fulfillment of the Old Testament revelation, which suggests at least an intrinsic relationship between them; second, Paul and Matthew agree that love of neighbor is the fulfillment of the Law and the sole criterion of divine judgment, which suggests that this love must involve also the love of God; and third, the statement of Jesus in Matthew 25.40 that a kindness to the least of his brethren is in fact done to himself requires that Jesus be seen as the embodiment of God's Reign and so implies that in him God and neighbor are inseparably the objects of our love.[10] While a professional exegete could probably have argued this case better than Rahner has done, he has at least accomplished enough to substantiate his claim. And this justifies our concluding in the matter of Jesus' love that, if his love of neighbor is the Holy Spirit sent by him upon the Church, his love of God must be the same Holy Spirit returned by him to the Father. The sacramental structure of the giving of the Spirit is explained by the fact that the Spirit whom Jesus sends upon us is the same as the Spirit returned by him to the Father, his contribution to the mutual relationship of love between the Father and himself. Thus our relationship to Jesus in the Spirit draws us into his relationship to the Father in the Spirit, a relationship of sonship (or daughterhood), and we become sons and daughters in the Son.

In bringing this step to conclusion, I emphasize the human character of the love of Jesus in each of these instances, his love of God and his love of neighbor. As was pointed out in note 3 of this chapter, this is not to say that this activity of Jesus is *purely* human. If the divinity of Christ is the supreme actualization of his humanity by grace, as in the Christology of Rahner, then the operation of the "God-man" is "theandric," that is, divine-human, or better, human-divine, which means that it is at base human. And if the two loves in Jesus are each to be identified with the Holy Spirit, then fundamentally by the word "love" here we cannot mean either his particular acts of love or the underlying virtue of charity in him, both of which he had in common with all graced men and women (even if to a greater degree), but a reality deeper still and unique to himself, and in his case the source of both his charity and his particular acts. This reality is the Holy Spirit precisely as appropriated by him, "humanized" in its radical reception by him. This appropriation I have not hesitated to call an "incarnation" of the Holy Spirit,[11] though the meaning of the word here is only analogous to that which it bears in the Incarnation properly so called. The matter might be accurately and succinctly expressed thus: in a way analogous to the Incarnation of divine being in human being in the person of Jesus, there is an incarnation of divine love in human love in the love of Jesus, this latter incarnation being the Holy Spirit.

Thus we are brought to the third step. If the conclusion that Jesus' love of the Father is the Holy Spirit as appropriated by him and returned to the Father seems somewhat doctrinaire, this impression should be removed once it is seen to be supported by at least two key texts of Scripture. The first is John 19.30, which reads, "When Jesus had received the vinegar, he said, 'It is finished,' and he bowed his head and delivered up the spirit" (RSV). It is generally recognized in the interpretation of John, as distinct from other more literal writers, that sometimes his statements are meant to be taken at two levels, one physical, the other spiritual. Such is the case here. At the physical level the latter part of this text means simply that Jesus died.

But the evangelist's choice of the unusual word *paredoken* ("delivered up," "handed over"), used in the Septuagint to express the death of the Suffering Servant in Isaiah 53.12, alerts us to the presence of a higher meaning. However, the differences between the two texts are significant. Where John says, "He delivered up the spirit," the Greek text of Isaiah has, "His soul was delivered up to death." Isaiah has the passive voice, emphasizing the inevitability of the servant's fate, while John has the active voice, which indicates the freedom of Jesus; Isaiah has "soul" (*psyche*), referring to natural life, where John has "spirit" (*pneuma*), which indicates life lived before God; and, most notably, Isaiah has the soul delivered up to death, where implicitly, and in line with Luke 23.46 ("Father, into your hands I commit my spirit" [RSV]), John has the spirit delivered up to God. In John, Jesus' embracing of his death is but the climax of the life of the Servant become Son, a life lived and ended in obedience to, and love of, God. However, the use of *paredoken* here suggests a further higher meaning, which is corroborated by John 19.34–35 in conjunction with John 7.38–39 and 1 John 5.6–8. This is that his death is the occasion on which Jesus sends the Holy Spirit on the Church in the persons of its representatives, his mother and the beloved disciple. This is the view also of Raymond Brown, though his labeling of this bestowal of the Spirit as "proleptic" (while that in John 20.22 is called "actual") does not seem correct.[12] Rather it seems that the bestowal of John 19.30 is fully actual, and that John 20.22 represents only the complete revelation of what is presented as an unadorned fact in the earlier text.

The second text is Hebrews 9.13–14: "For if the sprinkling of defiled persons with the blood of goats and bulls and with the ashes of a heifer sanctifies for the purification of the flesh, how much more shall the blood of Christ, who through eternal Spirit offered himself without blemish to God, purify your conscience from dead works to serve the living God" (RSV). Of the various alternatives, the best seems to be the interpretation of F. F. Bruce, according to which the writer's approach here is shaped by the figure of the Spirit-equipped Suffering Servant who "accomplishes every phase of his ministry, including the crowning phase in which he accepts death for the transgression of his people, filling the twofold role of priest and victim."[13] We conclude that this text shows how the obedience and love of Christ for the Father reached its perfection in his voluntary self-offering on the cross, and that this act, which gathered up and reexpressed the obedience and love that characterized his whole life, was performed in the power of the Holy Spirit conferred on him by God.

With these texts we have pinpointed Jesus' death as the moment at which he begins to pour out the Holy Spirit on the Church, and also seen that in his death he definitively gives himself over to the Father in love in the power of the same Spirit. We have already established the identity of love of God and love of neighbor, and seen that for Jesus the latter is identical with his gift of the Holy Spirit to the Church. We can now draw our final conclusion: just as Jesus does not simply give himself to the Church in the power of the Spirit (which anyone could do), but does this with a unique radicality expressive of his unique Sonship by giving the Spirit itself, so he does not just give himself over in love to God in the power of the Spirit (which is as far as the texts examined above take us), but likewise does this with unique radicality precisely by returning the Holy Spirit to the Father. The puzzling character of this last statement is overcome when it is realized that it alone is equal to the task of expressing the unsurpassable radicality of Jesus' self-gift to the Father in love in the power of the Holy Spirit. Thus we have the following structure: the Father bestows the Holy Spirit on Jesus as his love for him in a uniquely radical way in which Jesus is brought into human existence as his beloved Son. Jesus further appropriates this unique Gift of the Spirit and the divine Sonship which it brings about, in the course of his life through his unfailing obedience and answering love of the Father, and in his death definitively returns to the Father in love by returning the Holy Spirit to him (though not thereby losing it himself). From this truly biblical theology the Holy Spirit emerges as the mutual love of the Father and Jesus Christ, his Son, even though, as Augustine pointed out, nowhere does Scripture actually call the Spirit love. And here, for the biblical and hence also the immanent Trinity, we see the ultimate ground for my statement that the Holy Spirit, though a distinct person, does not have a personality distinct from the Father or the Son. In his very propriety as a person he is, from one of the two possible points of view, the medium of the Father's self-communication to the Son, and from the other, the medium of the Son's self-communication to the Father.

I conclude the whole argument with two brief comments. First, Jesus' answering love of the Father is the "missing link" between the Father's love of him and Jesus' own love of the Church (each one of which is in its own way the Holy Spirit). The standard way of speaking of this situation is to see it as a "chain of love," in which Christ's love of the Church is simply the continuation and revelation of the Father's love of him. Rather than simply reject this view, I point to its inadequacy in the light of the theology here presented. The Father's love of Jesus evokes from him in the first place an answering love of the Father. Christ's love of the Church is then seen as his love of neighbor (or as his love of his "bride," to invoke the image of Ephesians 5.25–26), which is the opposite side of the coin of his love of God. This view takes the humanity of Christ more seriously than does the alternative, in which it merely serves passively as a channel for the communication of God's love to the Church. And secondly, while the Holy Spirit is a bond between even ordinary Christians and the Father, it is in a much more radical sense a bond between Christ and the Father. The union between Christians and God is explained fully by their reception of the Holy Spirit from him and their consequent empowerment to love him, but Christ in receiving the Spirit from the Father appropriates it, and so returns it to the Father as his own Spirit, his personal love of the Father.

This argument enables us to see that the process of return to God is not just the simple inversion of the process of mission. The actual complexity of this process, which comes to light in the argument, is in fact masked by the simplicity of the order of its revelation with the taxis Father—Son—Holy Spirit. This taxis is taken from the epistemological order where it belongs, and simply applied, in inverted form, to the ontological order, to which it cannot do justice. Looking back from the vantage point of the Resurrection, the order of revelation identifies the earthly life of Jesus as the mission of the Son (or at least as its beginning) and sees the mission of the Holy Spirit (only recognized as "appropriated," that is, not proper to the Spirit, in the general Western Catholic tradition, which has remained unchallenged on this point until very recently) as starting only on the cross (following John) or at the

Resurrection (according to Paul) or at Pentecost (according to Luke). But in Western Catholic theology the possibility that the mission of the Holy Spirit be proper was opened up by Rahner's theology of the self-communication of God with its attendant category of quasi-formal causality. As long as God's work in men and women was understood just in terms of efficient causality, it had to be work *ad extra* ("to the outside") and hence common to all three divine persons, but because formal causality is assimilative, it draws the creature into the inner life of the Trinity through union by a special title either with the Son (in the case of the Incarnation) or with the Holy Spirit (in grace, the case of ordinary believers). More exactly, in each case the union is with *both* the Son and the Holy Spirit, though the special title remains: in the case of the Incarnation there is an utterly radical bestowal of the Holy Spirit, so radical that it summons the sacred humanity into existence ex nihilo ("from nothing") and brings about *unity* with the Son; in the case of grace the bestowal, being not so radical, effects simply a *re*-creation (in grace) and *union* with the Son. With this clarification, we can take Scripture and the Fathers on the Holy Spirit at their face value and understand his mission as proper.[14] My study has shown that the mission of the Holy Spirit began already with that of the Son, at his conception; that the mission of the Son was only partially and progressively revealed during his lifetime; and that what happened on the cross (or at the Resurrection, or at Pentecost) was that this mission was rendered fully revealed and effective, that is, that the Son was constituted "the universal sacrament of salvation" (to apply to him to whom it most properly belongs the expression which Vatican II used of the Church).[15]

The mission of the Holy Spirit does not follow that of the Son in temporal succession; the two missions are never separate from each other but stand in a relationship of mutual causation from their common inception, which is the beginning of Jesus' life. The Father bestows the Holy Spirit as Spirit of Sonship on Jesus in the creative act that initiated his human life. Thus begin, together, the missions of the Son and the Holy Spirit, though as yet they are not revealed, but hidden. As the humanity of the Son begins to develop, it begins to acquire its revelatory character, but in permanent dependence on the Holy Spirit who sustains it. At the same time Jesus begins to send the Holy Spirit himself, though in a limited and partial way, as he begins his work of establishing the Reign of God, upon which men and women enter through faith in him, a faith enabled by the Holy Spirit, now his own, who goes out of him in his words and deeds of ministry. With the death of Jesus his humanity stands, at the end of its history, fully realized, transparent in its universal efficacy. There is now no impediment to his pouring out the Spirit, *his* Spirit, fully on the Church and the world. This view of the distinct missions of the Son and the Holy Spirit and of their mutual relationship is to be distinguished from both the prevailing Catholic theology, in which a proper mission of the Holy Spirit is not acknowledged at all, and from the general Orthodox theology, in which the two missions are understood as successive, that is, that of the Son is seen to be terminated with the death of Christ and replaced with that of the Holy Spirit.[16]

Those in the Church, and those outside who are drawn to it, are confronted by the person of Christ living in its ministry. To them is offered the Holy Spirit as Spirit of Christ in visible acts of ministry (both ordained and lay) deriving from, and stamped by, his humanity, his personality. As they respond in faith, they begin to receive this Spirit as Spirit of Christ, the Spirit who draws them into union with him. But as I said before, the Spirit acting visibly as Spirit of Christ is the sacrament of the same Spirit acting invisibly as Spirit of God. Through the action of the Spirit as Spirit of Christ they are drawn into the ambit of the action of the same Spirit as Spirit of God, the Spirit of Sonship, the Spirit of the Father, the ultimate dynamism of whose action is to make Jesus the beloved and only-begotten Son of God, and thus they are *re*born, *re*-created in *this* Spirit, as sons and daughters of God the Father, sons and daughters "in the Son," Jesus Christ. As far as their relation to the Father is concerned, the process is essentially the same as for Christ, except that it lacks the radicality present in his case. The taxis of their union with God is Holy Spirit—Son—Father, but only because in their case (as distinct from that of Christ) the Spirit is mediated to them by the Son, not because the actual process of their return requires what appears as just a simple inversion of the traditional taxis. At the same time we see without difficulty why the taxis in the case of Christ himself is Father—Holy Spirit—Son. Scheeben's image of the lightning conductor is thus shown up as at best a rather misleading oversimplification.

The Two Schemes Compared

It is clear from all this that the New Testament offers not just one, but two models of the Trinity. Let us now consider each of them briefly. The first is one that has always been accepted, and which exhibits the taxis Father—Son—Holy Spirit. So far as the biblical Trinity is concerned, we may call it "the model of mission" or "the mission model," as it is structured according to the missions of the Son and the Holy Spirit from the Father.[17] Transposed to the sphere of the immanent Trinity, it becomes what is appropriately called "the model of procession" or "the procession model," because there mission necessarily gives way to procession. The procession model is common to both East and West, though there is an important difference between them in regard to its more precise formulation, as the West affirms, while the East denies, that the procession of the Holy Spirit is mediated by the Son. Its distinguishing feature is that it describes the outward movement of the Son and the Holy Spirit from the Father. In calling it a "model" we relativize it, that is to say, present it as only *a* way, rather than *the* way, of conceiving the Trinity. This will come as a surprise to many, as this conceptual mode has traditionally been absolutized, with the only variations admitted (and even then only de facto, and not de jure) being the Filioquism of the West and the Monopatrism of the East. For the economic Trinity, it reverts to its original name, "mission model."

In conclusion, I identify two problems that result from the wrongful absolutization of the procession model. The first, as we have seen, is that it was assumed that, in order to integrate biblical data relating to the return of Christ and believers to the Father with the doctrine of the Trinity, one simply inverts the taxis of the procession model. Because this is wrong methodology, it leads to factual errors. And the second problem is that no role was recognized for the Holy Spirit in the bringing about of the Incarnation. Any involvement of the Holy Spirit in this mystery was seen only as subsequent to it and hence as secondary and derivative. This has led to all sorts of impoverishments and errors, most notably to a downgrading of the Holy Spirit, not only in the West as is commonly noted, but in the East as well.

The second model has been known since the time of St. Augustine but only now is being presented as what it is, an alternative model of the Trinity.[18] At the biblical level (at least) its *taxis* is Father, Holy Spirit, Son, or, to state this fully, Father—Holy Spirit—Son—Holy Spirit—Father. This is the Augustinian "mutual love theory," according to which the Holy Spirit is the mutual love of the Father and the Son. At one time I called it "the bestowal model," because it had to do with the bestowal of the Holy Spirit by the Father and the Son on each other. Later, however, I dropped this name, not because it is incorrect, but because "bestowal" does not express any contrast to, or distinction from, the mission or procession model. Accordingly, I began calling it "the model of return" or "the return model," as it was concerned with the return of the Son and the Holy Spirit to the Father, or, more precisely, the return of the Son in the Holy Spirit to the Father. This is certainly a fitting name. But it is possible to consider a return no longer as a movement, but either as a moment along the way, for example, the union of Jesus with the Father at some given point in his life, or as the return fully accomplished, that is, in its eschatological completion. The name "return model" applies also to the immanent Trinity, but at this level too it is appropriate to consider the persons no longer as in a process of movement but as in a state of equilibrium (which would, of course, be a dynamic rather than a static equilibrium). In other words, this model can focus on the relations of the three persons as grounding their union with each other, where the procession model can concentrate on the same relations as grounding their mutual distinction. At all three levels, therefore, it seems appropriate to call the second model also "the model of union" or "the union model" in distinction from the procession model, which from this point of view can be known as "the model of distinction" or "the distinction model."

Comparing the two models, we see that the first covers only the outward movement of the Son and the Holy Spirit from the Father, whereas the second, dealing with their return to the Father, presupposes the outward movement from him. The first is therefore partial, while the second is comprehensive. Another contrast emerges from the distinction between "descending" and "ascending" theology. This distinction is a generalization of that which exists between descending and ascending Christology, Christology "from above" and Christology "from below."[19] The former is that which takes its point of departure from the heavenly sphere and moves thence to the world of men and women, the general Christology of the Fourth Gospel being the prime instance; the latter is that in which Jesus is apprehended as the man whose message and actions and ultimately whose Resurrection lead the well-disposed to discern his unique union with God, and in which, therefore, minds and hearts are raised from this world to the sphere of God. Examples would be, in general, the Christology of the synoptics, and in particular the very early Christology found in parts of Acts. This distinction can then be applied to other areas of theology to characterize the orientation of a particular methodology, whether from heaven to earth or from earth to heaven. Because the procession model of the Trinity describes the outward or downward movement from the Father to the Son and the Holy Spirit, the two divine persons who first come into contact with the world of men and women, the theological data capable of integration with it are those of the descending type; and, conversely, because the return model has to do with the return of the Son and the Holy Spirit to the transcendent Father from whom they originally came, it is with it that ascending data must be harmonized. Egregious errors are made when ascending data, with which theology is increasingly concerning itself, are forced into some kind of integration with the procession model, the only one hitherto recognized.

Because in the immanent Trinity the procession model deals with the unfolding of unity into diversity, it is the one more congenial to Western preoccupations. Conversely, because the return model, as model of union, has to do with the relations of the three divine persons among themselves, it corresponds better to Eastern emphases, even if in fact it is hardly accepted or even known in the East. In any case, because this model is more comprehensive, theologies of the Trinity that ignore it, as, for example, do Lonergan's and even Rahner's, will be judged ultimately inadequate, and, from the ecumenical point of view, unhelpful. A balanced theology of the Trinity, one that aims to be ecumenically constructive, must encompass *all* the biblical evidence and hence must employ both models according to the varying demands of the biblical data, as was intimated in the last chapter.

3

Models of the Immanent Trinity

My reflections thus far have resulted in two biblical models of the Trinity, which I have called the mission model and the return model. These in turn have led us to two corresponding models of the immanent Trinity, the procession or distinction model and the return or union model. In this chapter I reflect further on these models of the immanent Trinity in the hope that by continued comparison and contrast I shall be able in some measure to clarify certain issues that in the past have proved difficult and controversial. While doing this I bear in mind that, while the exercise is in a sense an end in itself, it does have a further and arguably more important end, namely, to enable us to return to the biblical data to appropriate them in a new way, a way that will be ontological rather than merely functional, and reflective rather than simplistic or fundamentalist. In what follows, for the sake of convenience certain words will be used that of themselves indicate a time sequence, for example, "then," "next," and so on. In every case, as so often elsewhere in this book, it will be a sequence of logical order, not of time, that is meant.

The procession model, dealing as it does with the outward movement of God to the world and therefore with his first contact with it in his self-revelation as triune (granted that before being revealed as triune he already stood revealed as having created the world and as being at work within it), necessarily presents a view of the Trinity as it were *ab extra*, "from the outside." This has an undeniable status as a revelation of the Trinity, but it is the very first revelation of it. While indispensable, it pales alongside the possibility of a further revelation, which we immediately affirm also as a fact, the revelation of the Trinity *ab intra*, "from the inside." This is where the return model begins to apply, for its work is precisely to chart the process by which, having first been contacted by God ab extra in the encounter of initial trinitarian revelation, we are led back, through our response, into God's innermost being, that is, by the Holy Spirit, through the Son, to the Father. As soon as we begin by faith to respond to this contact from outside we are drawn across the invisible line that divides outside from inside and we begin to live, by participation (not by nature), by the inner trinitarian life of God. From the inside much more can be seen and understood than ever was possible from the outside, not that the outside view was wrong or misleading in itself. It is merely inadequate by comparison. These remarks set the stage for much of what follows in this chapter. We shall see that certain statements made about the Trinity require to be situated against the background of the procession model, and therefore, though correct and even necessary, can never be the last word on the subject. Against the background of the return model another, more profound, and reconciling or at least balancing, view will emerge.

The Procession Model

Following as it does the order of revelation, the procession model logically takes as its starting point the unity of God taught in the Old Testament. This unity is then seen to unfold into diversity, however this unfolding be explained. This perspective is maintained also in the East, where, however, the original unity is not simply that of God, as in the West, but that of the Father, principle or cause of the other two persons. A problem that Western Catholic theology encounters at this point is that Augustine's psychological analogy, to which it generally adheres, has difficulty in maintaining the status of the Word and the Spirit precisely as persons, not inferior but equal to the Father in all things. They appear to be only expressions or products of an original and single divine mind, to which alone the status of person rightly belongs. The trinitarian theology of Lonergan is not immune to this criticism either, as all that he has done, as I noted that Anthony Kelly admitted, has been to transpose the psychological analogy into more modern categories. Such a theology could not expect to make much headway in the East. An even more fundamental problem, as I mentioned earlier, is that it can no longer claim the biblical foundation formerly proposed for it. Hence William Hill's contention that Rahner's "failure to appeal to the psychological analogy" is necessarily an "impoverishment" of his trinitarian thought should not be conceded.[1] In the first place, Rahner does not always fail to appeal to it (we shall see him appealing to it later in this chapter); but, second, to the extent that he does so fail, his "failure" could well be the opposite of an impoverishment. Of course the same objection could be raised against Gregory of Nyssa's image, already considered, of the Son as the Father's Word and the Spirit as the Breath accompanying that Word.

If the procession model starts with the unity of God, it ends with the distinction of the persons (and hence the alternative name I have given it, "distinction model"). Now as Mary Ann Fatula has shown, in the Western tradition, typified by Augustine, Anselm, and Aquinas, the dogmatic intent of the Filioque is the hypostatic distinction of the Holy Spirit.[2] From this we conclude that the Filioque belongs to the procession model, that is, it makes sense primarily against the background of this model. In any case it is obvious that historically the Filioque emerged from this model. Of course the East also employed the procession model, without arriving at the Filioque. Why was this so? Because, it seems, in starting with the unity of the Father instead of the unity of God, Eastern theology introduced a certain confusion into the model at the outset. Methodologically, the distinction of persons is its end point, not its starting point. It follows from this that in the economic Trinity it is not the Father who is to be equated with Yahweh of the Old Testament. Rather, it is *God* who is to be thus equated, God who differentiates out into Father, Son, and Holy Spirit, and this despite the fact that in the New Testament the word "God" nearly always refers to the Father.[3] In preempting the natural operation of the model as they did, Eastern theologians made it impossible for a valid midway position such as the Filioque to be reached. It is only a midway position, for, while the distinction of Father and Son has emerged clearly in the consideration of the first procession, it has become blurred again in the consideration of the second. But the situation could not have been otherwise. For the sake of the hypostatic distinction of the Holy Spirit, which, with that of the other two persons, is what this model is ultimately concerned with, the unity of his principle must be clearly stated; and if that unity resided purely in the Father, the Holy Spirit would not be distinct from the Son. Also, if the unity of principle of the Holy Spirit resided purely in the Father, the latter would have to have some additional name, as "Father," expressing only his relationship to the Son, would not be a sufficiently defining expression of his personal character or person-hood. It is only if Father and Son be not distinguished in regard to the production of the Holy Spirit that their traditional names would sufficiently define their respec-tive persons. By the same reasoning we see the need for a completely different term, which de facto and de jure was "spirator," to express their common character of constituting the aforesaid principle. I have already demonstrated the biblical ground for the assertion that the Son, as well as the Father, is the source of the Holy Spirit.

One way of expressing the truth I am here striving to articulate is to say that the Holy Spirit proceeds from the Father "through" the Son, and this is a way that has been found acceptable in both East and West. But it is not precise enough. It immediately invites the question: What does "through" mean here? Does it have a passive or an active sense? If the latter (as its biblical ground suggests), the Father and the Son together must constitute a single principle of the Holy Spirit, since in the immanent Trinity, in this particular circumstance, they can no longer be distin-guished, as, thanks to the humanity of the Son, they can be in the biblical and the economic Trinity.[4]

As I shall go on to show, the relationship of the Holy Spirit to the Father and the Son can be clarified further, but this can be done only with the help of the return model, not with the procession model and therefore not in regard to the Spirit's hypostatic distinction. In this latter respect, despite Augustine's famous rider that "ultimately" (*principaliter*) the Holy Spirit proceeds from the Father,[5] the Filioque, finally unsatisfactory though it be, is the best that can be done. With it we have come up against the limits of the only trinitarian model whose direct business is the hypostatic distinction of the persons.

The Return Model

Changing over to the return model, we find a quite different picture of the relation-ship of the Holy Spirit to the Father and the Son. In summary, the biblical theology is as follows: the Father bestows the Holy Spirit ad extra ("to the outside") as his love in a radical act that brings Jesus into being as the Son of God in humanity; Jesus in response returns the Holy Spirit as his own love of and to the Father; the Holy Spirit is the mutual love of the Father and Jesus his Son. An apparent problem arises at the level of the immanent Trinity, where also the Holy Spirit is the mutual love of the Father and the Son, or at least its "objectivization," as John Cowburn correctly reminds us.[6] Here it must be said that the Son proceeds from the Father without any participation of the Holy Spirit, and that then, not in temporal order but in the logical order required by the traditional taxis, the Father bestows the Holy Spirit, as his love, on the Son. The problem is the apparent contradiction of taxeis between the biblical and the immanent Trinity: in the former the Father bestows the Holy Spirit in a creative act that brings Jesus into being as the Son of God, while in the latter the Father generates the Son on whom he then bestows the Holy Spirit. The problem is solved when we see that, when in the immanent Trinity the Father by the most radical possible act bestows his love ad extra, this brings into existence a human being who by the very same act is drawn into the most radical possible union, that is, unity of person, with that divine being *in* the Trinity who there is and ever was the sole proper object of the Father's other-directed love, the Son.[7]

If the Holy Spirit is the outcome of the mutual love of the Father and the Son, the Spirit must be, in the first instance, the love of the Father for the Son, and only in the second instance the love of the Son for the Father. The Eastern tradition agrees in part with this, for it holds that the Son is the "Treasurer" of the Holy Spirit, that is, that the Spirit proceeds from the Father and rests on the Son.[8] In a remarkable text Palamas goes further, approximating to the Western position: "That Spirit of the most exalted Word is like an ineffable sort of love of the Begetter for that ineffably begotten Word, a love by which the very Word and Son beloved of the Father responds to the Begetter, but as having him [the Spirit] proceeding with him from the Father and reposing in him connaturally."[9] Two significant differences from the Western position are, however, to be noted. First, the Spirit is not said to *be* the Father's love for the Son, but only to be *like* that love, which in any case remains mysterious and ineffable. And second, instead of having the Son appropriate the Holy Spirit and return it to the Father as his own, Palamas has the Son return it simply as a mirror reflects a beam of light to its source. So, while the text leans toward the West in a striking way, it is not as Western as might at first appear, and in excluding the Son from all participation in the spiration of the Holy Spirit it contravenes the biblical ground of Western insistence to the contrary.

In the immanent Trinity the love of the Father for the Son, which is the Holy Spirit, is a love that logically follows, rather than precedes, the generation of the Son, as the taxis requires. St. Thomas has pointed out that "every agent, whatever it be, performs each action out of love of some kind (*ex aliquo amore*)."[10] This must apply also to the Father in the act of generating the Son. But the love of the Father with which he generates the Son can only be his self-love, not his love for a Son who according to the taxis (and to put the matter crudely) does not yet exist. This love, therefore, cannot be the Holy Spirit, since the Holy Spirit is the Father's love for *the Son*. As his self-love, this "first" love is identical with the Father himself. But acting in his total self-possession, which is his self-love, identical with himself, the Father generates the Son, whom he then loves with a "second" love, which is the Holy Spirit.

From this arises the question: If the Holy Spirit is the mutual love of the Father and the Son, how can we say that the love of the Father for the Son is the Holy

Spirit? Does not the mutuality of the love of Father and Son have to be completed by the Son's love for the Father before it can be said that the Holy Spirit is constituted as a person? This is the point made by the Filioque and the *tamquam ab uno principio et unica spiratione* ("as from one principle and by a single spiration") of the Councils of Lyons and Florence (though there is no talk here of love, let alone mutual love).[11] Yet it is undeniable that the Holy Spirit is, fundamentally, the love of the Father for the Son. This emerges as a necessary extrapolation of part one of the two-part biblical argument I presented in the last chapter. In any case, having the Holy Spirit proceed as it were in two stages is absurd and impossible. While, therefore, I sympathize with Jürgen Moltmann's effort to escape this impasse by saying that "the Holy Spirit receives from the Father his own perfect divine *existence*" and "from the Son his relational *form*,"[12] I cannot concur with this proposal. True, we have it from St. Epiphanius, as Moltmann points out, that the Holy Spirit "proceeds from the Father" and "receives from the Son."[13] Indeed, we have this not only from Epiphanius but from Gregory of Nyssa,[14] and ultimately from John 15.26 and 16.14,15. John, of course, is speaking of the biblical Trinity, where it is not difficult to see what the Holy Spirit receives from Christ: the ability to convey the presence of the glorified Christ to the community. He becomes Christ's gift of his love, of himself, to them, which, as we saw, presupposes that the Holy Spirit becomes Christ's gift of himself, of his love, to the Father. This latter attribute, therefore, is what primarily the Holy Spirit receives from Christ. But what does the Holy Spirit receive from the Son in the *immanent* Trinity? We must answer, correspondingly: He receives the attribute of being the Son's love of the Father, which completes that of being the Father's love for the Son, so that he thus becomes the mutual love of the Father and the Son.

But are we not now in the very impasse we were trying to avoid? St. Augustine comes to our aid here with the following observation, repeated in substance at Florence:

> As the Father has in himself that the Holy Spirit should proceed from him, so he has given to the Son that the same Holy Spirit should proceed from him. . . . His proceeding also from the Son is a property derived by the Son from the Father. For if the Son has from the Father whatever he has, then certainly he has from the Father that the Holy Spirit proceed also from him.[15]

We should, I suggest, integrate this principle with the theology of mutual love in the following way. The Holy Spirit, be it remembered, is precisely the objectivization of the mutual love of the Father and the Son. The initial personal love of the Father for the Son is identical with the Father's own person. Similarly, the purely personal answering love of the Son for the Father would be identical with the Son's own person, were it not for the fact that in the meeting of the two loves, their mutual love, the objectivization that takes place becomes a reality that transcends its constituent elements, that reality being the person of the Holy Spirit proceeding from the Father and the Son. Henceforth according to the taxis the Father's love for the Son and the Son's love for the Father are each to be identified with the Holy Spirit. This latter point is also the teaching of St. Thomas.[16] According, then, to the traditional taxis, *first* there is the generation of the Son by the Father, and *second* there is the coincident bestowal of the Holy Spirit by the Father on the Son and the bestowal of the same Spirit by the Son on the Father. It is only as the *mutual* love of the Father and the Son, or rather as its objectivization, that the Holy Spirit has his existence. As mutual, the double bestowal of love, that is, by the Father and the Son on each other, must be coincident and indeed must constitute a single bestowal and a single act (I shall return to this point). But the Father's love for the Son always has priority over the Son's love for the Father, and the latter is always an answering love. Anticipating the Son in existence, the Father anticipates him also in activity, in love. This *prevenient* act of the Father, however, is not to be identified with the Holy Spirit. As a prevenient act of the Father it is identical with the Father's hypostasis, with the Father himself. The love of Father and Son becomes mutual when the Son responds, and *as* mutual it, or rather its objectivization, is the Holy Spirit. While the Father's prevenient love of the Son is to be identified with the Father, the Son's answering love is to be identified with the Holy Spirit, not with the Son, because the Son's response is what renders the love mutual. In effect this means that, insofar as it is mutual, the love comprises constituent elements that are simultaneous and coincident; but insofar as these elements are personal and individual, they have an order, in which the Father's love for the Son remains prior to the love of the Son for the Father. In other words, the priority of the Father's prevenient love is imported into the mutual love without prejudice to the coincidence of its elements qua mutual.

There is no contradiction here, nor is the matter even surprising. An earthly comparison can easily be adduced. Let us say, for example, that a man begins to love a woman before she loves him. Eventually, she returns his love. As from that moment their love becomes mutual. As such, it contains but transcends (objectivizes) its constituent elements. It is no longer just his love (though it is also this), nor her love (though it is also this), but *their* love. In order to be one love, its constituent elements must be simultaneous, and indeed they are. But his love came first, and it does not lose this attribute through being imported into their mutual love. This analogy, of course, like all analogies, has its limits. For example, it is weakened by the fact that human beings in loving frequently exchange roles in regard to giving and responding. It is not thus between the Father and the Son, for the Son draws his entire existence from the Father and hence remains always in an attitude of response to him (though admittedly this response is also a giving, that is, the bestowal of the Holy Spirit, the return of the Spirit to the Father).

What I am doing here is making a distinction between two "stages" of the Trinity, *in fieri* (in the process of becoming) and *in facto esse* (as already constituted). This is a valid procedure from my point of view, and necessary because without it our understanding of the Trinity would be greatly impeded. It is necessitated by the fact that the Son and the Holy Spirit draw their origins from the Father. But a moment's reflection shows that this distinction cannot be real in God, with whom there is no succession of time. His being is paradoxically eternally the same and yet dynamic. What actually is the case with him is the eternal *factum esse*. Now the prevenient act of the Father of which I have been speaking belongs to the fieri stage. It therefore fulfills a purely formal role. Once the mutual love is seen to be established it plays no further part. Hence there is no actual love of the Father for the Son that is not the Holy Spirit. The prevenient love has one function only: to establish and secure the priority or order of the Father's love for the Son over the Son's love for the Father in their mutual love qua personal, without prejudice to the coincidence of these elements in their mutual love qua mutual. This done, the Father's love for the Son is thenceforward to be identified simply with the Holy Spirit, as is the Son's love for the Father. Each of these loves is to be regarded as a distinct modality of the mutual love, that is, of its objectivization.

This is more clear in the economic Trinity, where we human beings get caught up in the mutual love of the Father and the Son. We experience its constituent elements differently from each other, though we encounter them united in sacramentally structured acts. We experience the Father's love for the Son in that we become sons and daughters "in the Son"; and we experience the Son's love for the Father in that we experience its "reverse side," that is, Christ's love of neighbor as one (in "unity-in-difference") with his love of God the Father. If one chooses to view this model as comprehensive, and hence situate the procession model within it, one should locate the Filioque at the level of the coincidence of elements, as the necessary unity of principle is made possible precisely by the logical simultaneity of the double bestowal. This is an illustration of the fact that the Filioque is a mid-position, for upon its attainment we move on, as Augustine did with his principaliter, to the priority of the Father's love for the Son over the Son's love for the Father.

The Order of the Two Models

Logically, the procession model is prior to the return model; it is the foundation of the return model and its prerequisite. The Trinity has to be viewed ab extra before it can be viewed ab intra. The procession model can be considered in isolation, as is appropriate under certain circumstances, or it can be considered as contained within the return model, which, as we have said, is comprehensive. Conversely, the return model itself can be considered in isolation, in the sense that it can be used simply for clarifying the relations among the persons, their hypostatic distinction being already known from the procession model. Or, alternatively, it can embrace and view in a new light what is already known from the procession model. The Filioque emerges by a necessary process from the procession model correctly deployed, and therefore was rightly dogmatized at Lyons and Florence. Imported into the return model, it is there transformed, as I have shown, into a statement of the mutual love of the Father and the Son, and its basic demand that the Son constitute with the Father a single principle of the Holy Spirit is there respected by the statement of the logical simultaneity of the double bestowal of the Holy Spirit by the Father and the Son on each other. Put simply, the Filioque, which emerges from the procession model, is the mutual love theory of the return model, that is, the theology according to which the Holy Spirit is the objectivization of the mutual love of the Father and the Son. But lodged in the return model and already transformed in the process, it can be clarified further in the light of the priority of the love of the Father for the Son over the love of the Son for the Father. Accordingly, it must be said (and here I use a biblical and patristic formulation) that the Holy Spirit proceeds from the Father and receives from the Son. It was this truth, not sufficiently respected in the West, that Photius was trying to protect (though he did it in a rather extreme way) when he said that the Holy Spirit proceeds from the Father "alone." A truly balanced statement, possible only at this remove from the controversy, would be, first, the Holy Spirit proceeds from the Father and the Son as from a single principle; and second, by way of clarification of this, the Holy Spirit proceeds from the Father and receives from the Son. The formal logical contradiction between the two parts of the statement is removed once it is realized that, materially, correct methodology requires a progression from the procession model to the return model without prejudice to what has been established from the procession model, and that the first part of this statement emerges from a consideration of the procession model, while the second emerges from the final consideration of the return model. With the procession model via the Filioque we have established the hypostatic distinction of the Holy Spirit; with the return model we have clarified the relation of the Holy Spirit to the Father and the Son, respectively.

The Filioque

In an important sense Eastern Monopatrism and Western Filioquism are already reconciled by St. Augustine's *principaliter*. That is to say, the Holy Spirit proceeds from the Father and the Son as a single principle, but *principaliter* (ultimately) from the Father alone inasmuch as the Son himself proceeds from the Father. In this matter the West needs to be more mindful of the Monarchy of the Father, while the East needs to acknowledge to the Son a role in the origination of the Holy Spirit. What the return model can do, as a comprehensive model, is provide a context in which the various assertions made by both sides (that is to say, those of them that are true) can be seen as not contradictory but complementary.[17] I have already shown that this model accommodates both the Filioque and the formula "who proceeds from the Father and receives from the Son." It also explains the sense of the *per Filium*, that the Holy Spirit proceeds from the Father *through* the Son. But it can also be seen that the Holy Spirit proceeds, in a sense, from the Father *alone*. Is this a claim to have solved the Filioque problem? Certainly not in terms of a formula. The search for a fully reconciling formula is illusory, as no single formula can express the many-faceted reality of the procession of the Holy Spirit.

This raises the practical and liturgical question of what should be done about the creed. The problem with the original formulation ("who proceeds from the Father") is that it makes no mention of the Son in regard to the origination of the Holy Spirit, though it does not exclude such a role. In this respect it must be said to represent a purely Eastern perspective. After all, the Council of Constantinople, which delivered it to the Church toward the end of the fourth century, was a purely Eastern council with no Western input, recognized as ecumenical in the West only in the seventh century.[18] On the other hand, its formulation regarding the Holy Spirit was officially upheld in both East and West until the eleventh century, when Rome eventually sanctioned the Filioque. Clearly, there is an argument for reverting to the original conciliar formulation in the West. The problem with the Filioque is that its emphasis is purely Western, making no reference to the Monarchy of the Father. The form "who proceeds from the Father and receives from the Son," though it does not express the fullness of the Church's faith in regard to the procession, emphasizes the Monarchy of the Father, and, provided it is not taken in a sense exclusive of the Filioque, allows the Son a positive role in the procession, indeed a role that actually implies the Filioque. It is therefore a compromise that should appeal to both sides. One advantage it has over both the Filioque and the *per Filium* is that, unlike them, it has as its immediate reference the economic Trinity, ultimate object of Christian faith. Another is that, unlike the rather contrived formulations one sometimes sees, it is simple. And finally, it is both scriptural and patristic. On balance it appears to present more advantages than the original formulation, but obviously its adoption would need to be carefully negotiated, especially with those on the Eastern side opposed in principle to any change in the creed whatsoever. In this regard it should be remembered that the Council of Ephesus's prohibition against altering the creed was directed at the Nicene Creed, not the Constantinopolitan.[19]

The Unity of the Mutual Love

Let us now return to the point that the mutual love of the Father and the Son is a single act, an assertion that has not passed unchallenged in theology. Rahner, for example, writes, "[T]here is properly no *mutual* love between Father and Son (as this would presuppppose two acts), but rather a loving, distinction-grounding self-acceptance of the Father (and of the Son because of the taxis of knowledge and love)."[20] It is impossible to tell from this short statement exactly whence Rahner's objection arises. Is it just from the alleged duality of subjects, or is it from their mutuality taken objectively, that is, that each subject loves precisely the other? I shall consider both possibilities. In the light of the methodology that has been proposed, however, both parts of Rahner's statement must be judged as confused.

I note at the outset that here (at least) Rahner has invoked the psychological analogy. Despite the reservations about this analogy already expressed, let us go along with his argument for the sake of exposing another weakness in it. We can do this, as the sort of thing he says in the context of the psychological analogy could theoretically be said in that of *any* formulation of the procession model, and is not, therefore, just a feature of this particular formulation. When in my critique I speak of "essential" acts, that is, acts proper to *God* as such rather than to particular divine persons, it need not be specifically to acts of knowing and loving that I refer, though that is how the Augustinian tradition would automatically understand them. I *could* be designating by this term simply those acts by which the one God unfolds by nature into diversity, however they be named or even if they be left unnamed (because of there being insufficient ground for naming them). At least it is clear that they cannot, at this stage, be named "generation" and "spiration," since as so named they are proper to divine persons, respectively, the Father, and the Father and the Son, rather than to God as such.

If one is restricted, as Rahner is, to the procession model in its Augustinian formulation, according to which the one God unfolds into diversity of persons through acts of knowledge and love, this knowledge and love can only be *God's* self-knowledge and self-love, and not, as in Rahner's text, that of the Father and the Son. According to the psychological analogy, persons proceed in the one God through the divine self-knowlege and self-love.[21] The model is that of a single mind with its acts of knowing and loving. In traditional terminology, it is the "essential" act of knowing and the "essential" act of loving that give rise to the plurality of persons. In any formulation essentialism should be the *starting point* of the procession model; where it *ends* is with the statements that the Son proceeds from the Father, and the Holy Spirit from the Father and the Son as from a single principle. It starts with essential acts; it ends with "notional" acts.[22] In other words, an original statement about *God* as such should, in the process of the operation of the model, differentiate out into statements about the *persons* as such.

In regard to the first procession we have a clear distinction between the Father and the Son; with the second, however, for the sake of an equally clear assertion of the distinctness of the Holy Spirit, the divine unity has been only partly, not completely, differentiated, for it is said here, as it must be, that Father and Son constitute a single principle of the Holy Spirit. Their personal distinction, therefore, has become obscured. However, having arrived at this position, and still staying with the procession model, we need not, indeed should not, maintain the uncompromising essentialism with which we began. We should *not* say, therefore, as St. Anselm did,[23] that it is as at one in the divine essence that the Father and the Son produce the Holy Spirit. Rather, they do this as being at one in the *vis spirativa*, the "spirative power" to breathe forth the Holy Spirit that they have in common because the Father has communicated it to the Son in the act of generation, and that the Holy Spirit lacks.

This spirativity (let us so call it) cannot be an accident; it is not just something *possessed* by the Father and the Son. With John Bessarion (the outstanding Greek theologian who stayed in the Catholic Church after the breakdown of the union of Florence) we must say that it *is* the Father and the Son insofar as together they breathe forth the Holy Spirit.[24] It is this spirativity that we must identify as the "nondistinct subsistent" of which Louis Billot, taking his cue from St. Thomas,[25] spoke in reference to the Father and the Son as the single principle of the Holy Spirit.[26] His argument was that, whereas "person" must by definition be a subsistent that is both distinct and incommunicable, the single principle comprising the Father and the Son need only be a subsistent, and not, therefore, distinct or incommunicable.[27] (It must be a subsistent; otherwise, the Holy Spirit proceeding from it would not be a subsistent.) As only the persons comprising it need to be distinct, it does not need to be distinct in itself; and because the spirativity by which the Holy Spirit is produced has in fact been communicated from one comprising person (the Father) to the other (the Son), it, as subsistent spirativity, need not be incommunicable in itself. Being neither distinct nor incommunicable, it poses no threat to the doctrine of three, and only three, *persons* in the Trinity, even though it is, and must be, subsistent. John Beccos (the patriarch of Constantinople who remained loyal to the Second Council of Lyons and was in consequence deposed from office) was therefore correct in his assessment that the Filioque marked a mid-position between essentialism and personalism.[28] But this judgment by no means damns the Filioque; it merely points to its unfinished, unresolved nature.

One completes the journey to personalism by having recourse to the return model, as I have shown. But as long as one stays with the procession model and therefore with the Filioque as presented above, one is obviously held in what is meant to be a transitional stage. It is incorrect to speak, as Rahner does, of a loving, distinction-grounding self-acceptance of the Father and the Son, even if he means by this (as he surely does, though his choice of words does not bring it out clearly) a single act of self-acceptance. To be faithful to the psychological analogy, he should have said that the loving self-acceptance that grounds the distinction between the Father and the Son on one hand and the Holy Spirit on the other is the loving self-acceptance of God as such. When this statement is differentiated at the conclusion of the operation of the model, where the Holy Spirit is seen to proceed from the Father and the Son as a single principle, there is nothing more that can be said to clarify the relation of the Father and the Son without having recourse to the return model. But when one does this (and now we come to the first part of Rahner's objection), it becomes clear that it is as the *mutual* love of the Father and the Son that the Holy Spirit proceeds.

We are now purely in the realm of the personal; the essentialism and the semi-essentialism of the procession model have been left behind. Here, if the Father and the Son are said to love, there are only two alternatives: either each loves himself, or each loves the other. But the love by which the Father loves himself is identical with his own person, as is the love by which the Son loves himself. These loves are not person producing or, to use St. Thomas's term, notional. Therefore, the love of the Father and the Son that is productive of the Holy Spirit can only be what we have already shown it, on biblical grounds, to be, namely, their mutual love. It remains now only to show, against Rahner, that this is a single act.

Rahner, I presume, would have no difficulty accepting St. Thomas's statement that in the Trinity there are *duo spirantes* ("two who spirate") but only *una spiratio* ("one spiration").[29] As the spiration takes place by way of love, he could just as easily have said *duo amantes sed una amatio* ("two who love but one act of loving"). This deals with Rahner's objection at its subjective pole: there is no problem inherent in having two divine persons love with a single love. As for the objective pole, the following must be said, in the context of the return model. The Father communicates spirativity to the Son in the act of generation. The Father then loves the Son, and at the same moment in the taxis (this is important for the singleness of the act) the Son loves the Father. Because the power of spiration is complete in each of them, each breathes forth the Holy Spirit, but because this power is strictly one in both, having been communicated from the Father to the Son, its act, which is spiration, must also be one, even though there are two who spirate and they do so not together (over against some third) but over against each other. Even here, therefore, in the return model (where we are dealing with mutual love), there are *duo amantes sed una amatio*.

At this point it is appropriate to add a reflection on the fact that while the property of generation is expressed by the Father's name, no additional name exists for the Father and the Son in reference to the spirativity that they possess in common. The reason is that this property is sufficiently expressed by the names Father and Son. These names express the fact that the Son is generated by the Father. Now according to St. Thomas generation is characterized by "likeness in the nature of the same species."[30] This is not the case with the procession of the Holy Spirit, which is universally acknowledged to be *not* generation. We have already seen that, while all three trinitarian persons are "like" each other in respect of the divine nature, only the Father and the Son are "like" each other as persons. The Son is said in the Bible to be the "image" of the Father, a statement that is never made about the Holy Spirit. Spirativity, then, is based in the likeness that the Father communicates to the Son in generation. Speaking precisely of the procession of the Holy Spirit, St. Thomas said that "likeness is the principle of loving."[31] Hence the personal likeness between the Father and the Son is the principle of their mutual love, which gives rise to the Holy Spirit.

Rahner's objection is one that is dealt with also by St. Bonaventure, and indeed in a remarkably succinct way.[32] Bonaventure puts the objection in its briefest possible form: *si mutuus non unicus*, "if mutual not single," that is, if the love be mutual, it cannot be a single act. His answer is that this would hold in the case of lovers whose loves were different (human lovers, for example), but not in the case of God. What is different with God, so he tells us in another place,[33] is that there the lovers, Father and Son, are strictly at one in the "fecundity" of the divine will. The Holy Spirit is at one with them in the *possession* of the divine will, but not in its fecundity, because only the Father and the Son are *improcessibilis*, that is, not able to proceed (in the Eastern sense of the word). Not able to proceed themselves, they cause another to proceed. This fecundity of the divine will, which is identical with spirativity, is strictly one in Father and Son, and therefore its act, which is their mutual love, is also strictly one, without being simply identical with the divine essence. However, Bonaventure's argument is incomplete: he needs to explain why the divine will is fecund only in the case of the Father and the Son, which he has not done just by saying that only they are improcessibilis. The divine will is fecund in their case because only they share the likeness based on generation that gives rise to their mutual love. Also, Bonaventure's basis for distinguishing the two processions, nature (for the first procession) and will (for the second), which he took over from his teacher, Alexander of Hales (and ultimately from Aristotle), is at best rather suspect, as it seems to predicate determination for the first procession and contingency for the second. Thomas contrasted will with intellect, but in contrasting it with nature Bonaventure was using the word in a different sense and venturing on dangerously anthropomorphic ground.

In Father and Son mutual love is strictly one act because, to use St. Thomas's terms, the duo spirantes give rise not just to una spiratio but to *unus spirator* (Billot's subsistent spirativity),[34] as in respect of breathing forth the Holy Spirit their perfect likeness based on generation rules out any "opposition of relation" between them, and hence the adage applies, "In Deo omnia sunt unum ubi non obviat relationis oppositio." Only in respect of generation does an opposition of relation exist. Further, in this matter one can take a psychological line, different from the metaphysical one above. It can be argued that even in human love the mutual love of two lovers is a single reality, transcending the individual loves that comprise it. Therefore, while St. Bonaventure may have been correct in conceding the objection in the case of human love, the experienced psychological unity of the mutual love of human beings is at least a pointer to the deeper ontological unity that obtains in the case of the mutual love of the Father and the Son in the Trinity, and to that extent is worth bringing forward.

As well as Rahner, another prominent critic of the mutual love theory is Yves Congar, who is content to endorse the negative judgment of H. F. Dondaine, whom he quotes at some length. The following excerpt expresses the heart of Dondaine's objection:

> [T]he metaphor of love as the "bond between lovers" cannot be raised above the image. What two friends have in common to unite them is not the reality experienced in their act of love. Each experiences his own act, which makes two loves, two acts of loving. What they have in common is the object and their common good. . . . But it is to this one object, their community in good, that they adapt their two hearts and their two wills by two loves.[35]

Below I comment only on that aspect of this criticism not already addressed in my treatment of Rahner. Evident in the quotation is the influence, on both Congar and Dondaine, of St. Anselm, and a reaction, perhaps an overreaction, against the theology of Richard of St. Victor. It is a strange concept of friendship here presented. Most people today would, I think, agree that what friends adapt their hearts to is not their "one object, their community in good," but each other. This older theology, for the reasons just indicated, shied away from any true personalism, taking refuge in a more or less thoroughgoing essentialism, which happily is now overcome in Catholic theology. In the Godhead, so perfect is the adaptation of Father and Son to each other in their mutual love that they become unus spirator of the Holy Spirit, remaining, however, always distinct as Father and Son, duo spirantes. It is in *this* adaptation, based on the personal likeness between Father and Son arising from generation, that, to use St. Bonaventure's word, the divine will becomes "fecund."

In conclusion, it should be pointed out that in the light of the gospels the criticism of the mutual love theory by Rahner, Congar, Dondaine, and others appears highly inappropriate. It is no exaggeration to say that the most basic and important fact revealed in the gospels is the unique love and intimacy obtaining between Jesus and his God. It was precisely this relationship that enabled Jesus to address God in prayer as his "Father," and to preach to others the blessings of the "Kingdom," the Reign, of God in the first instance in their hearts and thence in their world on the basis of a loving submission in faith. It was the contribution of the Synoptics to point out that this relationship was created, sustained, and fostered by the Holy Spirit of God bestowed by the Father in all fullness on Jesus at his conception. The reality of Jesus as presented in the gospels, then, is trinitarian, and its most basic feature is the mutual love existing in the Spirit between the Father and the Son. Yet when we come to a study of the Trinity, which we can only know on the basis of precisely this revelation, we are asked to accept that this love is either secondary, irrelevant, or even nonexistent. Surely, any and all such theology has to be gravely mistaken and inadequate.

The Consciousness of the Divine Persons

A further question that needs to be pursued here is that of the consciousness of the divine persons. Clearly, a mutual love of the Father and the Son is impossible unless each is conscious of himself as subject and knows the other, at least in some sense, as object. The passage from Rahner's *Trinity* on which I have been commenting at length is immediately preceded by the words:

[W]hen *we today* speak of person in the plural we think because of the modern meaning of the word almost perforce of several spiritual act-centers, spiritual subjectivities and freedoms. But there are not three of these in God. This is so not only because there is only *one* essence and therefore *one* absolute self-presence in God, but also because there is only *one* self-utterance of the Father, the Logos, who is not the one uttering but the one uttered, and because . . . [the passage then continues as quoted earlier].[36]

This passage from Rahner appears to be quite confused. For one thing, he makes a category error in linking together the three concepts, act-center, subjectivity, and freedom. He is right in saying that there is only one subjectivity (consciousness) and one freedom in God, each identical with the divine essence. But there is no reason that each person should not be a distinct *subject* (as distinct from subjectivity, i.e., that by which a subject is a subject) and therefore a distinct act-center. Indeed, each of them must be such, as the notional acts by which they produce and/or are produced are spiritual, and therefore conscious and deliberate. Also, while it is true that there is only one *absolute* self-presence in God, this does not prevent there being three relative self-presences in him. And the fact that the Logos is, over against the Father, uttered rather than uttering is totally irrelevant to the question of whether he is a distinct subject, and this quite independently of the fact that Rahner here takes the psychological analogy more seriously than usual and more seriously perhaps than it merits.

The opinion of Lonergan on this matter has found much wider acceptance and is the one I wish to propose, with the single qualification (which applies also to the next quotation, from Kasper) that it would be better in this context to restrict the term "conscious" to the subject's subjective self-awareness, rather than allow it to include, as here, their objective knowledge as well, as it does in the popular usage, as, for example, in the sentence, "I was conscious of another person in the room." Lonergan's opinion is summed up succinctly as Assertion no. 12 in part two of his *De Deo Trino*: "Through one real consciousness, Father, Son and Holy Spirit are three subjects, each conscious both of himself and of each of the others, and of his act (of being), both notional and essential."[37]

There is an important aspect of this question that I must leave to the next chapter, namely, whether subsistence in God is single or threefold. Postponing this, let me conclude the present consideration of the question by quoting with approval, slightly qualified as above, a passage from Kasper, who bases his opinion on Lonergan:

[A]ccording to the traditional terminology, we must say that the one divine consciousness subsists in a triple mode. This means that a triple *principium* or subject of the one consciousness must be accepted and, at the same time, that the three subjects cannot be simply unconscious but are conscious of themselves by means of the one consciousness (*principium quo*). This assertion follows, on the one hand, from the fact that the divine persons are really identical with the one being and consciousness and, on the other hand, from the fact that they proceed from spiritual acts of knowledge and love, so that between them there exists a spiritual relationship which by its very nature cannot but be conscious. We have no choice, then, but to say that in the Trinity we are dealing with three subjects who are reciprocally conscious of each other by reason of one and the same consciousness which the three subjects "possess," each in his own proper way.[38]

Inadequacy of the Procession Model

The mutual love with which we are concerned in the return model is notably different from the love involved in the procession model. The first is personal, or, better, interpersonal, love, the love that binds two persons together, while the second is personal only in the sense of an operation, even if the supreme operation, of a single spiritual subject, and directed to the self; that is, it is self-love. At the beginning of the operation of the model the love in question is simply the self-love of God; at the end it is the self-love of the Father, with which he generates the Son. But in either case it is self-love. This would be so even if the psychological analogy were not utilized, for whether the agent were simply God or the Father he would still be acting *ex aliquo amore*, out of love of some kind, which could only be self-love. Normally, in the case of human love, love of neighbor is the first-given explicit experience of love, with love of God as its implicit transcendental dimension.[39] This love of God can itself become explicit and categorial, with the aid of the concept of God (given us by society, usually through religion). But also implicit in this first experience of love is the affirmation of the self of the lover, that is, self-love, which also can become explicit, through the process of self-objectivization. Here again we find a reversal of order between the experiential and epistemological, on the one hand, and the ontological, on the other. If in the epistemological order love of neighbor occurs first and love of self second, in the ontological order, with which we are here concerned, it is the other way round: here the primary datum is self-love, and it is given as the ground of possibility of love of neighbor (and of God). Therefore, when in the *divine* sphere we isolate the procession model, and thus give it momentarily an independent reality (though in fact it exists only as a preliminary phase of the comprehensive return model), it is divine *self*-love with which we are confronted. But when we move on to the return model, we find that the love there operative is "love of neighbor," and indeed as reciprocated, that is, the mutual love of the Father and the Son. What was given as a ground of possibility in the procession model has been realized in the return model.

These reflections show up the inadequacy of the procession model in whatever form. There is something unsatisfactory, even narcissistic, about self-love so long as it remains unincorporated into the larger and altruistic project of other-directed love, as was pointed out by Richard of St. Victor.[40] I emphasize that this critique includes Lonergan, for the only answer available within his system to the question With whom is God, as Being-in-Love, in love? is Himself, as his being in love with humankind can only be a description of his contingent relation to us and not the definition of his immanent being.

The Self-Communication of God

Finally, I now re-present the theology of the return model in terms of the concept, borrowed from Rahner, of "the self-communication of God."[41] This is a rich and pregnant concept, which Rahner has presented in detailed form several times in his writings.[42] It will be necessary to speak here of the economic Trinity (rather than the immanent Trinity alone), because this is where the weaknesses in Rahner's theology show up. It is clear that Rahner himself did not think the concept through thoroughly. Otherwise he would not have written that in the economic Trinity the self-communication of God involves "a quasi-formal causality in which the three divine persons 'act' strictly as such and can communicate themselves."[43] The difficulty with this is that in the biblical (and hence also in the immanent and the economic) Trinity the Holy Spirit does not communicate himself but is only communicated by the Father and the Son. In any case, if each divine person could communicate himself, then self-communication would be something common to the three persons, and therefore proper to the divine essence, the divine unity, as such rather than to the persons as such.[44] This in turn would mean that, contrary to Rahner's own understanding, the causality they could exercise on human beings by this activity would be only efficient, and not quasi-formal, causality.

Another defect in Rahner's understanding of the concept appears in his assignation of it, as it occurs in his Christology, to descending rather than ascending Christology. Tracing the development of Rahner's thought in Christology, John McDermott writes:

> [H]e developed a central insight of his system, the meaning of the "real symbol." This was expanded into a Christology from above and into a Trinitarian theology in which the economic Trinity was affirmed to be the immanent Trinity. Then as Scriptural exegesis won a more independent position vis-a-vis dogmatic theology, Rahner turned to problems resulting from studies about the historical Jesus. . . . There was need of showing how even the meager results of historical criticism permitted an ascending Christology, or a Christology from below, that accorded substantially with the traditional dogmatic affirmations about Jesus. After emphasizing for more than 10 years the ascending Christology, Rahner's last major work, *Grundkurs des Glaubens* (*Foundations of Christian Faith*), tried to synthesize his descending and ascending Christologies.[45]

In the Christology section of this work (the English translation, *Foundations*, pp. 176–321) it is clear that the ascending Christology is summed up in the phrase "active self-transcendence," while the descending Christology is termed the "self-communication of God." This is why Rahner was able to write, on page 198, "In its ultimate and highest phase this self-transcendence is identical with an absolute self-communication of God, which signifies the same process as seen from God's side." It is clear that for him the two expressions denote exactly the same reality viewed from two different standpoints, that of the world rising to God and that of God coming to meet the world.

In this, I suggest, Rahner was mistaken. "Active self-transcendence" on the part of the humanity of Christ certainly represents ascending Christology. But so does the "self-communication of God." The reason for saying this is that, as distinct from efficient causality, quasi-formal causality, the scholastic concept that led Rahner to the idea of the self-communication of God, has to do with assimilation and union, and even, in the case of Christ, with the unity (of person) that God (the Father) establishes, through the radical bestowal of the Holy Spirit, between the humanity of Christ and the preexistent divine Son. But here the emphasis is on the immanence of God in, and working up from, his creation, rather than on his transcendence. Oddly, this latter point is one that Rahner himself showed he appreciated when he called his ascending Christology a "Christology within an evolutionary view of the world" (see the heading on p. 178 of *Foundations*). Our model for understanding this should not be that proposed by Rahner, namely, the same reality viewed from different perspectives, but rather the cooperation, postulated by Catholic (and Orthodox) doctrine and theology, between divine grace and human effort in the achievement of a supernatural end. For "grace" here, understand God the Father acting by the power of his Spirit (therefore "uncreated" grace); and for the human element, the humanity of Christ in its active self-transcendence. If an imaginative depiction is desired, picture two arrows, moving not in opposite directions on a collision course (as Rahner would have it),[46] but in the same direction, with the first and larger one powerfully bearing the second to its destination. And, as has been explained on other occasions (I address a hesitation that McDermott expresses in regard to Rahner's ascending Christology), the view presented here should not be suspected of Adoptionism, as the self-communication of the Father spoken of is so radical that it establishes the humanity of Christ in hypostatic union with the Son from the very first moment of its existence (it brings it into existence *as* the humanity of the Son of God), so that the self-transcendence remaining for that humanity to achieve (under the ever-present grace of the Incarnation) is simply that which is necessary for its historical human and spiritual development as an authentic and integral humanity, through a continually active response to the challenges of life from infancy through to adulthood and, ultimately, to a freely embraced death.

That here divine self-communication and active human self-transcendence belong alike to ascending Christology is important for us, since, as we have already established, ascending data should be integrated only with the return model and descending data only with the procession model. Admittedly, the ascending data here are philosophical rather than biblical, but this does not affect the principle just enunciated. Self-communication has to do with return, as the communicator does not just reach out to the other but, having done this, admits the other to their own life, their own world. In doing this, they elevate the other from within so that the latter can participate in this life, this world. This elevation will always involve a new creation in and of the other, and viewed in isolation, this can be seen as a work of efficient causality. But, seeing the creation as integrated into the self-communication, Rahner explains this phenomenon in terms of the inclusion of efficient causality within quasi-formal causality as its own "deficient mode."[47] As long as one remains exclusively concerned with God's reaching out (in revelation), that is, with descending data, the correct trinitarian model to use is the procession model, but when one moves on to his self-communication, the correct model becomes the return model. Hence the task I have set myself here, the re-presentation of the return model of the immanent Trinity in terms of the self-communication of God.

In the immanent Trinity, the self-love of God brings about first of all the differentiation of Father and Son, in that, acting out of this self-love, which is his own self-love, the Father generates the Son. This act must be identified as a self-communication of the Father to the Son. In it the Father communicates to the Son everything that the Son will have, including the Son's power to love his other, the Father. The act of the Father is a notional act, eternally positing the Son in existence as the Son of the Father. The Son thus receives himself at the hands of the Father. The Son is not identical with this self-communication, but rather is its term.

Next, the Father communicates himself again to the Son, this time not acting out of his self-love but out of his love for his other, the Son. At the same time the Son returns his love to his other, the Father, thus communicating himself to him (we explained earlier how simultaneity and return of love are possible in this situation). This mutual love, the self-communication of the Father and the Son (to each other), is a single act, not just because its two components occur simultaneously in the Godhead, but because the Son's power to love (the other) is identical with the Father's power to love (the other), each being identical with the divine essence precisely as communicated by the Father to the Son (and not, therefore, with the divine essence precisely as such), that is, as communicating a perfect personal likeness. This act of the Father and the Son is a notional act, productive of the Holy Spirit, who is the objectivization, or, better, the personalization, of their mutual love. Note that with this statement the Filioque is affirmed. The Son receives the first self-communication, but the Father and the Son receive the second self-communication, the Holy Spirit being the one received by them. Whereas the Son is the outcome of the self-communication of the Father (to the Son), the Holy Spirit is the outcome of the self-communication of the Father and the Son (to each other). But neither the Son nor the Holy Spirit is identical with the self-communication of which he is the outcome: whereas the Son is the term of his, the Holy Spirit is the objectivization of his. In regard to the self-communication of God, the property of the Father is to be its *Giver*, that of the Son is to be its *Receiver*, and that of the Holy Spirit is to be the *Gift* itself, the *One Given and Received*.[48] A point of similarity between the two self-communications is that each is notional, that is to say, divine persons as such posit another divine person eternally in existence.

Within the mutual love, however, there is a certain priority of the Father's love for the Son over the Son's love for the Father, for the Father precedes the Son in all things. The Son's love for the Father, therefore, as operating (and not just as bestowed, as a power), is an answering love, evoked by the Father's love for him. It is the Son's return to the Father in love. The Holy Spirit as returned by the Son to the Father is the Holy Spirit appropriated by the Son. Within the concept of the Holy Spirit as the mutual love, it is possible, therefore, to identify the Spirit now as the Father's love for the Son, now as the Son's love for the Father. In this perspective the statement of St. Gregory of Nyssa, that the Holy Spirit proceeds from the Father and receives from the Son, should be affirmed. What the Holy Spirit receives from the Son is the character of being the Son's love for the Father. The Father's love for the Son can be called a self-communication of the Father, in that he communicates himself to the Son by his love for him; likewise the Son's love for the Father can be called a self-communication of the Son. However, neither of these self-communications on its own is notional; it is only combined as a unity, that is, as constituting the mutual love of the Father and the Son, that it is notional.

From this it can be seen that each of the loves that operate in the Trinity, self-love and love for the other, is notional. True, the Father *generates* the Son, but in so doing he acts *ex aliquo amore*, out of love of some kind, and the love out of which he acts is self-love. Father and Son then love each other, and this love, their mutual love, is constitutive of the Holy Spirit. Where the procession model in the form of the psychological analogy has the divine knowledge and love as notional, the return model has as notional the two kinds of love, love of self and love of the other. But even in the return model the Son is produced by generation, though it is the generation of a Son rather than a Word.[49]

Returning to the economic Trinity to complete the critique of Rahner, we see that the Incarnation is the self-communication of the *Father* to Jesus of Nazareth, and as such is the revelation of the Father and therefore the expression and image of the *Father*, and not the expression of the Word (the Logos) as Rahner constantly asserts. Jesus is established in hypostatic union with the Son because Jesus coincides ontologically with the Son, being the one who perfectly receives the self-communication of the Father in the world as the Son does in the immanent Trinity. The divinity of Jesus, the same as that of the Son (though in human nature), is the Godhead in receptive mode, as stated above. The divine Sonship of Jesus is, as Wolfhart Pannenberg asserts,[50] indirect and known indirectly. We see here also the most profound reason why of the three divine persons only the Son can become human: only that person can perfectly receive the self-communication of God in the world whose property it is to do so in the Godhead.

Further, since the Holy Spirit is Christ's *human* love of the Father, and since human love of God is identical (in distinction) with love of neighbor, as Rahner teaches, the Holy Spirit sent by Christ upon the Church as his own, as well as being the self-communication of Christ to the Father, is his self-communication to his brothers and sisters in the Church. The Holy Spirit is received in the Church as the self-communication of both the Father and Christ as united in a structured sacramental relationship, therefore not as either separated or undifferentiated, and hence he is received as the economic self-communication of the Father and the Son, that is, according to this economic transposition of the Filioque, in his hypostatic distinction as a person, though acting in two roles or modalities, namely, as Spirit of Christ and Spirit of God, corresponding to his double role in the immanent Trinity as love of the Father for the Son and love of the Son for the Father.[51] In grace we have the communication (by the Father and the Son and therefore not the *self-communication*) of the Holy Spirit, Gift in the economic Trinity as he is in the immanent Trinity.

A final word in criticism of Rahner is that, though in *The Trinity* he is able to speak (always in the context of the procession model)[52] of the self-communication of God as being in reality two modalities of the self-communication of *the Father*,[53] he is all too ready to persist with the undifferentiated terminology of the self-communication of *God*. But as we have seen, in the return model, where the theology of self-communication rightly belongs, both essentialism and semi-essentialism have been left behind in favor of pure personalism. While it may be acceptable to *begin* discourse about divine self-communication with the general term, the self-communication of God, the actual theology demands precision from essence to persons; and, as we have seen, the self-communication, in the case of the immanent Trinity (and therefore in the economic Trinity as well), is that either of the Father alone or of the Father and the Son together. In the case of the economic Trinity, for the reason stated earlier, there must be added the self-communication of the Son, or of Christ, to his brothers and sisters in the Church. Strictly speaking though, this is not a simple addition; it is the complementary aspect of the self-communication of Christ to the Father, inasmuch as human love necessarily contains these two distinguishable but inseparable dimensions: love of God and love of neighbor. The Incarnation, then, is the self-communication of the Father to the world in the person of Jesus Christ, the Son of God; and grace is the self-communication of the Father and Christ his Son to us, in the person of the Holy Spirit. Through the theology of the divine self-communication and the attendant philosophy of quasi-formal causality, the long-standing Western objection against the possibility of personal (as distinct from essential) divine action ad extra, based as it is on the axiom "In Deo omnia sunt unum ubi non obviat relationis oppositio" (In God all things are one except where the opposition of relationship rules this out) and the philosophy of purely efficient causality, is transcended.[54] Thus the way is opened to an understanding of the relevance of the doctrine of the Trinity to the mystery of salvation, that is, by the Father, through Christ, in the power of the Holy Spirit.

4

Persons, Divine and Human

It is time now to take a critical look at the concept of person, which hitherto I have been using rather uncritically. On this subject, both in general and in regard to the Trinity, there exists an extensive body of literature, only a small part of which can be invoked here. But, despite the fact that many others have labored over the subject, I need to address it anew, as for all its apparent obviousness and simplicity it remains a puzzle and a challenge. To give just one example of its elusiveness, and a striking one at that: though Rahner addressed it constantly in the course of his theology and even devoted two lexicon articles explicitly to it,[1] he failed to convince his critics that he had really mastered it.[2]

We can cut a path through many of the difficulties that beset the question by observing that all attempts to come to terms with it try to integrate two fundamental and apparently opposed concepts, individual and relation. The person is the ultimate individual: whatever makes them the person that they are is distinct and incommunicable to any other person or any other being for that matter. While every individual being is unique in its own way, persons, as we realize as we come to know them, are vastly more unalike than are any other same-species beings in the entire scale of being. Yet at the same time persons are essentially in relation to each other: "Without Thou the I is impossible."[3] And, as we are bound to say when speaking theologically, the person is essentially related to God. While every being exists in relation to every other being, the relation of the person to other individual beings and to the world in general is of an altogether higher order, being spiritual by nature; and the relation of one person to another, of an I to a Thou, is higher again and absolutely unique, being not only spiritual but mutually so, and also constitutive of the person as such, as the quotation above asserts. Paradoxically, therefore, the being that by definition is most isolated in the world of beings is, at the same time and (as I hope to show) by that very fact, the one most intimately connected to, and involved in, that world.

Let us now look, in the light of these observations, at a recent attempt, by Petro Bilaniuk, to describe the concept of person. According to Bilaniuk, "person" is:

an impenetrable and divine mystery of a being, which is a substance possessing either aseity, or at least inseity, the essence of which is not only a supposit, but also a rational subsistence which makes it possible for it to lead a self-conscious and free existence as a self-standing, self-possessing and autonomous center of attribution; it is incommunicable, indestructible, and unique in its individuality, and in its positive transcendental relationship to being, to the ground of all being, to existence, and to becoming.[4]

This description is clearly theological as well as philosophical, and it ranges well beyond what I have written here so far. However, I wish to endorse it at the outset and to express the intention of catching up with its assertions in my own way in the course of this chapter. At this stage it will be sufficient to point out that everything in it down to and including the phrase "unique in its individuality" can be categorized under the heading "individual," and everything from there to the end under "relation." This illustrates the fundamental importance of these two categories for the concept of person.

As Wolfhart Pannenberg has pointed out, "person" is a specifically Christian concept.[5] It was acquired in the course of the formulation of christological and trinitarian theology and doctrine in the first five centuries of the Christian era as the functional categories of the New Testament needed to be translated into ontological ones borrowed from Hellenism and then to be developed within this new context. If today we speak of an "ancient" concept of person in which individuality predominates, and a "modern" concept in which relation does, we need to remember that this is only a matter of emphasis and that both aspects were present from early times.

Admittedly, it was the first aspect that came to the fore at the Council of Chalcedon, where it was given the additional nuance of "subsistence." It was necessary to do this because it was then realized that the humanity of Christ, while possessing individuality, was not itself a person. This was because it lacked its own subsistence, subsisting by the subsistence proper to the divine Son and Word. Hence the council called it a "nature" rather than a "person." In this situation only the divine Son could be called a person. Philosophy had not found it necessary to make this distinction, but it was now imposed on theology by the unique case of Christ. The council had to struggle to find appropriate words in Greek to express the new concept. It finished up choosing two complementary terms: *hupostasis*, literally, "subsistence" ("inseity," to use Bilaniuk's term), but here individual, concrete, subsistent being ("supposit"), which could be used just as well of a purely material being, such as a tree or an animal; and *prosopon*, the mask worn by an actor in the theater, and therefore "character," which overcame (in a nonphilosophical way) the limitation of hupostasis by expressing the spiritual dimension of this being. Putting these two concepts together, we get "person" in the sense of individual, concrete, spiritual, subsistent being, or spiritual supposit. Though Latin theology, through Tertullian's doctrine of *persona*, has been credited by some with reaching this point two centuries earlier, the fact is that, far from anticipating Chalcedon, it fell well short of it, as the relation of nature and person had played no part in Tertullian's considerations.[6] All this reflection bore fruit in the sixth century with the lapidary and influential definition of Boethius, *rationalis naturae individua substantia*, "individual substance of a rational nature."

Pannenberg has observed that, with the accession of psychological thinking in modern times, what changed was that this understanding was translated from metaphysical into psychological categories: "The conception of person as spiritual individuality continued to apply right into modern times, particularly in humanism and the Enlightenment. The latter saw the kernel of spiritual individuality in self-consciousness."[7] Bilaniuk's description, as a Catholic understanding respecting traditional elements while being open to new developments, has no problem with affirming both options simultaneously. The second is to be seen in the words "a rational subsistence which makes it possible for it to lead a self-conscious and free existence as a self-standing, self-possessing and autonomous center of attribution." In the developing concept of person, that which is to be characterized as modern is not the conception of person as relation as such, but rather the psychological reinterpretation referred to above, which is summed up in the single word "subject," which in the last chapter we saw Lonergan affirming (for the persons of the Trinity) and Rahner rejecting. Of course the concept of relation also underwent modernization, as it too began to be understood in psychological as distinct from metaphysical terms; and here too it was possible to affirm both possibilities together.

The metaphysical concept of relation, which since St. Augustine has been characteristic of Western trinitarian thought, actually began with the Cappadocians, and principally with St. Gregory of Nazianzus: " 'Father' is a term neither of essence (*ousia*) nor of energy (*energeia*), but of relation (*schesis*), of the manner of the Father's bearing toward the Son or of the Son's bearing toward the Father."[8] There is good reason to believe that it was in Gregory that Augustine, despite his lack of proficiency in Greek, discovered the concept of trinitarian relations.[9] The Cappadocians had reached the point of realizing that the divine persons (*hupostaseis*) were each identical with the single concrete essence of God and differed from each other only by their mutual relations.[10] Though this doctrine was capable of being developed into that of "subsistent relations" later attained by the scholastics, the Cappadocians themselves never took this step and neither did the Greek tradition after them. Thus we find the twentieth-century Orthodox theologian John Meyendorff, having just identified "hypostatic characters" with "internal relations," quoting with approval the statement of Palamas, "The hypostatic characters are not the hypostasis, but they are the characteristics of the hypostasis."[11] In the quotation given earlier from Gregory of Nazianzus we see him, in response to the Eunomians, who were using the distinction of essence and energy to conclude that the Son was different in essence from the Father, pushed to transcend this distinction (not that of substance and accident as Eugene TeSelle asserts).[12] But what is the outcome of this forced move? What exactly is relation in God if it transcends the distinction of essence and energy? It is obvious to a Western mind that despite its good points there remains in the thought of Gregory and in the subsequent Greek tradition a certain lack of clarity and precision. Thus, of Palamas and Meyendorff one could reasonably ask: If a hypostatic character is not identical with its hypostasis but only characteristic of it, how does it avoid being an accident inherent in the hypostasis?

It was precisely this question that St. Augustine took up. In book 5, chapter 3, of *De trinitate* he addressed the Arian objection that, as distinction in God must be according to substance since it cannot be according to accident, the Son must differ from the Father by substance and therefore not be truly divine.[13] In chapter 5, though he concedes that many relations among persons or objects in the world are accidents and as such are impossible in God, he insists, first, that there can be no distinction in God according to substance, and second, that the distinctions that do exist, those among the persons, pertain to relation, which must therefore be a different kind of relation, a nonaccidental kind.[14] He concludes: "Therefore, though being the Father is different from being the Son, there is no difference in substance, as this statement is made not according to substance but according to relation, which relation, however, is not accidental."[15] It remained only for Augustine to say that these relations must be subsistent and identical with the persons: if they are not accidental, that is all they can be. Nowhere, however, did he actually say it. It fell to St. Thomas to provide this final flourish, which he did in several places in his works but principally in the *Summa theologiae*, 1, q. 40, a. 2, where he says in the ad 1 as plainly as one could wish, "The persons are the subsistent relations themselves."[16]

Fichte and Hegel

According to Pannenberg, it was Fichte, taking his point of departure from individuality interpreted psychologically as self-consciousness, who, in 1798, first transposed the ontological category of relation into its psychological correlate, forging in the process an argument against the possibility of a personal God: "[I]f God were infinite, he could not be a person: self-consciousness always presupposes the existence of another, from whom one distinguishes oneself, thus becoming conscious of self. Therefore, if God were a person he could neither be infinite nor be the creator of all things."[17] There is no reason to challenge Fichte's basic stand insofar as it applies to *human* persons; but, as we shall see, its application to God is another matter. However, Fichte has made an important point: at the psychological level individuality—now self-consciousness—and relation—now spiritually experienced interpersonal relation—are not two unrelated, merely juxtaposed aspects of the person; they are intrinsically related and they condition each other. If this is so at the psychological level, is it not likely to be so also at the underlying ontological level? This is a question I shall explore in this chapter.

Pannenberg reports that Fichte's objection against a personal God was answered by Hegel, and with the two following arguments. First: "It is the essence of a person to surrender themselves to another and precisely in the other to discover themselves. The unity of God is comprehended as the unity of love bringing itself to perfection in the mutual surrender of the three persons."[18] And second, Hegel responded "with the thesis, similar to it (the above) in structure and stated with emphasis, that God is *subject*."[19]

Let us now consider Hegel's line of argument. One notes first the common ground between Hegel and Fichte, the shift to the psychological plane and the concentration on person as relation. As Pannenberg points out in the same place, via Feuerbach the influence of Fichte and Hegel extended right into the twentieth century in the persons of Ferdinand Ebner and Martin Buber, the last-named being almost synonymous with the concept of person as psychological relatedness. But where Hegel takes issue with Fichte is over the assertion that God has no other from whom to distinguish himself. Certainly, no created person could fill this role, for that would make God dependent on his own creation. But God in himself, says Hegel, is no undifferentiated unity: within the Godhead and constituting it are the three persons, each of whom is constituted as a person over against the others by a mutual surrender of love. Thus, Hegel invokes the concept of triunity to save the personhood of God. On this argument, if God were not triune he would not be personal at all.

Pannenberg tells us that "theology did not appreciate this service of Hegel's."[20] And well it might not! In its undifferentiated treatment of the three persons, Hegel's first reply is a purely philosophical construction bearing no relation to the biblical data. Taking my point of departure from the two biblical missions, I was able to show in the last chapter that the notional or person-constituting loves of God are not the loving surrender of each person to the others, but, first, God's self-love, which brings about the distinction of Father and Son, and, second, God's love-of-the-other, the mutual love of Father and Son, which brings about the distinction of the Holy Spirit from them. This is not to deny that in fact each person surrenders himself to the others in love, but only that this undifferentiated love is notional. Further, both Fichte and Hegel take too anthropomorphic a view of God. To say that each divine person becomes conscious of himself in his distinction from the others is to speak in a way that today can have no currency outside Process thought. Nevertheless, in grounding God's personhood purely and simply in his triunity, Hegel issued an important and abiding challenge to the received theology.

Reconciliation of the One and the Three

There is, however, in this matter another aspect that must be taken into account, and I present it in the light of a summary account by Franz Diekamp.[21] He asks how the naturally known single personhood of God can be related to the Trinity of persons. We could ask even more pointedly how the single (nontrinitarian) personhood of Yahweh revealed in the Old Testament can be related to the Trinity of persons revealed in the New, a question that I broached earlier, in chapter 3: "[I]n the economic Trinity it is not the Father who is to be equated with Yahweh of the Old Testament. Rather, it is *God* who is to be thus equated, God who differentiates out into Father, Son, and Holy Spirit, and this despite the fact that in the New Testament the word 'God' nearly always refers to the Father." Diekamp summarizes the discussion since St. Thomas in terms of one absolute subsistence and three relative subsistences. Thus, Durandus (fourteenth century) held that the only subsistence in God was absolute and was communicated to the three persons. This view Diekamp rightly rejects on the ground that despite its terminology it in fact would allow only one person in God. The next opinion is that of Vasquez and De Lugo (seventeenth century), who with many others maintained that there was in God no absolute subsistence but only the three relative subsistences. And finally, there is the view of Cajetan (sixteenth century) and the Thomists, with whom Diekamp agrees, that in God there are one absolute and three relative subsistences.

Between the last two opinions, however, Diekamp discerns only a difference of terminology, not of substance. According to him, the apparent difference depends on whether subsistence is understood to include incommunicability or not:

[T]he word "subsistence" is taken by some in a stricter and by others in a broader sense. In the strict sense, that is, for the being-of-an-individual subsistent in itself and incommunicable, it cannot be predicated of the divine substance as such, for the latter subsists in three persons. To admit such an absolute subsistence would be to profess a quaternity. But taken for the subsistent being of an individual, prescinding from incommunicability, subsistence can be attributed to God absolutely.

Diekamp goes on to observe that St. Thomas allowed the broad sense of subsistence and quotes him accordingly: "[In God] there are several things subsisting if the relations are considered, but only one if the essence is considered"[22]; and "The supposits of the divine nature . . . are not the principle of the subsistence of the divine essence, for the latter subsists of itself."[23]

We saw earlier that philosophy found no reason to distinguish between individuality and subsistence. Provided it was not an accident, an individual was understood thereby, from the very fact that it *was* an individual, to subsist. It was theology that made the distinction, obliged thereto by the Chalcedonian doctrine of Christ. It was now understood that a concrete individual did not thereby have to subsist, at least with its own subsistence. But the converse was not thereby logically imposed, that a subsistent being does not have to be thereby an individual. Indeed, there was still no reason to call into question the principle that whatever subsists is thereby an individual. And whatever is individual is thereby incommunicable. We can therefore continue to hold without any qualms that whatever subsists is thereby both individual and incommunicable.[24] Even the doctrine of the Trinity suggests nothing to the contrary. The contribution of Billot, availed of in the last chapter, helps us here, though it is necessary to modify his argument. The Father and the Son, so he tells us, together constitute subsistent spirativity in regard to the spiration of the Holy Spirit. This spirativity is not a person, because it is not distinct, but it is individual (because Father and Son here constitute a single principle) and subsistent (because the Holy Spirit who proceeds from it is subsistent). Against Billot, however, I should add that it is incommunicable, for it cannot be communicated to the Holy Spirit, nor to any other being; that is to say, it cannot be communicated outside the "nondistinct subsistent" with which it is identical. Of course, I agree with Billot that it is communicable insofar as it can be communicated, and in fact is communicated, from the Father to the Son; but then, as such, it is not subsistent. The Father is not subsistent spirativity on his own (on his own he is only subsistent Fatherhood); the spirativity that he communicates to the Son is that whereby *together* they spirate the Holy Spirit, and this despite the fact that spirativity is complete in both the Father and the Son.

Diekamp's distinction between a strict and a broad sense of "subsistence," therefore, is incorrect. There is no subsistence without incommunicability. What is necessary is to distinguish between various senses of "incommunicability." There is the normal sense, in which it denotes the quality of ultimate individuation possessed by a supposit that is a concrete individual instance of an abstract essence capable of unlimited multiplication. Clearly, in this sense it does not apply to God at all. Then there are two special senses that apply to God, imposed on us by trinitarian considerations. First, there is an absolute sense, which applies to the concrete, single, divine essence as such and says that this essence cannot be communicated *outside itself*, that there cannot be more than one God.[25] And second, there is a relative sense that applies to the persons as such. This recognizes first of all that the divine essence possesses a relative communicability *within itself* and that in fact it is communicated from the Father to the Son and from them together to the Holy Spirit. But then, and most importantly, by this sense it is asserted that the persons as such are *incommunicable*: Fatherhood, which is the same as the Father,[26] is *not* communicated to the Son or the Holy Spirit, and neither is Sonship, nor Spirithood (to coin, with apologies, a necessary term), to either of the others. And just as John Beccos rightly situated the Filioque midway between trinitarian essentialism and personalism (I drew attention to this in the last chapter), so there is a mysterious incommunicability (from one perspective) that is also communicability (from another) that characterizes the "subsistent spirativity" of the Father and the Son as together constituting the single principle of the Holy Spirit.

The upshot of all this is to rule out the opinion of Vasquez and De Lugo and affirm that of Cajetan and the Thomists, that in God there are one absolute subsistence and three relative subsistences.[27] The two quotations from St. Thomas can be interpreted in this sense. Diekamp's remark about subsistence-cum-incommunicability as implying a quaternity in God is specious, as the three relative subsistences imply only three corresponding relative incommunicabilities, which cannot be counted along with the absolute incommunicability of the essence but are contained within it. In fact, we can generalize here and say that, apart from the divine names and their equivalents and also apart from spirativity, *whatever* is predicated of God can be predicated in two ways: absolutely and singly, as regards the essence; and relatively and three times over, as regards the persons.

In saying this, we have removed Diekamp's basis for asserting that, even though there is only one absolute subsistence in God, we cannot say that there is one absolute *person* in him (and, by implication, three relative persons) as here " 'subsistence' is not used in the strict sense demanded for the notion of person strictly understood, which includes incommunicability." We must conclude, therefore, that, as with subsistence and incommunicability, so with person: in God there are one absolute person and three relative persons. And thus we answer the question with which we set out: how to reconcile the one person of God of the Old Testament with the three persons of the New. Diekamp rather reluctantly admits that there are many theologians who espouse the view rejected by him, and that they can quote St. Thomas in their support: "If through our intellect we exclude the personal properties, there remains in our consideration the divine nature as subsistent and as a person."[28]

We are now in a position to see that Hegel's two arguments are mutually incompatible in the form in which they stand. In regard to the subject matter of the first, we recognize that the persons are in certain notional ontological relations with each other, which ontological relations logically ground psychological ones. These ontological relations are, respectively, those that obtain between the Father and the Son, and between Father and Son on the one side and the Holy Spirit on the other. They are to be identified simply as the persons, but only in the relative sense of this word. In this sense, then, God must be affirmed as truly personal. As for the second argument, as Hegel has here said "subject" rather than "subjects," it depends on our understanding "person" in the absolute sense in which it is used of Yahweh in the Old Testament. In the light of the distinction-cum-compatibility of absolute and relative subsistence established above, the incompatiblity that we observed between the two arguments can be overcome. However, I must note that in answering Fichte as he does, Hegel has embarked on a wrong course. It is not sufficient for him to draw attention to the relative (trinitarian) personhood of God, as in his first argument; to answer Fichte properly he would need to deal with the latter's objection against the possibility of an absolute divine personhood on its own terms. Clearly, with my talk hitherto simply of divine subsistence, I have not done this either, as yet.

I said earlier, and I repeat, that faith assigns no priority of the unity of God over his threeness (or vice versa). It is the prerogative of theology to do this if it so chooses, but such a decision, as made by a particular theology, could never be normative. It is therefore impossible to say whether the absolute personhood of God is more important or more basic than the three relative personhoods. What we *can* say is that the progress of revelation itself leads us from Yahweh of the Old Testament to the Father, Son, and Spirit of the New, and that therefore we attain a more profound knowledge of God when we penetrate beyond the absolute personhood to the relative personhoods contained within it.

Relatedness of God

I now take up Fichte's challenge to the possibility of an absolute personhood in God. This personhood, being simply identical with his essence, remains utterly mysterious and hidden from us. But this does not mean that we must conceive it as wholly nonrelational as the Thomistic tradition would urge. In chapter 1, building on the position of Thomas Weinandy, I argued that God's relation to creatures was transcendental, "superreal" rather than nonreal. This actual relation to contingent being must rest on a relational tendency in the being of God. But how can this be?

Let us begin, with the help of Etienne Gilson, at the most fundamental of all concepts, *esse*, "to be."[29] Gilson speaks of the "intrinsic dynamism" of this act of being.[30] He writes, "Not: to be, then to act, but: to be is to act. And the very first thing which 'to be' does, is to make its own essence to be, that is, 'to be a being.'"[31] Between this act of being and its essence we must posit a basic, indeed a "transcendental," relation, which is the fundamental expression of the dynamism here spoken of. (Here, of course, I use the term "transcendental" in a somewhat different sense from that in which it was used in the last paragraph.) As distinct from a categorial relation, which is an accident supervening upon two already existent beings, such as, for example, the friendship of two friends, a transcendental relation is not an accident but "a relation so necessary or essential to a thing that the being cannot be without it and removal of the relation would imply a change of essence or the destruction of the being."[32] In the present context I am speaking of such a relation, not between one being and another, but *within* a finite being, the relation that co-ordinates its most fundamental components. Relationality, therefore, is not something tacked on subsequently to finite being; of its very nature it is relational. Indeed, we can go further and assert, on the basis of the essential relationality of its esse, that its relationality is prior to its substantiality, for, as Gilson says, esse is "the ultimate root of all being."[33] Gilson continues, "[T]he next thing which 'to be' does, is to begin bringing its own individual essence somewhat nearer its completion."[34] There are three things to say here. The first is that finite esse itself must be some kind of limitation of the infinite esse of God. The second is that the action here spoken of is simply a consequent exercise of the primordial dynamism of the act of being, "channeled" now via the essence (and hence no longer primordial) as the latter realizes itself through, and only through, its own proper activity. In Thomistic terms, it is a case of "first act" and "second act." The third comment is that, as a channeling of the act of being, which, as we have seen, is essentially relational, this activity, whose first action is the "to be" of the essence, is itself essentially relational, relating the being actually (though categorially, not transcendentally) to all the beings in its environment to which it belongs and with which it interacts, and thus to all other beings in the world.

The difference in the case of God is that with him "to be" does not "make its own essence to be," as his essence already *is*, for his essence is simply "to be." Nor does it have to realize itself through consequent activity; indeed it cannot, as it is already given in total self-existence. Gilson again: "Fully posited by its 'to be,' essence here (in God) entails neither limitation nor determination. On the contrary, finite essences always entail both limitation and determination, because each of them is the formal delimitation of a possible being."[35] Here, then, there can be no channeling of the dynamic act of being via the essence, relating God for the purpose of self-realization to the world of finite beings. Dynamic it is, but its dynamism requires only what it already meets, what it already has and is, in the all-perfect divine essence, and it requires nothing beyond it. This dynamism is the foundation of God's relationality. It *becomes* relationality only when creatures are taken into account, and in their regard. In the case of God it is meaningless to speak, as we do of creatures, of a transcendental relation between existence and essence, for in him they are identical. Therefore, if created beings exist, they do so by God's *free* decision, and, while they are necessarily expressions of the dynamism and relationality of the divine being, they are not necessary, but only contingent, expressions of it. By their existence, they bear witness to the excess, abundance, and non-necessary overflow of the divine being, into the world of contingent being. All this confirms the conclusion reached earlier that the absolute personhood of God, far from being nonrelational, or being really related to the world in a way that would demand its creation for the realization of his essence, possesses a relationality that comes to a non-necessary expression in his superreal relations to creatures.[36] What has enabled our perception of this is our appreciation of the innate dynamism of the divine esse, which has its necessary expression in the divine essence, "to be."[37]

The relationality of God's absolute personhood does not, of course, solve the problem of how there can be such a personhood, since by definition there can be no other divine person in relation to whom it can define itself. It is only the relative divine persons, *within* the Godhead, who are such in relation to other divine persons, the Father and the Son in relation to each other, and the Holy Spirit in relation to the Father and the Son together. Yet God in his unity (Yahweh) is revealed as truly personal in the absolute sense. How can this be?

The answer to this question rests on the distinction, or lack of it, between essence and existence. In the case of human persons, where this distinction is real, essence, and with it personhood, undergoes initial actualization at the first moment of existence and then further actualization through the forging of psychological relations, and thus the realization of its underlying ontological relations, with other human beings and ultimately, as we shall see, with God. For our purposes let me analyze, very briefly, the ontology of the human person. We need to start with God, unlimited esse. The human esse can only be a created participation in this esse of God. As I said earlier, the dynamism of the human esse comes to expression in its transcendental relation to its essence, and is then channeled via the essence, specifically through its being and proper activity, into categorial relations with other creatures, particularly with other human beings. But its relationship with *God* is not categorial; rather, it is a transcendental relation to God as absolute spirit. I must leave this all-important point for detailed treatment later in the chapter, but for the moment suffice it to say that the fundamental ground of this is the unique character of the human person as a spiritual entity, or, more precisely, relative spirit or spirit by participation. The word "spirit" denotes, in this case, that qualified transcendence and independence of matter that allows its possessor to be and to become a "subject," in Bilaniuk's terms, "a self-standing, self-possessing and autonomous center of attribution." As a *capacity*, this is bestowed at the moment of initial actualization, at the moment of creation. In human beings, then, the real distinction of essence and existence posits the essence, along with its task of self-realization, in a transcendental relation to God as absolute spirit.

In the case of God, where essence and existence are identical, the essence is given already as complete and unlimited self-existence, simply "to be." (It is not appropriate to speak here of "self-realization" or "self-actualization," in regard to that which because of its perfection is incapable of realization or actualization.) Here there is no qualified transcendence or independence of matter, but one that is simply unqualified and infinite. God is not *related* to absolute spirit; he *is* absolute spirit. He is not merely *a* subject, or the residue of three relative subjects; he is absolute subject, fount of all subjectivity. This is why it is possible for him to be, and why he is, absolute person, not standing for the sake of his personhood in relation to any other person, but nevertheless related to all other persons through relations that are superreal. This is why Fichte's argument is fundamentally wrong and why Hegel was wrong to accept its premises. Both conceived God too anthropomorphically.

The question inevitably arises whether the existence of relative persons in God bespeaks some limitation in him, on the analogy of human persons. But the answer must be that it does not, because the divine persons do not have to be actualized over against each other; indeed they cannot, as they are given, each of them, in total *identity* with the divine essence, the distinction between each of them and the essence being merely "virtual" (in the Thomistic school) or "formal" (in the Scotist).[38] Let me be clear that they are persons by virtue of their relations to each other (and so not to God as absolute spirit); but these relations are not actualized, they are simply given as three (really) distinct modalities of the one divine essence.

Given what we know of being in general, it should come as no surprise to learn from revelation that the divine being is internally relational. But, as I have shown, this is not something we could ever deduce from the innate dynamism of the divine being. Hence the intrinsic bond that we identify between substantiality and relationality in the case of finite being, with, as I have argued, the latter taking precedence over the former, cannot be perceived at all in the case of God, though it is there, since there can be nothing in the being of God that is not necessary. This means that there is no known philosophical principle that can be used to integrate absolute personhood and relative personhood in God in a single vision. All we can do is to proceed on the basis of the negative principle that they are not contradictory. Thus we can say: the absolute personhood of God is given in three relative persons; or, pace Rahner (as I noted in the last chapter): in God there is one subjectivity (or absolute subject) but three (relative) subjects.

Because we human beings realize our personhood through relations, the relative personhood of God is more interesting and relevant to us than is his absolute personhood. This is so particularly as his relative personhood becomes accessible to us in the revelation-event of Christ, who is set before us as a model, and whose life's challenge can be expressed as the task of realizing his personhood, that of the divine person of the Son within the confines of human nature, over against God (the Father). In the case of the immanent Trinity we speak of ontological relations logically grounding psychological ones; in the case of human persons we speak of psychological relations drawing ontological ones in their train as their efforts at forging appropriate psychological relations actualize and develop the capacity they have for ontological relations from their creation as spiritual beings; and in the economic Trinity, where Christ is the paradigm, his human efforts at the level of spiritual action over against the Father allow the preexistent divine Son to become progressively expressed (incarnated) in the created human nature as such actions (under grace, that of the hypostatic union itself) render the latter an ever more apt medium for the expression of divinity (in it).

Human Personhood

We now take up the question of human personhood in terms of relation with God. In Pannenberg's article one of the most arresting and challenging statements is the following:

> In contrast to Thomas Aquinas, who because of his distinction of *esse* (existence) and *essentia* (essence) saw the act of being (the *esse*) as the constitutive element of human personhood, Duns (Scotus) understood only *relationship* to God as constitutive of the human being as a person. According to Duns, there are two ways in which a human being can be a person: in self-assertion against God or in devotion in openness to him.[39]

Clearly, Pannenberg's own ideas on person as expressed in the article are shaped by this doctrine, which he learned through an early work of Heribert Mühlen, *Sein und Person nach Johannes Duns Scotus* (Being and Person According to Johannes Duns Scotus).[40] In the remainder of this chapter I shall be drawing on this work of *Mühlen's*, and I present the material in three points, as follows.[41]

First, Christian anthropology is an exercise that is both philosophical and theological. While it must strive to do justice to the data of revelation, its method must remain philosophical. Second, for the human person a Christian anthropology cannot be satisfied with a material principle of individuation only, such as suffices for material beings in general, namely, "quantified matter," in this case the "body." To this it will insist on adding a formal principle that respects the unique nature, the "spirituality," of the human person. In the words of J. F. Donceel, "[M]an is individualized basically through the relation of his soul to quantified matter, secondarily through his own personal history, as written in him by his immanent actions, especially by his free decisions."[42] In other words, the human person is individuated materially by their body, which is proper to themselves, and formally by their unique personal history lived in and through the body, especially as this history is shaped by their free decisions and consents as distinct from events undergone simply passively (which, however, also have an individualizing effect). Moreover, unless for our theology of the afterlife we are prepared to accept the Platonic-style dualism inherent in the theology of the "intermediate state" (not to mention its accompanying mythology), it is necessary to embrace something like the "resurrection-in-death" theology of G. Greshake and G. Lohfink (who build on certain ideas of Rahner).[43] Greshake writes as follows:

> The perfection of the human being in death is not to be thought of as the migration of a disembodied soul which leaves bodiliness and world behind, but rather as the definitive coming-to-self of the human spiritual subject in and at the world and in and at bodiliness, whereby matter has been interiorized and transformed into an abiding dimension of the perfection of the spirit, even if this is beyond our imagination since for us materiality is known only in the form of sense-perceptible visibility.[44]

Such a theology has the advantage of permitting Donceel's twofold principle of individuation to operate consistently, for the afterlife as well as the present life.

The third point is that the human person is characterized by two transcendental relations, the first that of their spirit to their body, and the second that of the person as a spiritual being to God. The first is identified as their primary principle of individuation (which then provides the possibility of their secondary principle of individuation), the second as their principle of subsistence, of their very being as spiritual. The first relation mentioned above is clearly transcendental, for in the human person spirit and body are not external or extraneous to each other, but, though distinct dimensions of human being, are, quite simply, intrinsically ordered to each other, essential to each other, and intertwined in an indissoluble unity of being, the unity of form and matter. The second relation mentioned above is also transcendental, because the human person must be understood as a spiritual being (and not only as a being with spiritual activities) and ultimately this demands that they be understood as a created participation in the God who is Absolute Spirit. According to Mühlen, though the ingredients of this idea are also found in St. Thomas, it was Scotus who first explicitly elaborated it,[45] and we recognize it (together with its genesis) in the quotation given above from Pannenberg.

Here, then, we have a vision of the human person: as spirit, created spirit, existing (subsisting) by virtue of two fundamental transcendental relations. Let us now, however, invert the order from the logical to the ontological, that is, to the order of constitution. Here the first relation is that by which the human spirit is related to God its creator, that by which its very existence as spirit is bestowed and sustained, that by which its transcendence over the world is expressed; and the second is its relation to matter, to the body, by which it is individuated and "anchored" or "hammered down" in the world, shown to be immanent in the world (so that it truly is "spirit in the world," to use Rahner's phrase). These two relations are not just things that the human person *has*; they are what he or she *is*. Therefore, like the divine persons, the human person is to be understood as a subsistent relation, though in this case the term of the relation is God as absolute person (at least in the first instance—I shall refine this position later).[46] But unlike the divine persons, the human person is to be understood in terms also of the second transcendental relation mentioned above.

Before proceeding, we need to deal with the following difficulty concerning this comprehensive concept of person. *Every* finite substance, whether personal or infrapersonal, is a creature, and therefore as such can be characterized in terms of a transcendental relation to God and so can be designated a subsistent relation. Since this designation is not specific to the person but applies to every finite substance, and since a definition covers only what marks off what is to be defined from other kinds of being, it cannot serve as a definition of the person. Scotus does not address this precise difficulty, as he did not take the step here taken from transcendental to subsistent relation, but he does deal with it at the level of transcendental relation, though not, apparently, satisfactorily. In a text in his Oxford Commentary on the Sentences, on which Mühlen comments, he gives a rather baffling answer to the question whether the transcendental relation of creaturehood should be included in the definition of a thing. In the answer he uses the word *perfecte* ("perfectly") twice, and Mühlen makes sense of the text by taking the two usages as different in meaning. I cannot comment on the legitimacy of this solution (to the question of what Scotus meant), but simply report Mühlen's interpretation: if we aim at precision (knowing *perfecte* in the first sense) and therefore consider only the common nature, which belongs to the realm of logic and comprises genus and specific difference, the transcendental relation is not included, but if we aim at depth (knowing *perfecte* in the second sense) and therefore embrace the concrete existence of the thing, the transcendental relation is included.[47] As an answer to the actual question, this seems to be invalid, as the transcendental relation clearly belongs to the common nature (i.e., it pertains to the *nature* of this thing to be, at least at its lowest and therefore most widely shared level of being short of being itself, a creature) even though it is omitted in the definition, which understandably restricts itself to the highest property held in common with other species (the genus) and the (specific) difference, which marks off its species from them. So neither Scotus nor Mühlen helps us much here. However, from Scotus we take the point that it is not only persons who possess the transcendental relation of creaturehood or dependent subsistence but all finite substances, and so we must acknowledge the original difficulty as real and as still requiring an answer. Let me now address this problem.[48]

Whatever has been created by God exists by virtue of the transcendental relation of creaturehood it bears toward him. This relation is identical with the finite, created being of the thing. If it were not a creature, it would not exist at all; and it is precisely as a creature that it does exist. But it does not just exist; it subsists, and does so as this relation. It is therefore a subsistent relation. However, if it be a material being, it is not *defined* as a subsistent relation, since it is adequately defined "from below," that is, on the basis of its properties, either evident or accessible, which suffice to mark it off according to genus and specific difference from other kinds of being in the world. Furthermore, in its case "subsistent relation" cannot be a defining concept, as it applies indiscriminately to everything. The fundamental argument, however, comes from St. Thomas. Creatures other than rational ones, he tells us, "do not reach anything universal, but only the particular, insofar as they share in the divine good either merely by existing, the case with inanimate beings, or also by living and knowing particulars, the case with plants or animals."[49] In other words, their end is purely immanent in the material creation, and for this reason they can *only* be defined from below. It is otherwise, however, with human beings. As St. Thomas goes on to say, "the rational nature, however, insofar as it knows the universal meaning of good and being, has an immediate relation to the universal principle of being." Note that in this text St. Thomas moves, as we also do, from operation to being, without, however, acknowledging that the relation in question must be transcendental. In other words, the human person does not just *have* this relation to God, but *is* this relation. Therefore, in the subsistent relation to God we have a new definition of the finite person to God. But for it to become a definition of precisely the *human* person (as distinct from angels) we would have to add the second transcendental relation of which I spoke earlier, that of the human spirit to the body. As we would then be defining human nature in the determinate mode of particular existence, we would be defining the human person as such, though not from below.[50] Furthermore, only this definition is adequate, as only it penetrates sufficiently both "upward," to God as the goal of human transcendence, and "downward," to the individual, to the human being who has been adequately individuated.

The divine persons of the Trinity, as we have seen, are also defined as subsistent relations. How is this so? The answer is that because of their spirituality and identity with the divine essence it is impossible that they differ by anything absolute. They therefore differ only by the relations that obtain among themselves, and indeed they are identical with these relations. Hence they are subsistent relations, and this is their definition. But they are not relations of creaturehood toward God, as is the case with human beings and angels. They are relations of equality and of mutual (ontological) opposition, of the Father over against the Son and of these two together over against the Holy Spirit, within the single, concrete, divine essence. Hence the divine persons are relations that, though transcendental and subsistent, as are those of human beings and angels toward God, differ very much from them.

My presentation thus far could give an impression of the human person as an individual essentially isolated from the world and everything (and everyone) in it and related to God alone. To correct this I need to bring to the fore the structure of the human person as spirit precisely "in the world," which characteristic is secured by its transcendental relation to matter.[51] This means that the self-realization of the human person before God takes place through activity, specifically love (with all that this entails), which is directed in the first instance to other human persons in the world, who because of their own spirituality provide for this person in their other-directed love a transcendental horizon that is truly their opening to God. This is why Rahner is able to write both,

> The act of personal love for the human Thou is therefore the all-embracing basic act of the human being which gives meaning, direction and measure to everything else,[52]

and,

> The categorial-explicit love of neighbor is the primary act of the love of God, which in the love of neighbor as such intends God in supernatural transcendentality un-thematically, but really and always; and even the explicit love of God is still borne by that trusting-loving openness to the whole of reality that is enacted in the love of neighbor.[53]

These statements of Rahner, taken from his essay "Reflections on the Unity of the Love of Neighbor and the Love of God" embody the theological anthropology that he first enunciated in his major early work *Spirit in the World* (*Geist in Welt*), from 1957.[54] In the brief analysis of love given in the last chapter I added another element to this Rahnerian scheme, self-love. Human love is determined by *three* coordinates, love of neighbor, love of God, and love of self; in the explicit love of neighbor both the love of God and the love of self are affirmed implicitly; and these two latter loves are rendered explicit in respectively different ways, the former by social means (principally, religion), and the latter through reflection and increasing self-knowledge. Therefore, when we call the human person a subsistent relation, we indicate the transcendental relation of the finite spirit to the infinite spirit of God, that is, the former's complete dependence on the latter for its existence, it being presupposed that this finite spirit is individuated through its other transcendental relation, that which it bears to matter (the matter out of which, in a sense, it rises[55]). This relation to matter both grounds it firmly in the world and gives it the task of achieving itself before God (i.e., its primary transcendental relation) through the relation of love of neighbor. Thus, the succinct expression "subsistent relation" sums up very suitably the complexity of the being and the task of the human person.

Conclusion

If I look back from this vantage point at Bilaniuk's description of person, I see that I have now done what I set out to do, catch up with all its assertions in my own way, which was to show how all the various aspects of person are included in the concept "subsistent relation." From the time of St. Thomas Aquinas it has been widely accepted in Catholic theology that this is how the persons of the Trinity are to be understood, but this teaching brought with it its own problems: it appeared to widen the gulf between the divine persons and human persons, who are the only ones we know directly; and it appeared not to do justice to the richness of content of the idea of person. This latter perception lies at the heart of the rejection of the Thomistic doctrine by Orthodox theologians, who seem not to appreciate how close to it their own Cappadocian Fathers came. As Kallistos (Timothy) Ware writes, "Orthodox thinkers find this a very meager idea of personality."[56] With the present treatment I have responded to both these problems. In particular, my disquisition on the human person in the context of a theology of the Trinity is explained and justified by a desire to show that, given that all our positive knowledge of God is had by analogy to earthly correlates, Catholic theology remained in an impasse as long as, on the one hand, it asserted that in God "person" meant "subsistent relation," and, on the other, admitted that this expression had no application to human persons as we know them. We are in a much better position if we can say that we *expect* divine persons to be subsistent relations because that is what human persons are, even if the two respective ways of being such a relation differ dramatically from each other.

I said earlier that the human person was a subsistent relation over against God conceived at least initially as absolute person. I now propose to explain the reason for the qualification contained in this statement. To say that the term of this transcendental relation is God conceived as absolute person would be how the matter would be expressed in terms of the one God of the Old Testament. But when we place this statement in the context of Christianity, it has to be formulated anew. First, we need to remember that in the actual divine dispensation in which we live the realization of personhood is not just a matter of nature but of nature enabled and assisted by grace. And second, we need to apply our knowledge that grace is the Gift of the Holy Spirit and that the work of the Spirit is to unite us to Christ and thus bring us into union with the Father. When we contemplate Christ, who is the very visibility of grace, we appreciate that his whole life as Son of God incarnate can be understood as the realization by him of authentic personhood, the realization of the divine person within the confines of human nature, by his human efforts aided by the Holy Spirit, not over against God as absolute person, but over against precisely God the Father. This helps us to understand our own case. Thus we are brought to see that the trinitarian character of grace changes what would otherwise be a relationship with God as it were from "outside" to one enacted within the Trinity, where we, through the power of the Holy Spirit, Spirit of sonship and daughterhood, become identified with the Son (that is, we become sons and daughters *in the Son*, to use the patristic phrase). Hence, while initially we may be tempted to see our relation to God as terminating in him merely as absolute person, from the trinitarian perspective of grace, which should never be omitted in a theological consideration, we come to see this relation as actually terminating in the Father, and we learn to understand our achieved personhood in terms of our faith, that is, to identify it with our sonship or daughterhood of God, which is unique to each one of us. And we would want to say essentially the same for the personhood of non-Christians and nonbelievers. Though they do not confess Christianity and we accept and respect this fact about them, as Christians we can only understand their achievement of authentic personhood in our own terms, as enabled and assisted by grace and so also as consisting of a relation (albeit unconscious or, to use Rahner's term, "anonymous") to God the Father.[57]

I now resume an earlier theme, the juxtaposition of individual and relation in the conceptualization of person. In the course of our considerations we saw that at the psychological level these two aspects, appropriately transposed, revealed an intrinsic relationship and I voiced the suspicion that the same might be true at the underlying ontological level. We also saw that the Christological dogma necessitated, for the person of Christ, a further determination of the concept of individual, so that this was changed to "subsistent." Thus instructed, we are brought by our reflections to the point of seeing that the suspicion mentioned earlier is in fact the case: the person simply *is* a relation, a relation, therefore, that subsists, the relation, namely, of spirit to spirit, of created spirit to uncreated spirit. This means that individual is subsumed into relation and becomes concretely indistinguishable from it (though they remain conceptually distinct). Because in the case of the *human* person the person belongs to a species (human beings, "man" as we used to say), this person needs to be individuated through a *logically* prior transcendental relation, that of the human spirit to matter, where matter, or the body, is the primary principle of individuation. However, what is *ontologically* prior, because constitutive of the person as such, is the transcendental relation to God; if it were not for that, the being in question would still be a subsistent individual, a hypostasis, an animal, but not a person.[58] Following the Thomistic doctrine,[59] we can go on to say that whatever determination or perfection the material dimension of the person has is imparted to it by the created spirit, by which the person stands in a transcendental relation to God.

If, on the other hand, we conceive person principally in the perspective of individual with relation seen as secondary (a not incorrect but less satisfactory conception, since it considers only the relationality that is consequent upon substantiation and not the relationality, deriving from esse, that is prior to it and that is channeled through it), we contemplate an isolated being, indeed the most isolated in the universe, which is then rescued from its isolation through relation. This view is brought to expression in various ways. For example, Rahner notes that to the individuality of the person comes universality (in the sense of "orientation to being as a whole"), seeing here, however, "a contradiction in formal logic."[60] Contrast there may be, but not contradiction, for spiritual individuality *implies* an orientation to, and in a sense an actual possession of, the whole of being, with the conscious self situated at its center. This is what lay behind my statement at the beginning of this chapter that the being most isolated in the world of beings is by that very fact the one most connected to that world. As a commentator points out, Teilhard saw a similar contrast, which he expressed in terms of, on the one hand, "granulation" ("of the species into isolated individuals on account of the growth in the psychic autonomy of its single members") and, on the other, "the bias towards convergence due to the merging of cultures."[61] And Mühlen, presenting the mind of Scotus, paints a detailed and vivid picture of the *ultima solitudo* ("ultimate solitude") to which the person would be condemned if they did not allow themselves to be "saved" from it by giving themselves over to the Son of God, as Jesus did in unique radicality, thus becoming the model for us all.[62] Apart from the excesses of the last-mentioned view (understandable in its historical context), one cannot question the validity, at a less profound level, of views of this kind. They may be said to constitute the prevailing approach. But I have here argued for another view, one that awards precedence to relation over subsistence or individuality (without, however, abolishing it), claiming it to be more adequate to the facts. And it has the undoubted advantage, very important from the point of view of our present study, of bringing Christian anthro-pology and the theology of the Trinity into line with each other.

Finally, we ask: In regard to person, where does relation come from? If we see each being as exemplifying the problem of the one and the many, for the case of person we can correlate individual with the former and relation with the latter. Human beings are persons because they stand in a transcendental relation to another than themselves, to God, and they achieve their personhood before him through relations with other human beings in the world. God himself, if viewed in his unity as absolute person, is without relation, precisely because there is no other, nor could there be, for him to relate to, and in this sense his personhood remains an impen-etrable mystery to us. But in God too there is plurality, of persons. Though we could not know this fact with certainty except from revelation, plurality of persons in God is not something contingent, but, like everything to do with his being, necessary with a necessity of nature.[63] But the ground of this necessity is hidden from us, though its fittingness is clear. With plurality in God known, person (apart from God's absolute personhood) is seen once more to be relation, and necessarily so. Relation, then, expresses the essential social dimension of all spiritual being. I add that it is only individual, subsistent beings that can have, or be, actual relations. What we have here, therefore, in this case, is subsistent relations.

5

Change in God

In this chapter I propose to examine the question of "change" or "mutability" in God. As we proceed, we shall see that the important *religious* question for us is one that depends directly on the possibility of a relational and loving, truly personal, God. I say "possibility" because the perfection and transcendence of God, taught in Scripture, safeguarded by the teaching of the Church and expounded by a continuous theological tradition, are increasingly being perceived as incompatible with the God of traditional Christian piety, with a God, that is, who truly loves us, is affected by our suffering and responds to our prayers. In this confused situation there are some who, feeling faced with a choice, prefer to sacrifice the divine transcendence rather than risk losing this God of piety, not realizing, however, that they thereby abandon the God of revelation in favor of a human creation. My task therefore will be to show how these two conceptions of God can be held together without contradiction. Because mutability in God is a key proposition of Process theology, a movement that has been conspicuously successful, particularly in the English-speaking world, I shall critically examine what this school has to say on this subject. I shall then look quite briefly but critically at what the Eastern Orthodox Palamite tradition contributes to the discussion. This critical work will favorably position me to argue more positively for a view of my own, one that I hope will give due place to all the relevant elements of the tradition.

Process Theology

I turn, then, to Process theology and choose as principal spokesman for it the Catholic theologian Joseph Bracken. But I can hardly speak of Bracken without first considering, however briefly, Charles Hartshorne, who over a long career has been a prolific writer on the various themes of Process philosophy and theology.[1] And since his thought, as that of Bracken, can be understood only against the background of the metaphysics of Alfred North Whitehead (1861–1947), the initiator of Process thought, I must begin by stating the fundamental principles of the latter's system.

Alfred North Whitehead

Whitehead began his academic career as a mathematician at Cambridge and later expanded his interests to include physics as well as philosophy. In the latter field he devised a comprehensive cosmology that included in its sweep everything from subatomic particles to God. His postulation of the existence of God provides a basis for comparison between his and other modern European theistic philosophical systems, for in all of them God is not in the first instance the God of revelation, but a "God of the philosophers," a guarantor of the integrity of the system in question. In this case, God ensured that the overall direction taken by that which is judged most basic in reality, the creative process, is positive and progressive rather than negative and regressive. For where other systems saw substances as the fundamental existents of the universe, and process as, at best, their inherent dynamism, Whitehead, taking his cue from modern physics, saw energy, or process itself, the "creative" process just mentioned, as the most basic reality of the universe. This process is constituted by a vast number of interrelated "energy events": these emerge, by "prehension," from preceding events caught in the act of perishing; they come, by "concresence," into actuality; and they perish as in turn they give rise to new events. Existents that give the impression of being enduring substances are in reality nothing but clusters, or "societies," of energy events, whose stability is only relative. God fits into this pulsating process as the one who gently persuades it forward by continually offering and making available to it "initial aims," fruitful possibilities for conversion into actuality.

If this system, with its foundations in science, seems rather mechanical and hence unable to cope with the reality and mystery of persons (a suspicion that may still turn out to be correct), it needs to be remembered that a second starting point for Whitehead was the phenomenon of human experience. Admittedly, the term "experience," as also "enjoyment" and "satisfaction," was used by him to characterize all energy events, even those occurring below or outside consciousness, but this was because he saw conscious human experience as the model for the actual structure of all energy events and for our understanding of them. In this limited sense, then, his system may be described as personalist (though clearly he did not understand "person" in the usual way, as inclusive of a sense of enduring identity). While it is not normal to use these terms ("experience," "enjoyment," and "satisfaction") analogously (and to do so sounds a little strange to unattuned ears), this is precisely what Whitehead did: for him they did not necessarily presuppose consciousness. In Whitehead's system God transcends all else in the universe, but at the same time is immediately related to, and affected by, it and all that is in it. From one point of view, he is to be described in the traditional way as Infinite Being (though preferably not in personal terms), and in this perspective is seen as the provider of the endless possibilities available for actualization in the universe. From another viewpoint, however, that of his actuality, he is to be judged as limited, as preserving, in a superior way suitable to himself ("eminently"), all the positive actual accomplishments of the universe. This view of God is necessary for the support of a human sense of meaning and value in the world and in life. And it is this view that opens up the possibility of change in God, a possibility that becomes actuality in this system. The contradiction that appears in God himself is allegedly resolved by discerning a polarity in his very nature, the first point of view in this paragraph representing his "primordial," and the second his "consequent," nature. Clearly, implicit in the system is a form of panentheism, though it is only a relative panentheism, not an absolute one, for ultimately the destiny of the universe is that it end as an entity in its own right and pass completely into the consequent nature of God. If the discernment of process rather than substance as the basic reality of the universe is Whitehead's first major departure from the European philosophical tradition, the discernment of a dipolar nature in God is surely the second. These two features constitute the hallmarks of his system.

Charles Hartshorne

It was this system that was inherited and in respectively different ways adapted by Hartshorne and Bracken. Hartshorne defends his right to add to the mass of writings on God by claiming to bring to the task a needed "logical rigor."[2] I shall bear this in mind when I come to assess his contribution. He modifies Whitehead's system in several significant ways. For instance, retaining the concept of a dipolar divine nature but preferring to speak of its primordial aspect as "abstract" and of its consequent aspect as "concrete," he firmly emphasizes the latter, in that, in line with Aristotle's general principle that the abstract is contained in the concrete, he asserts that the abstract divine nature is included in the concrete nature and only there becomes real. Note, though, that not only the concrete nature but the abstract nature is declared to be real, though they are "not on the same ontological level."[3] By "abstract," then, Hartshorne does not mean conceptual, or belonging to the mental order or the order of abstraction. Rather, by this word he denotes the open range of possibilities available for actualization in the future of the event (or "occasion") in question, as distinct from those already actualized in the past and those being actualized in the present. God, then, is conditioned by temporality as is any other event.

In the abstract nature, God is immutable; but as actual, in his concrete nature, he is mutable and indeed changing. However, there is no contradiction here, for the opposites are predicated of him in different ways, in regard to the different poles of his nature. And his mutability is not to be equated with ours, for it is in keeping with the uniqueness of his nature. For example, the fickleness of human nature is in no way to be predicated of him. He is completely reliable in all his ethical qualities, for example, his fidelity and justice. He is mutable in the sense that he can respond to us and undergo new experiences, but he is immutable, even in the concrete nature, in regard to ethical goodness (though he becomes even better through his experiences). God is unsurpassable, and indeed it is this quality that makes him the proper object of worship, but this only means that he cannot be surpassed by any other entity. He always remains *self*-surpassable. The Christian religion rests on the biblically revealed foundation of God's love for us, but if he were unchanging he would have to be uncaring and indifferent in our regard and therefore could not "love" us in any acceptable sense of the word.

But the Bible is right: God does love us; indeed he *is* perfect love, and this is the only metaphysical idea that provides a truly satisfactory explanation of the universe.[4] This perception marks a second modification of the Whiteheadian system:

God is to be conceived primarily as person, with personal attributes, foremost among which is love.[5] This means that God really cares for us and undergoes change in responding to us, rejoicing in our joys and grieving in our sorrows. Thus he exemplifies, albeit in a unique way, the general meaning of love as "sympathetic dependence on others."[6] God's transcendence is not compromised by this position, as even in the concrete nature he cannot be surpassed by any other entity. This attribute serves to guarantee his transcendence, though it needs to be remembered that he possesses a "dual transcendence,"[7] his "other" transcendence being that of the abstract nature, the divine transcendence as traditionally understood.

Hartshorne does not hesitate to draw the conclusion that in the concrete nature God is in a state of potency, moving constantly from potency to act. He rejects the notion that God is "pure act"; indeed, even the idea of *actus purus* he rejects as self-contradictory, since it affirms the logical coexistence of what he calls "incompossible values," actual values that by definition exclude other actual values.[8] If it be thought that this problem might be solved by an appeal to the doctrine of the "divine eminence," it is clear that for Hartshorne it does not, even though he has such a doctrine.[9] The reason is that for him God's eminence is nothing more than his unsurpassability in his concrete nature.

Joseph Bracken

Like Hartshorne, Joseph Bracken adopted Whitehead's philosophy with modifications of his own, and in turn he has been influenced by Hartshorne. This philosophy he has developed in a theological direction, and in so doing has been at pains to accommodate it to the requirements of Catholic doctrine. Thus, while affirming Hartshorne's insistence on the personal nature of God, he has gone beyond him by emphasizing the trinity of divine persons as taught in the early Church councils. He has contributed a number of books and articles on the trinitarian character of God.[10] Not surprisingly, his thought has undergone considerable development over the years. Here we shall be concerned only with its more recent formulation, in which the following two important new features appear.

First, Bracken has borrowed from Wolfhart Pannenberg's recent writings the concept of "dynamic field" as a highly suitable means for depicting the divine nature. From modern physics Pannenberg had taken over the notion of "cosmic field" and adapted it to this end and in the way indicated in the way just indicated.[11] In having recourse to science for a concept with which to revitalize Process thought about God, Bracken was certainly proving faithful to the spirit of his physicist-philosopher mentor, Whitehead. Bracken expresses in the following way his new understanding of the trinitarian God and the world in their mutual relationship :

> [I]f larger fields by definition contain smaller fields that are still governed by their own laws or patterns of activity, it should be possible to reconceive the God-world relationship in terms of interrelated fields of activity within which the three divine persons and all their creatures continuously come into being and are related to one another.[12]

Each divine person, then, coconstitutes his own field operating coextensively within the more comprehensive field that is the divine nature and which encompasses creatures as well. In an earlier statement, Bracken had nominated "Creativity" as "the underlying nature of God, that is, the power of divine intersubjectivity whereby the three divine persons at every moment come into existence and are related to one another as an all-embracing structured society."[13] In the light of the new field-approach, however, this means that "[e]ach of the divine persons is a subsistent field of (intentional) activity and that their ongoing interaction with one another results in a common field of intentional activity, which I would identify as the extensive continuum within Whitehead's categoreal scheme."[14] This "extensive continuum," which is "broader than the space-time continuum proper to our own cosmic epoch since it is not restricted by the patterns of order already established within the latter,"[15] should, on this reasoning, says Bracken, be recognized to "co-constitute with Creativity the underlying nature of the triune God."[16] Creativity and the extensive continuum are "distinguishable but inseparable dimensions of the ultimate ground of the universe," which for Bracken is God, the divine nature as presented here.[17]

The second new feature of Bracken's thought is his association, if not identification, of the Holy Spirit with what Whitehead calls in his major work, *Process and Reality*, the "superjective nature" of God.[18] There Whitehead describes the superjective nature as "the character of the pragmatic value of his [God's] specific satisfaction qualifying the transcendent creativity in the various temporal instances." Obviously, these are not easy words to interpret. Robert B. Mellert understands them in the following way:

> God is thus the repository of all reality because he is the unique subject that prehends every actual occasion. But just as this reality contributes to the reality of God, so also, is it the data for all further development in the future. In this sense, therefore, God contains the data out of which the world is continually being renewed. The fact that God contributes what he is in his consequent nature to the on-going process of reality is the meaning of his "superjective nature." This contribution is unique in that God passes back to the world not only the stubborn facts of history, but a sense of what perfected actuality might have been. God can do this because, in addition to prehending the totality of actuality, he also prehends the totality of possibility. In his superjective nature, then, God offers back to the world everything that is of value from the past for the formation of the future.[19]

Is the superjective nature meant to be a third divine nature or a third pole of the one divine nature? Mellert thinks that neither of these alternatives is likely. Given the infrequency of reference to it and the fact that normally Whitehead speaks only of the primordial and the consequent natures, the most likely hypothesis, in Mellert's view, is that it is nothing more than "an aspect of the consequent nature."[20] Although Bracken is clear that each divine person shares in both the primordial and the consequent nature, Whitehead's at least nominally tripartite distinction allows Bracken to associate the Father specially with the primordial nature, the Son with the consequent nature, and the Holy Spirit with the superjective nature, so that "the Spirit appears to be the hypostatized Superject of the ongoing relationship between the 'Father' as representing pure potentiality and the 'Son' together with all creatures as representing actuality here and now."[21]

Though anxious not to destroy the divine unity by distinguishing too sharply between the roles of the divine persons, Bracken is willing to provide two accounts of these roles, in terms, respectively, of creativity and the extensive continuum, the two constitutive aspects of the divine nature. Thus, on the one hand, the Father proposes from the primordial nature initial aims for the Son and the whole of creation; the Son from the consequent nature responds together with the creation with an unqualified assent to these aims; and the Holy Spirit from the superjective nature prompts the Father to offer these aims, and the Son and the creation to respond to them, thus mediating creativity both in the divine community and in creation.[22] And, on the other hand, the Father is specially associated with "the field of possibilities that constitutes the extensive continuum"; the Son is associated with the space-time continuum (which, as we saw earlier, is not identical with the extensive continuum) insofar as the former is "a partial actualization" of the Son in the divine community; and the Holy Spirit is associated with "Creativity as the dynamic principle whereby at every moment the extensive continuum is being actualized or concretized in terms of the relations between entities in the space-time continuum."[23]

In all this it is abundantly clear that each of the divine persons is time-conditioned and is not only mutable but undergoes actual change in the kaleidoscope of altering relations that obtain among the persons themselves, on the one hand, and between the persons and the creation, on the other. Twice in this presentation I have mentioned Bracken's view of a continuous "coming-into-being" of the three divine persons along with their creatures.

Assessment of Process Theology

By way of assessment of Process theology, particularly in regard to its doctrine of God and divine mutability, I shall proceed by first outlining briefly its attractive features and then offering a critique, which will be first theological and then philosophical. In some respects Process theology may be seen as a beneficial challenge to classical religious thought. If the latter can be characterized as presenting a remote, uncaring (perfect, immutable, and unrelated) God presiding over a static universe (though many would see this as a caricature), Process thought is claimed to present us not only with a universe that is dynamic and in which everything is related to everything else (a view that commends itself strongly to scientists as well as to many other people) but with a God who is fully immersed in all this action and interaction, who is caring, responsive, and loving, who rejoices in our joys and suffers in our sorrows, and at the same time is provident in our regard, though fully respecting the freedom that distinguishes us as human, in short, a God who corresponds far better to the biblical depiction than does the God of classical theism.

Theological Assessment

In moving on now to my theological critique, I can profitably begin by taking up this last point. Certainly, the Bible presents us with a God who is involved with us and loves us: indeed we are told in 1 John 4.8 that "God is love." This God also "grieves" over our sins (Eph 4.30) and is capable of "wrath" against those who persistently resist him (Rom 1.18). But we know that the Bible often speaks in simple religious language, which it would be simplistic to take too literally. What the Bible is telling us by such statements is that God is a person and that he is loving and provident in our regard; but, while it is not always harmful to think about God anthropomorphically, there are occasions—and the examples given are among them—when we do better to exercise caution. For the same Bible teaches, in its own way, the transcendence of God (his "holiness"); and there is a long biblical tradition, running through both testaments, that he is unchanging and immutable. This tradition reaches its zenith in James 1.17, where it is stated that "every good endowment and every perfect gift is from above, coming down from the Father of lights with whom there is no variation or shadow due to change" (RSV). The "lights" here are the heavenly bodies, which emit differing degrees of brightness according to time and season. But God their creator is not like them, for in him there is no change at all. That is why his continued generosity and the excellence of his gifts can always be counted on. Note that the argument concludes to God's ethical constancy, but that the ground invoked for it is his general and absolute immutability. The first set of biblical statements, therefore, needs to be balanced by the second and to find a solution beyond the pages of the Bible, a solution that only theology and ultimately Church teaching can supply. And until recently there has been a consistent theological and doctrinal tradition, witnessed to by (among many others) Augustine, Anselm, and Aquinas,[24] and expressed succinctly in the statement of the First Vatican Council that God is simply *incommutabilis* ("unchangeable").[25]

We observed earlier that Whitehead's God is a "God of the philosophers" rather than the God of revelation, and this remark seems true of Process theology in general. With this body of thought one cannot avoid the impression that what is paramount is the philosophical system itself, into which, then, theological facts are made to fit if and to the extent they can. The clearest instance of this is the difficulty experienced with the very idea of the Trinity, given the essentially binary character of Process thought. In portraying the role of the Holy Spirit in the light of God's superjective nature, Bracken, it is true, does find some resonances with the theological tradition; but we may well ask how seriously we are meant to take the superjective nature in Whitehead's thought, for there it pales into insignificance beside the primordial and consequent natures, and indeed, as we saw, may be meant as nothing more than an aspect of the latter. Does this mean that the Holy Spirit is less important than the other two persons, or that his real distinction from the Son is unclear? There seems to be a certain desperation about Bracken's seizing onto the superjective nature, as though it provides the only possible avenue for a theology of the Trinity in Process thought, since, as every grade-school child knows, "three into two won't go." The same difficulty is evident in Lewis Ford's well-known article "Process Trinitarianism," which is one of the more serious attempts of Process theology to confront the question of the Trinity.[26] Of this, William Hill writes: "In the end, Ford's interpretation of the God of Christian experience in Whiteheadian categories is unitarian, not trinitarian. It represents a unipersonal God who interacts with the world on the basis of his own dipolarity of nature."[27] It is clear that in both Ford and Bracken it is extremely difficult, if not impossible, to recognize the Father, Son, and Holy Spirit of the New Testament, or even a construct of thought based on this foundation.

A further difficulty, and a serious one, is the place of person in this system of thought. It is often remarked that Aristotelianism suffered from the same defect and for the same reason: its categories were drawn from the infrapersonal world and hence could not do justice to the reality of the person. In the case of Process thought, the point of departure is mathematics and physics, and it is questionable whether it does or even could get beyond them. But its denial of the possibility of any ultimate or perduring identity in the face of superficial change places it more profoundly at odds with personalism than Aristotelianism ever was. We noted that Whitehead used personal terms like "experience," "enjoyment," and "satisfaction" of all energy events, but our judgment must be that even an analogous use of such terms can only stretch as far as animals and perhaps plants, but certainly no further. It is clearly an abuse of language to speak of subatomic particles as undergoing experience, enjoyment, or satisfaction in any sense at all. Therefore, Whitehead's attempt at personalism, halfhearted as it was, must be counted a failure.[28]

Nor have subsequent Process writers been any more successful with the concept of person. Thus, Hartshorne, who erects it into the principal characteristic of God, can only understand love, its supreme manifestation, as "sympathetic dependence on others." This appears a legitimate understanding within the confines of Process thought, but it is not the full reality of love as understood in mainstream philosophy or traditional Christian thought, where it would be identified only as the carnal *amor concupiscentiae*, the "love of desire," selfish love, as distinct from the more spiritual *amor benevolentiae*, "the love of benevolence," by which the good of the other is willed for their own sake. Likewise, Bracken's recourse to the concept of dynamic fields to explain the reality of persons invites criticism. Perhaps this concept has a legitimate use as a humble metaphorical way of illustrating how several (not necessarily just three) persons can possess the one numerical nature, but that would be the limit of its usefulness. Pushed further, it becomes, because of its inherent materialism, incompatible with the spiritual character of the person.

I now move on to assess, from a theological point of view, the Process assertion of the dipolarity of the divine nature. As this assertion is essentially philosophical, the most appropriate place for its consideration will be the philosophical critique, but I must consider it here too, since it has implications that are theological. Obviously, it would be wrong to reject it simply on the grounds that it is nowhere directly taught in Scripture or the ecclesiastical or theological tradition, for this could be just a feature of its "second order" nature. Despite its absence from the sources, it could be theologically justified if they required it in the service of a contemporary hermeneutics. Just such an argument was used, be it remembered, to justify the term "homoousios" in the emerging doctrine of the Trinity at the Council of Nicaea. But it is a proviso of such new terms that they do not contradict the sources of revelation either explicitly or implicitly. Certainly, "homoousios" does not offend in this way, and neither does "person," but alas, the same cannot be said for dipolarity, for it cannot be reconciled with the divine transcendence as taught in these sources.

Process theologians, of course, are prepared for this objection. They point out that their system upholds the divine transcendence in the traditional sense so far as the primordial nature is concerned. Even in the consequent nature, they aver, they affirm it in a certain sense, that of the unsurpassability of God by any other entity. But, they continue, it is precisely because *absolute* transcendence is lacking to the consequent nature, that God can enter into real relations with human beings as taught in the Bible. Therefore dipolarity, far from being theologically objectionable, is a postulate of the biblical teaching about God.

In reply it has to be said that the sources require for God a doctrine of unqualified absolute transcendence, nothing less. Otherwise God would cease to be God. It is not enough to say that he is absolutely transcendent in the primordial but not in the consequent nature. Such an assertion does not amount to much if it is remembered that the primordial nature lacks actuality and exists only as a range of pure possibility. To some extent the biblical depiction of God as personal, involving, as it does, spiritual limitations and imperfections such as irascibility, vindictiveness, irresolution, and so on, is to be explained by the anthropomorphism of the biblical writers, which sometimes is unconscious, at other times consciously adopted for dramatic effect (e.g., Gen 18.16–33). This being said, however, it must be asserted that the biblical teaching of God as truly personal and relational is to be maintained at all costs. The Christian religion, not to mention the Jewish, depends on it. Therefore theology must accept the challenge of defending and explaining it without, however, having recourse to illegitimate stratagems like dipolarity, which solves the problem by sacrificing the divine transcendence. As we saw in the last chapter, the reality (in the sense of "superreality") of God's relations with creatures is not threatened by the doctrine of his actual absolute transcendence, but how this reality of relationships works in practice we shall have to leave to the next chapter, though its *content* is clear enough already from the Bible.

According to Hartshorne, as an actual entity God is limited and passes constantly from potency to act. His rejection of the idea of God as *actus purus* shows up his inadequate concept of God's "eminence" and hence, in turn, of his transcendence. Hartshorne fails to appreciate that values that he calls incompossible are in fact integrated in God according to the traditional understanding of the divine eminence, which asserts that they are affirmed of him really but in a way exceeding our comprehension. Irreconcilable at the level of the world, in God they are truly reconciled. This traditional understanding stems from St. Thomas, specifically from his much misunderstood theory of the "analogy of being," which is ably presented by Henri Bouillard, to whose treatment I now turn.[29] In St. Thomas analogy is a mode of attribution ("being is *said* analogically") rather than a property of concepts. Hence the concepts by which we grasp reality in no way *represent* it. Citing Gilson, Bouillard points out that "[o]n the level of concept and of representation, analogy is confused in practice with resemblance."[30] Concepts do not *represent* reality; they *signify* it. Now because we know directly only creatures (and not God), the concepts by which we signify the attributes of God are true and meaningful only because and insofar as God is the *transcendent cause* of corresponding qualities in creatures. That God is good, therefore, we know, not by any direct knowledge of him, but because we know directly both the goodness of his creatures and the way in which they are good. But of the way in which God is good we know nothing. Our knowledge of God, therefore, involves thesis, antithesis, and synthesis: God is good; God is not good (in the way creatures are); but God is good (in an eminent way that we do not know), and therefore, we might say, "supergood." "It is through the thesis that the synthesis offers a content of thought and affirms something."[31] To this Thomistic theory there needs to be added, Bouillard observes, a further element, deriving from

St. Augustine and not sufficiently emphasized in St. Thomas, to save it from being mere projection, namely, a sense of the presence of God in the soul: "If God were not present to our spirit we would be unable to know that he transcends our spirit. We would not know that God is the totally other if he were not the secret principle of all knowledge in us."[32] These reflections amply demonstrate the inadequacy of Hartshorne's concepts of the divine eminence and transcendence, and reveal the root of his problem to be the lack of a theory of analogy in his system. It is because he understands human predication of God *univocally* that he speaks at all of incompossible values. With such a deficiency, it is not possible that he do justice to God's eminence and hence to God's transcendence.

Another indication of Process theology's failure to comprehend the divine transcendence is the fact that it makes God in his inner being subject to time. That it does this for the consequent nature requires no demonstration, but even in the primordial nature Whitehead's exclusion of God from temporality is an exclusion only from the time that is constantly perishing, not from all time.[33] In an article entitled "Does God Know the Future?" William Hill deals with this matter in a Thomistic perspective that to me is convincing in all but one respect.[34] He sums up St. Thomas's position as follows:

> All free human activity that is yet to eventuate in time, then, first of all originates as predeterminations of the divine will in its transcendent creative freedom. Next, identity of divine intellect with divine will means that God knows all such determinations of His will. Lastly, eternity as an attribute of Being that is uncaused explains that all finite occurrences are present to God not sequentially but actually. Future events are before Him in the mode of presentiality, and thus are not known as merely possible but are "seen" in a true *scientia visionis*.[35] Eternity grounds, within divine existence, the simultaneity of all time—past, present, and future—so that events that have not yet occurred historically and which thus lack all *temporal* actuality nonetheless possess eternal actuality within the divine intentionality.[36]

He points out that, in regard to future events flowing from free human decisions, Thomas, in opting for divine "foreknowledge"[37] according to transcendent causality, has considered and rejected the alternative of foreknowledge of things in their proximate causes, on the grounds that as the human wills in question have not yet determined themselves, the outcomes of their decisions are not actual, and hence "there is no future to be known other than a merely possible one, about which there can only be conjecture."[38] According to Hill, this limitation of alternatives, however, reflects a Greek dichotomy between pure necessity (in the realm of the perfect) and pure contingency (in the realm of the imperfect, i.e., the human) that Thomas had already overcome in principle through his acquisition, over a long period, of the idea of human freedom as self-determination. This opens up the possibility of a third, intermediary alternative, which Hill then presents as the actual case, a

> dialectical encounter, wherein God, from His ontic situation outside history, enters it and interacts with men on the level of temporality. Without introducing temporality within His own inner reality, God (kenotically, as it were) opens Himself in and through the creature to an order of time and succession. This dialectical relationship is something directly intended by God in giving existence to a creature

whose beingness formally participates in that of God Himself, scil., a beingness that is personal and free.[39]

This reasoning appears unexceptionable. Further, it bears out a central point made in the last chapter, that God's relation to the world is real, or rather, superreal. Indeed, the reality of God's relation to the world is the condition of possibility of the encounter of which Hill speaks.[40] However, he goes on to depart from St. Thomas's view by asserting, in two places,[41] that God's knowledge of future free events is not actual but only possible, since it depends on human decisions not yet made. This seems, however, not to be imposed by the development just considered, and indeed to be incorrect. True, God kenotically enters history in his dialectical encounter (interaction) with human beings, and his knowledge is modified by the actual contingent realities that result. As Hill says,

> [T]he area of determination regards not God's nature but His intentionality, not God in Himself but in His chosen relationality towards creatures. It is His knowledge and love which alter, not as subjective activity constituting divinity, but in terms of what objectively terminates and specifies that activity.[42]

However, it seems that, in denying actuality to God's knowledge of future free events, Hill is not maintaining consistency with his statement in the previous quotation. God's nature, be it noted, remains completely unchanged. His contingent knowledge, despite its contingency, is still the knowledge of *God*, and is therefore possessed by him in his own proper way, according to the requirements of the divine nature and therefore *actually*, as is all his knowledge. God's knowledge of the future of the world, whether of events predetermined in their natural causes even if unknown to us (e.g., earthquakes), or of free human decisions and their outcomes, or even of random events (e.g., the behavior of certain subatomic particles), is all actual and "in the mode of presentiality,"[43] because present to him precisely in his eternity.

This *signifies* the more basic fact that God's transcendent causality is at the same time all-encompassing and not threatening to human freedom, even if we cannot understand *how* this is so. However, let me point out that what has just been said is generally accepted without demur by Christians in regard to the divine sovereignty and human freedom in the context of grace, which, after all, is simply a particular instance of the general principle under discussion. In the matter of grace and free will, Rahner has argued, convincingly on my view, that the only satisfaction available to the human mind is that it can understand *why* it cannot understand.[44] We conclude, therefore, against Process thought, that, though God is affected by time both in the exercise of his transcendent causality and in his knowledge of what results from this, he is not thus affected in his inner being. His transcendence remains intact.

Philosophical Assessment

I now move on to the philosophical critique of Process theology, particularly its concept of God. Since the philosophy underlying Process theology is Process philosophy, this critique, being specifically philosophical, will naturally focus on it, particularly on its statements about God, and most particularly on the alleged dipolarity of his nature. The most thorough existing such critique I am aware of is that of the Lonerganian philosopher Michael Vertin, which concentrates on Hartshorne.[45] But as this critique can legitimately be extended to all Process theology in regard to the aspects named, we can invoke its help in our present project.

In essence, Vertin's critique is that Hartshorne's philosophical revision suffers from being truncated and incomplete:

> [I]f Hartshorne is keenly aware that the metaphysics of God systematically presupposes a general metaphysics, he appears to be almost completely unaware that a general metaphysics in turn, insofar as it is not simply dogmatic, methodologically presupposes a cognitional phenomenology—in the limit, a phenomenology of the cognitional activity of the very person asserting the metaphysics.[46]

This defect is the reason for the fact that "Hartshorne overlooks the fact that one grasps a full cognitional term not immediately, in direct and unmediated awareness, but rather through the mediation of questions and answers."[47] This oversight in turn gives rise to two serious confusions. The first is a confusion of "data," "descriptive intelligibility," and "explanatory intelligibility," that is, respectively, of the thing or property "merely as given," "as understood in relation to me as a concrete sensing/imagining subject," and "as understood in relation to other things or properties." The second is a confusion of intelligibility and affirmability, on the one hand, and the abstract and the concrete, on the other, so that in regard to a thing or property the difference between it as merely hypothetical or as verified is reduced to the difference between it "as taken apart from any particular spatiotemporal location" or "as taken here/there and now/then."[48] These confusions in their turn underlie "Hartshorne's erroneous (albeit largely just implicit) phenomenological supposition that that toward which one's cognitional awareness is fundamentally oriented, and which thus at least performatively is defined as the actual, is concretely spatiotemporal."[49] So much, then, for Hartshorne's claim to "logical rigor" reported earlier in this chapter!

The Lonerganian definition of the actual, on the other hand, is "whatever intrinsically is intelligently understandable, reasonably affirmable, and responsibly evaluable," and since my a priori wonder about these qualities is without restriction, I cannot without self-contradiction deny a priori that actuality is *more* than the mere concretely spatiotemporal, that it has a non-spatiotemporal, immaterial, and spiritual dimension as well.[50] Given also the limitations of my knowing, of which I am aware, namely, that I am only primitively self-present in a nonreflexive way, only partly self-constituting, and only in process toward the achievement of knowledge, I cannot exclude a priori the possibility of the existence of a subject simply free of these limitations and therefore fully self-present, totally self-constituting, and not at all in process, "because it would already possess the fullness of all that it could possess," a subject, therefore, of which the very suggestion of a dipolar nature is absurd.[51]

Similar reasoning can be used to strike at the heart of the Process system, at the principle of creativity itself:

> [S]ince I have no performatively incontrovertible warrant for asserting that creative self-determination is intrinsically characteristic of whatever I desire to know (rather

than of merely one kind of knowable), neither does it follow philosophically that every element in the concrete actual universe is creatively self-determining.[52]

Therefore, "[t]he claim of universal creativity is either an utterly uncritical—i.e., dogmatic—philosophical assertion, or else it is a mere empirical hypothesis, to be established, if at all, through the usual procedures of empirical verification."[53]

In *Insight* Lonergan, through a long and involved argument, arrives at the existence and nature of God on the basis of the complete intelligibility of the real.[54] Upon ruling out the possibility of a complete material or abstract intelligibility, he concludes that what he seeks resides in a spiritual intelligibility that is complete because it "cannot inquire because it understands everything about everything."[55] This unrestricted understanding is "the idea of being." He has already shown that its primary component, "the unrestricted act's understanding of itself," possesses all the attributes of God,[56] and by this means concludes that by nature God is "an unrestricted act of understanding." Vertin adds that God is at the same time "an unrestricted act of affirming and loving."[57] The implications of this are that

> [t]his act is fully self-present in a non-reflexive way and, moreover, it is totally self-constituting. It is completely one, simple, self-identical in nature. It is purely immaterial, strictly spiritual, diversified neither spatially nor temporally. It is totally necessary. And it is wholly immutable and changeless—not, however, as though suffering under some constraint but rather as free from any need, already possessing the fullness of all that it could possess.[58]

It is obvious that the idea of God that emerges from this critique is totally at odds with that of Process theology. In particular, the alleged dipolarity of God's nature is ruled out, and the traditional understanding of his transcendence, his changelessness and his immutability in himself, is reaffirmed.[59]

The general metaphysics on which Process theology's metaphysics of God rests is gravely defective in seeing change, process, creativity, rather than being, as the fundamental reality of the universe. As Norris Clarke aptly points out, in the history of thought the dynamic, relational aspect of being (to which I devoted considerable attention in the last chapter) was lost through Descartes's conception of the isolated, unrelated substance, to which conception further disabling restrictions were added by Locke and Hume; it was against such "distortions" that Whitehead reacted.[60] It was appropriate for him to do so, but the correct methodology would have been to recover and develop the authentic concept of being, rather than attempt to replace it with a concept simply unable to do its duty. For if, as John Wright says, we find it necessary to ask why this changing universe, rather than nothing at all, exists, and are not satisfied simply with analyzing the process of change that we observe as characteristic of it, we are affirming being rather than change as the fundamental reality.[61] Indeed, the phenomenon of language itself defeats Process philosophy and theology. For if there exists an isomorphism between language and the world (and we can philosophize only on the assumption that there is), grammar, the very structure of language, with its nouns, verbs, prepositions, adjectives, and adverbs all arranged in logical order, confirms the view that being rather than change is what is fundamental. For example, the expression just used, "changing universe," reveals by its structure that change is a feature of, and therefore subordinate to, the universe that actually exists. If against this simple argument it is replied that language rests on convention dictated by common sense rather than on the way things really are, it can be said that, if this be so, the convention should be corrected, at least for the benefit of those able to cope with so major a change; but because of the contradiction it involves, it is *impossible* to construct a coherent grammar on the basis of Process philosophy; and until someone has successfully done so, we can continue to maintain this argument against it.

Wright brings a further argument against Process philosophy, the contradiction he considers to be involved in Whitehead's position on the "phases of concrescence."[62] Wright summarizes Whitehead on this in the following way: "These phases are not temporally successive, but simultaneous. Each of them occupies the entire quantum of time during which the entity exists."[63] In objection to this, Wright puts the following five questions (which are here recast to some degree in different words): 1) How is the priority of the initial phase over the final phase of concrescence to be understood? 2) How can an entity be exercising freedom if its ultimate satisfaction is simultaneous with the conformal feelings and the initial aim? 3) How can the later phases be causally dependent on the earlier ones, since on Whitehead's own admission things that are simultaneous are causally independent? 4) If, as Whitehead accepts, there is no temporal interval between actual entities, how can he maintain his understanding of an enduring event as a society of only relatively stable component events? Would not actual entities, along with their phases of concrescence, have to be continuous with each other, and would not therefore an enduring event have to be a continuous process rather than, as claimed, a series of individual atomic events? 5) If the whole process is conceived as resulting in a growth in intensity and satisfaction for both God and the world, how can creativity lead to such continual self-surpassing? How can the greater come from the less?

Whitehead took up the position to which Wright objects because he felt constrained thereto by certain arguments that go back to Zeno's "arrow in flight." He found it necessary to reconcile the two following statements: 1) in a becoming, something becomes; and 2) "every act of becoming is divisible into earlier and later sections which are themselves acts of becoming."[64] He sets forth the following case:

> Consider, for example, an act of becoming during one second. The act is divisible into two acts, one during the earlier half of the second, the other during the later half of the second. Thus that which becomes during the whole second presupposes that which becomes during the first half-second. Analogously, that which becomes during the first half-second presupposes that which becomes during the first quarter-second, and so on indefinitely.[65]

This gives rise to an unwelcome conclusion:

> Thus if we consider the process of becoming up to the beginning of the second in question, and ask what then becomes, no answer can be given. For whatever creature we indicate presupposes an earlier creature which became after the beginning of the second and antecedently to the indicated creature. Therefore there is nothing which becomes, so as to effect a transition into the second in question.[66]

To avoid this conclusion, he assumes the position "that in every act of becoming there is the becoming of something with temporal extension; but that the act itself is not extensive, in the sense that it is divisible into earlier and later acts of becoming which correspond to the extensive divisibility of what has become."[67] He concludes succinctly "that the creature is extensive, but that its act of becoming is not extensive."[68]

This in turn obliges him to distinguish between "genetic" and "coordinate" division, understood thus: "Genetic division is division of the concrescence; coordinate division is division of the concrete,"[69] of the actual event. Coordinate division takes place in "physical" time, time as normally understood, while genetic division takes place in "epochal" time.[70] Whitehead spells out what he means by this kind of time (and we are now in a position to understand why he would think thus): "Temporalisation is not another continuous process. It is an atomic succession. Thus time is atomic (*i.e.* epochal), though what is temporalised is divisible."[71] Because epochal time is successive rather than continuous, within a given epoch occurrences that might appear to be successive are in reality simultaneous in a distinctive sense of this word: "An event in realising itself displays a pattern, and this pattern requires a definite duration determined by a definite meaning of simultaneity."[72] In his list of objections Wright does not appear to take account of this distinction of Whitehead's between physical and epochal time. Where Whitehead for his own reasons speaks of epochal time, Wright interprets this as physical time. Hence the first four of Wright's objections would appear to miss the mark, though the fifth, which arises from other considerations, seems valid. It is identical in content with Lonergan's famous critical observation, cited already in note 59, that in Process philosophy "God is the first accident." The question, however, remains: Is Whitehead's distinction of epochal from physical time valid? If it is not, Wright's first four objections would have to be allowed to stand after all. It is this question that we must now, in conclusion, address.

In Whitehead it is the endurance of objects that necessitates for him the category of epochal time. Admittedly, it is also tied up with the question of the relativity of space and time, which for him is a multiple relativity: "[I]t seems that the observed effectiveness of objects can only be explained by assuming that objects in a state of motion relatively to each other are utilising, for their endurance, meanings of space and time which are not identical from one object to another."[73]

However, this seems to be a separate question, which we can leave aside in this context.[74] Unable to have recourse to a philosophy of substance in order to explain endurance, Whitehead does so in terms of enduring "patterns." He understands an "event" as "the grasping into unity of a pattern of aspects,"[75] and continues:

> If the pattern endures throughout the successive parts of the event, and also exhibits itself in the whole, so that the event is the life-history of the pattern, then in virtue of that enduring pattern the event gains in external effectiveness . . . The event constitutes a patterned value with a permanence inherent throughout its own parts; and by reason of this inherent endurance the event is important for the modification of its environment.[76]

As events are actualized in time, Whitehead is led to a consideration of duration, which he understands as "the field for the realised pattern constituting the character of the event."[77] It is here that considerations from Zeno, detailed earlier, are brought to bear, and they reveal themselves as all-important. Via Immanuel Kant, they draw him to the conclusion that a duration is an "epoch," that is, an "arrest."[78] He continues: "Accordingly we must not proceed to conceive time as another form of extensiveness. Time is sheer succession of epochal durations."[79] Presumably he is here speaking of "physical" time, as in *Process and Reality*. In other words, contrary to what we might think, time as we know it is not extensive, that is, continuous, but is a succession of epochal durations. By these words Whitehead expresses his understanding of the relation of epochal time to physical time.

It seems that the weakness of Whitehead's position here is that, given the starting point of his system, creativity, which is exclusive as well as inclusive, it cannot really account for the phenomenon of endurance. For him endurance consists in a pattern that persists throughout the history of an event and also throughout its successive parts. When the event perishes and is succeeded by a new event, this will be because a new pattern has established itself and has persisted throughout *its* successive parts. But on Whitehead's own principles does not this endurance have to be an illusion? In reality does not the pattern have to be changing all the time, continuously, with minute and therefore imperceptible changes, which over time become perceptible because they add up to something significant, so that eventually it has to be recognized that a new pattern has emerged and replaced the old? In other words, does not the endurance of which Whitehead speaks have to be, on his principles, in the eye of the beholder rather than in the reality observed? It seems that Lonergan's principle that a false position cannot long maintain itself without beginning to contradict itself is exemplified here.[80] The inescapable fact is that endurance can only be explained by a philosophy of substance. But Whitehead had barred himself from access to such a philosophy through his understandable but excessive reaction to the distortions introduced into the idea of substance by Descartes, Locke, and Hume.

In Process philosophy we encounter a protest movement that went about its protest the wrong way. In identifying creative process as the basic reality of the universe, it limited itself unnecessarily, cutting itself off from all possibility of dealing satisfactorily with the phenomenon of endurance, with the concept of person and with the transcendence of God, to name just three key problem areas. Such disadvantages could have been avoided and its positive aspirations fulfilled by a return to a revitalized philosophy of substance, in which the latter was presented as dynamic, relational and active. Employed in the service of theology, particularly trinitarian theology, Process philosophy reveals itself an unprofitable servant. Already unable adequately to handle persons, it runs, because of its binary conception of the divine nature, into further difficulties when it attempts to cope with a trinity of divine persons. And as we saw in the case of Joseph Bracken, Process theology of the Trinity turns out to be less an illumination of the New Testament revelation of the Father, Son, and Holy Spirit than an extension of the system of Process philosophy.

As we saw in both this and the last chapter, a renewed philosophy of substance can clear the way for a notion of God that supports the biblical teaching of a God who is personal, dynamic, and relational. According to such a philosophy, God, though immutable in himself—in his nature—nevertheless changes in his relationships with creatures, and, being absolute divine person in relationship with human persons, has relations to and with them that are truly personal, expressible analogically across the gamut of human emotional and spiritual relations, for example, love, joy, pity, anger, sadness, suffering, compassion, and so on, only those relations excepted that are incompatible with his ethical perfection. That God relates to us in these ways requires no biblical demonstration; indeed the biblical foundations for this statement are only too well known. But it raises the important *philosophical* question: How is God's relatedness reconciled with the philosophical datum (which is also biblical) of his perfection and immutability? Allow me to recall, in the ensuing paragraph, words written in the last chapter that could provide a key to the sought-after philosophical reconciliation. In God there can be no channeling of the dynamic act of being *via* the essence, relating God for the purpose of self-realization to the world of finite beings. Dynamic it is, but its dynamism requires only what it already meets, only what it already has and is, in the all-perfect divine essence, and it requires nothing beyond it. This dynamism is the foundation of God's relationality. It *becomes* relationality only when creatures are taken into account, and in their regard. In the case of God it is meaningless to speak, as we do of creatures, of a transcendental relation between existence and essence, for in him they are identical. Therefore, if created beings exist, they do so by God's *free* decision, and, while they are necessarily expressions of the dynamism and relationality of the divine being, they are not necessary, but only contingent, expressions of it. By their existence, they bear witness to the excess, abundance, and nonnecessary overflow of the divine being into the world of contingent being.

The new ontological relations thus set up from God to creatures are the ground of the genuinely personal and interpersonal relations that he has with those of them that are persons. Hence what has just been said provides the ground of the words of William Hill cited earlier in this chapter, words that are highly relevant to the issue under consideration:

> The area of determination [i.e., of God by human beings] regards not God's nature but His intentionality, not God in Himself but in His chosen relationality towards creatures. It is His knowledge and love which alter, not as subjective activity constituting divinity, but in terms of what objectively terminates and specifies that activity.

The only objection we might make to this quotation is that "determination" is not quite the right word, being rather too mechanical. Because they are free, persons are "affected," rather than "determined," by other persons. God in his personal stance toward us is therefore not so much determined, as affected, by our stance toward him and by our free actions and unfree passions (i.e., that which we simply undergo, e.g., our suffering), though an appropriate noun form in English for the state of "being affected" is hard to find.

From what has been said it will be evident that God's status as actus purus is nowise threatened by his changing personal relations to human beings, for these relations are no more than an expression of the "overflow" of the all-perfect divine being into the contingent world that he has freely created. At the same time one can sympathize with Hartshorne's dislike of the expression "pure act" as applied to God. Though true in itself, it falls so far short of adequacy as a statement of God's personhood (which is characterized by pure love) that it cries out for complementation and improvement. On its own it can only mislead, conveying the impression of an impersonal God conceived along the lines of the Aristotelian First Mover. In the realm of the personal, as Norris Clarke reminds us, receptivity should be recognized as a *positive perfection*. He writes:

> Here the ontological value of receptivity, as not a defect or inferiority but a positive perfection of being, emerges more and more clearly into the light. There is indeed a side of imperfection included, insofar as change is involved, that is, a passage from prior non-possession of my friend's love to later receiving it, or from potentiality to act. But if we analyze this, it becomes clear that this imperfection is solely due to the change or temporal aspect, not to the very nature of receptivity as such, which at the level of personal love is not passivity at all but an active, welcoming receptivity, that is purely positive in nature, a relation of act to act rather than of act to potency.[81]

However, valuable though this be, it is only part of the answer, not the whole. For in his dealings with us God does enter kenotically into time and hence into change, and so there is a need for us to explore and try to explain, as both possible and actual, his changing relations with us and our world.

Further, this divine receptivity should not be confused with powerlessness, a point well made by Elizabeth Johnson in regard to divine suffering. A powerless God is just as open to objection as a God who is immutable and omnipotent. Johnson sees the answer in compassion, which is "neither power-over nor powerlessness" but "akin to power-with."[82] In her view this line of thought leads to "a resymbolization of divine power not as dominative or controlling power, nor as dialectical power in weakness, nor simply as persuasive power, but as the liberating power of connectedness that is effective in compassionate love."[83]

In maintaining that God is unchanging in himself but changing in his relations with creatures, I might be seen to be aligning myself in some way with either Process theology or Palamism. To take Process theology first, is not the distinction suspiciously like that of Hartshorne between God's abstract nature, in which he does not change, and his concrete nature, in which he does? To this I should answer: only superficially. I have already presented and upheld the theological and philosophical objections against Process theology's distinction of natures in God. After this negative exercise I face the task of trying to achieve from my own more traditional perspective Process theology's objective of finding a theology of God that allows him to be personal, related, and involved in the world. Hence my distinction of the nature of God and his relations precisely in its situation in the scheme of the essential dynamism of the divine being and the contingency of creatures. This, of course, does not answer the pressing question: What *kind* of distinction is meant here, real or only logical? As the same question occurs in regard to Palamism, I defer answering it until my consideration of that system, to which we can now pass.

Palamism

Several times now I have had occasion to observe how convenient it would be to use Palamas's simple distinction of the essence and the energies of God rather than become enmeshed in the complex terminology that a Western approach seems to impose. Of course, against Palamas's formula can be raised the awkward question of the kind of distinction intended. If it is a real distinction, the simplicity of God is compromised and other unfortunate consequences flow, particularly, as Catherine LaCugna points out, the exaltation of the divine essence over the three persons.[84] If, on the other hand, it is meant as only logical, there seems little point in making it at all. Like many other Western writers, LaCugna proceeds on the assumption that Palamas intended a real distinction. However, as was pointed out in chapter 1, Palamas never gave a precise account of the distinction, preferring to eschew such scholastic subtleties. John Meyendorff quotes him as saying, "In a certain sense essence and energy are identical in God, but in another sense they are different,"[85] which certainly does not sound like a real distinction. However, in the end LaCugna may be right. The demotion of the three divine persons over against the divine essence, an unfortunate fact the existence of which I do not question,[86] is understandable systematically only on the basis that the distinction is real, Palamas's subjective and conscious hesitancy about it notwithstanding. But as long as it is not claimed to be real, Palamas's distinction seems a useful way of expressing in simple language a phenomenon that is very difficult to express clearly and succinctly. Also, because of its foundation in the theology of the Cappadocians it is more traditional than the formulation offered here or those offered in the past. It would be good if we in the West could adopt it without further ado. But we would have to be careful not to fall into the same trap as Palamas, to erect it into a total theological system.

If one is going to commend the use of Palamas's distinction, one should at least try to say of what kind it is. In this connection the suggestion of George Scholarios and others, including Gérard Philips, that in Western terms the distinction that comes closest to what Palamas wanted to say is Scotus's formal distinction *a parte rei*, the distinction between different but inseparable formalities of the one object, deserves serious attention.[87] To those who question the possibility of such a distinction, it must be pointed out that there is a case in trinitarian theology where it, or something like it, is imposed, namely, the distinction of a divine person from the divine nature. It is clear that, while each person must be identical with the nature, there must also be a distinction of some kind, and it can be neither simply real nor simply logical.[88] Of this distinction and its application in this case, Leonardo Boff writes:

> In this formal distinction, the reality is not multiplied, but it is possible to grasp three distinct modes in which this same reality subsists. These three modes do not originate in our minds but in the reality itself. This is precisely what is meant by "formal" distinction: the same essence, nature or reality is mediated through different "formalizations." Applied to the Trinity, this means: the reality (nature) of God is understood as realized in the formalizations of Father, Son and Holy Spirit; it is an attempt at expressing the inner dynamic and richness of this one and only divine reality.[89]

In the case of Palamism I suggest that the two formalizations between which this distinction is made are God in relation to himself and God in his relations to us, or God as he is in himself and God as creator of the world. Rowan Williams, in the admirable article already referred to in chapter 1,[90] does not challenge the validity of the Scotistic distinction (to which he does not explicitly refer), but argues against a real distinction between essence and energy in God on the grounds that energy is nothing other than essence in act. Any distinction, then, would have to be logical only ("epistemological" in his terminology). He touches my exact point when he criticizes John Meyendorff's presentation of it from Palamas in the following terms:

> [I]t is no answer to this to say that God's *ousia* ("essence") is immutable and His *energeiae* ("energies") mutable, as this drives a very considerable wedge between the two terms: what is true of one "mode" or aspect of God is *not* true of another. The unity of God is far more gravely imperilled by this than any Palamite or neo-Palamite seems to have grasped; it is the purest Neoplatonism, an affirmation of two *wholly* distinct orders of reality in God.[91]

In speaking thus of two "modes" of God Williams is giving a fairly exact account of what is meant by the formal distinction, but he confuses it with a real distinction and proceeds to draw appropriately dire conclusions. More basically, he is proceeding on a mistaken idea of what energy is. It is not just essence in act; it is the divine essence in act in relation to us, as distinct from the same essence in act in relation to God himself. A formal distinction would permit precisely that, in the sense just enunciated, "what is true of one mode or aspect of God is not true of another." It would allow God to be immutable in his essence and mutable in his energies *without* imperiling the divine unity, just as the same kind of distinction allows the Father to be identical with the divine nature without the latter's thus becoming the principle of the Son. (One admires the perspicacity of the remark of Martin Jugie, made in 1913, that "in this matter Scotism is, as it were, Palamism *in fieri*.")[92] Strangely, Williams declares that "we know God only in so far as he acts upon us, as he is 'present' to us, never as he is 'present' to himself," and goes on to say that "this is not peculiar to our knowledge of God."[93] He is excused of inconsistency here only through a determined effort of interpretation. Presumably he means that in regard to God as indeed to all objects of our experience, as there is no real distinction between the two modes and the first is what we actually undergo; the second, if it is postulated at all, remains just that, a baseless postulate. He then goes on, however, to point out the difference that exists between our knowledge of God and our knowledge of other objects, namely, that while they can be known fully, comprehended, by us, God, because of his transcendence, cannot. This is precisely why I take the position that while the two modes are only logically distinct in the case of our knowledge and experience of objects in the world, in the case of God the distinction has to be more than simply this, yet it cannot, for the reasons adduced, be real. To recall a key word used by William Hill in a quotation deployed earlier in this chapter, in his relations with the world God acts "kenotically." This is the precise point overlooked by Williams. It cannot be said of the relations of any being in the world to any other being in the world. God's transcendence means that even in his relations to us he is not comprehended by us, as beings in the world are, but is known only partially and analogically; and as he is in himself, for example, in his triunity, he cannot be known by us at all save by revelation. With Williams's overall judgment of Palamism as a system, however, that it is "a piece of dubious scholasticism,"[94] one must, sadly, agree.

On the matter of formal, or virtual, distinction in God, Rahner makes a point that is worth heeding. In regard to the distinction between a given divine person and the divine essence, he points out that it does not solve the problem simply to invoke the term "virtual" or "formal."[95] Such terms in their normal sense only approximate to what in God is a unique kind of distinction, between the same reality considered first absolutely and then relatively. A similar caution should be exercised in the present case as well. There is no exact name for the distinction between God in his own being and God acting kenotically, as the situation itself is absolutely unique. With Palamas we should refuse to say that it is either real or logical. And if we say "formal" or "virtual," that is only that we may speak in a technical way of the mystery of God's kenotic action. If it is a formal or virtual distinction, it is a unique one, only analogous or approximate to those we know from ordinary experience. It is nothing more than a device for saying that it is not demonstrably impossible for God to act kenotically, just as in the previous case it is nothing more than a device for saying that it is not demonstrably impossible that in God the relatively distinct persons be really distinct from each other despite the fact that, absolutely, each is identical with the single essence. In neither case does the distinction bestow positive intelligibility on the situation under consideration.

Finally, the reader will note that I have not appealed to the trinity of persons as the ground for change in God. This approach will be considered in the next chapter. If change in God can be predicated at the level of trinity, this is because it has first been grounded in his unity, in God as absolute person, which has been the business of this chapter. Quite apart from Christian considerations, the problem of a personal, relational, and even changing God presents itself also for the one God, Yahweh, of the Old Testament and the Jewish religion, and demands to be solved first at that level.

6

Recent Theology

Moltmann

In this chapter and the next we shall consider four theologians, two Protestant, two Catholic, with whose work on the Trinity my own invites some comparison. The purpose of the exercise is partly to contextualize my work, partly to discover what can be learned from them. Then will follow the conclusion, which will sum up what I have to say at present about the doctrine of the Trinity. The Protestants are Jürgen Moltmann and Eberhard Jüngel, and the Catholics, Heribert Mühlen and Hans Urs von Balthasar. What we all share is that, following Karl Barth, our reflections on the Trinity take their point of departure from the New Testament statements about Jesus Christ, Son of God, about the God to whom he prayed as Father, and about the Holy Spirit sent by him from the Father upon the Church, rather than from the psychological analogy of the Trinity pioneered by St. Augustine and completed by St. Thomas Aquinas.

My interlocutors have at least two other points in common, the first of which is that they can be classified as "Paschal Mystery" theologians of the Trinity.[1] This title indicates that they read off their theology of the Trinity precisely from Christ's death, resurrection, ascension, and sending of the Spirit, that is, from the trinitarian structure of these events. Of course the Paschal Mystery can be so defined as to embrace the entire mystery of Jesus Christ,[2] and in that sense I too could be considered a Paschal Mystery theologian of the Trinity. But it seems that such a definition is too general. On it, the expression loses the specificity that constituted the reason for its introduction in the first place. On this reasoning it is better to limit its meaning in accordance with its original Christian designation, which in the first place was the liturgical celebration of Easter as the "Passover" of Jesus, and then, by extension, the climaxing historical events of his life as enumerated above. This last sense is the one intended here. On this reckoning I should not be considered a Paschal Mystery theologian, as my work lays considerable stress on the beginning of Jesus' life and the beginning of his ministry, that is, on the Lucan material relating to his conception by the Father through the power of the Holy Spirit, to his baptism, his "anointing" by the Father with the Holy Spirit, and to his ministry. True, it climaxes in the

Paschal Mystery as defined above, but even if in eschatological perspective it awards primacy of place to the end of Jesus' life, it avowedly seeks the revelation of the Trinity in the whole of his life, its beginning and its active period as well as its end.

The second point these theologians have in common is that all interpret the cross of Jesus in some kind of positive relation to the type of soteriology known as "penal substitution." While elements of this are to be found in Luther, it is in Calvin that we first find it thought through as an explicit soteriology. Here is F. W. Dillistone's summary of Calvin's thought on the matter:

> God has given man his Law: he therefore stands condemned at the bar of judgment and no punishment is conceivable except eternal death: yet the Son of God has become man and has stood *in man's place* to bear the immeasurable weight of the Wrath, the Curse, the Condemnation of a righteous God: Christ in fact "was made a substitute and a surety in the place of transgressors and even submitted as a criminal, to sustain and suffer all the punishment which would have been inflicted on them" (*Institutes*, 2:16:10); so man's guilt was obliterated: God has opened the way for man to accept his release, to be justified by faith, to become accepted in the Beloved.[3]

Dillistone immediately adds, "This picture, with minor variations, remained dominant in Reformed theology until well into the nineteenth century."[4] Even though there was then a reaction against it, it has remained influential in Protestant circles, and also in some Catholic ones, to the present day.[5] I refer particularly to the tendency to interpret the cry of Jesus on the cross, "My God, my God, why have you forsaken me?" (Mk 15.34), in terms of an actual abandonment of Jesus by God because of Jesus' identification with sinners in the manner of his death. This tendency finds its logical context in the penal substitution theory. Clearly, if our four theologians are influenced by this theory, this will have a significant impact on their trinitarian theology.

There is no particular reason for treating Moltmann first; but I devote an entire chapter to him because in the case of the first theologian treated it is necessary to deal at some length with the soteriology that underlies the trinitarian theologies of all four theologians. On his work as on that of the others the penal substitution theory has left its characteristic mark. However, our critical exercise needs to be done only once. Thereafter it can be taken for granted, and this means that the remaining theologians can be considered at less length, even, indeed, in a single chapter.

Presentation of Moltmann's Theology

Some Preliminary Points from Moltmann

Let us turn, then, to Jürgen Moltmann. In the first place, he holds that the doctrine of the Trinity is necessary as a response to the protest of atheism against a God who because he is one and simple cannot suffer and therefore cannot love.[6] And second, the Trinity is necessary to discredit the system of monarchy, whether political or clerical, that is implied in unqualified monotheism.[7] To take these points in turn, first, God's simplicity does not allow of distinction in him, and therefore does not allow of change. The impossibility of change rules out the possibility of suffering, which in turn rules out the possibility of love. This remote, uncaring God inevitably provokes the kind of atheism that we encounter in the world today. And second, the one, all-powerful God of religion tends to be reflected in the social order, politically in the rule of despots, and ecclesiastically in the authority structure of the Catholic Church, against which, of course, Protestantism rebels. Each of these defects is countered by the doctrine of the Trinity, the first through the introduction of distinction in God, and the second through the relativization introduced by the community of three divine persons, a "community free of dominion" (Hasenhüttl).

Moltmann is accused by some of having rejected the distinction of immanent and economic Trinity.[8] The accusation appears justified in the case of his earlier work, but responding to criticism in *The Future of Creation*, he revises his position, saying that his rejection holds only insofar as "the distinction 'God in himself—God for us,' as well as the distinction between immanent Trinity and economic Trinity, both start from a general (metaphysical) concept of God, and make use of the difference between idea and appearance."[9] If this were really what the distinction was meant to do, one could only endorse Moltmann's rejection of it. But as was explained in chapter 1, the distinction can be used in a quite different and indeed very constructive way. Applying Lonergan's three levels of knowing, one starts not from a metaphysical concept of God but from the biblical data of Father, Son, and Holy Spirit, and proceeds to the level of reflective understanding, to the immanent Trinity, only to return thence to the original data to affirm them in the light of this understanding, that is, to the economic Trinity (and, in the sense 1 explained, to the immanent Trinity as well). As is clear from Moltmann's words, he himself adopts part of this scheme, its first two levels. Thus he has no problem about "pushing back our question from the starting-point of the history of God on the cross into the conditions of possibility for that history in God; so that the event of the *derelictio Jesu* [abandonment of Jesus] can lead us to the eternal *generatio filii* [generation of the Son]."[10] However, as Richard Bauckham points out, Moltmann remains unwilling to surrender his basic idea of the historicality of God, and in still later work appears to have landed himself back in the original difficulty, which arises from his determination to situate the economic Trinity between two phases of the immanent Trinity, a Trinity "in the origin" and a Trinity realized by the eschatological future, a Trinity in which the being of God ends up being determined by historical events.[11] This seems a rather confused approach. And it appears to compromise the divine transcendence.

Moltmann's Theology of the Cross

As intimated at the beginning of the chapter, it is to the cross of Jesus that Moltmann looks for the supreme revelation of the Trinity. In his numerous works he has restated this theme several times, which is an indication of the high importance he attaches to it.[12] Moltmann's theology of the death of Jesus is acknowledged by him as a variation on Luther's theology of the cross.[13] But Moltmann does not fully subscribe to Luther's theory. One important difference is the different role in which he casts the Father:

How is the death of Christ on the cross to be understood as atonement? It can be understood as atonement for the sins of the world only if we see God *in* Christ. So in this context Paul is always stressing that Christ is the Son of God. But the consequence of that is that Christ's suffering is divine suffering and that his death is the death endured by God as the representative of all sinners who have fallen victim to death. Therefore it is wrong to assume that through his representative suffering, Christ has reconciled God's wrath over human sin, or that like a sadist God has crucified, or has had crucified, his own Son. The crucified Christ has nothing to do with a God of vengeance or a divine punitive judge. Such notions are completely contrary to "the Father of Jesus Christ."[14]

In this passage we see an identification of Christ and the Father, such that where Christ is the representative of humanity, the Father also is this,[15] and where Christ is the atoner, the Father also is this.[16] In the light of this the Lutheran wrath of God becomes merely the "wounding of his love for his creatures,"[17] and the Father does not punish Christ. Both "bear" the sins of the world.[18] All this notwithstanding, alienation takes place between God and Christ, and to this extent the penal substitution theory survives in Moltmann:

What did Christ suffer on the cross that can be called "atonement"? . . . What he suffers are his particular pains over God: his experience of praying unheard in Gethsemane and being abandoned by God on the cross. Because the one who had experienced the nearness of God as "Abba" in such an incomparable way that he knew himself to be the messianic child, the Son of God, experiences being forsaken by God, he experiences the pain of divine love for sinners and accepts it. The suffering of Christ on the cross is human sin transformed into the atoning suffering of God. Therefore nothing can limit Christ's experience of being forsaken on the cross. As the young Luther stressed so emphatically in his theology of the cross, it is the experience of *hell*. Paul, too, took this view of the godforsakenness of Christ on the cross: "For our sake he made him to be sin who knew no sin" (II Cor.5.21). Christ became "curse for us" (Gal.3.13). The Son of God, abandoned, cursed and damned, hangs on the cross. He hangs there "for us" that we might have peace. Through his wounds we are healed.[19]

Moltmann has deliberately used the word "representative," rather than "substitute," of Christ: "Understood as substitution, representation alienates men. But personal representation has within itself an element of liberation."[20] The liberation to which he refers comes from the fact that Christians do not experience "death and hell in solitude," as Christ did, but rather "in his company."[21] Our comment on this, however, is that the experience of liberation on the part of Christians is something consequent upon Christ's redemptive act; it does not change the nature of that act, which in Moltmann's theology remains substitution in the sense in which this term is usually contrasted with representation, a contrast of passivity with activity. Certainly, in its physical reality the cross is something undergone by Christ rather than something positively accomplished. But in its spiritual and theological essence, what happened to Christ on the cross is seen by a theology of representation as a positive act on his part, whereas for a theology of substitution (as understood above) it is a passive undergoing of godforsakenness, though of course it is recognized that the latter is embraced by Christ in a positive spiritual act. The vital question that emerges from this is: Was Jesus actually abandoned by God on the cross, or not?

In the theology of Luther and Calvin and of Moltmann, Jesus' death-cry, "My God, my God, why have you forsaken me?" (Mk 15.34), is interpreted as a sign of his abandonment, his rejection, and his being cursed by God in death. For Luther and Calvin, Christ, though sinless, as the substitute for humanity attracts on the cross the full punishment of God's wrath, the pain of hell, and hence averts it from those who by their sins deserve it. Moltmann, as we have noted, revises this theology, but is able to quote Luther in support of his revision:

> To be forsaken by God is to go from life and salvation into the distant country of death and hell.—Not only in the eyes of the world and his disciples, nay, in his own eyes too did Christ see himself as lost, as forsaken by God, felt in his conscience that he was cursed by God, suffered the torments of the damned, who feel God's eternal wrath, shrink back from it and flee.[22]

Operating out of this context and utilizing the exegetical work of Wiard Popkes,[23] Moltmann exploits the double *paradidonai* of Pauline theology, two particular occasions, Romans 8.32 and Galatians 2.20, when Paul uses this word, which means "to deliver up," "to hand over." We have already encountered the word in chapter 2 in the text of John 19.30, where it carried a positive sense, in that Jesus is there said to deliver up the spirit (his life, to God, in the basic meaning). As used in Romans 8.32, which reads, "He who did not spare his own Son but gave him up [*paredoken*] for us all, will he not also give us all things with him?" (RSV), while it retains the same meaning, it has a negative sense in that the Father is said to give up Jesus his Son to death, and indeed to the shameful death of the cross (he did not "spare" him). Moltmann backs up this point from Paul by two other quotations, 2 Corinthians 5.21 ("For our sake he made him to be sin who knew no sin, so that in him we might become the righteousness of God" [RSV]) and Galatians 3.13 ("Christ redeemed us from the curse of the Law by becoming a curse for us—for it is written, 'Cursed is everyone who hangs on a tree' "). Moltmann finds further support in the statement of Hebrews 2.9 that Jesus died "apart from God." However, he is on doubly insecure ground on this text, as I shall point out in detail in my critique. According to Moltmann, Jesus was not just the object of the Father's "giving-up," but voluntarily became the subject of his own. It is most significant that Paul, in Galatians 2.20c, uses the same word, *paradidonai*, to express the spiritual attitude with which Jesus went to his death: "The life which I now live in the flesh I live by the faith of the Son of God, who loved me and gave himself up for me." Paul's double paradidonai expresses the deep conformity and unity of will that exists between the Father and the Son. It existed throughout Jesus' life and ministry and particularly in his passion (witness the agony in Gethsemane: "[n]ot what I will, but what you will" [Mk 14.36c]). But most of all it is evident in his death:

> [T]his profound community of will arises at precisely the point when the Son is furthest divided from the Father, and the Father from the Son, in the accursed death on the cross, in the "dark night" of that death. On the cross the Father and the Son are so deeply separated that their relationship breaks off. Jesus died "without God"—

godlessly. Yet on the cross the Father and the Son are at the same time so much one that they represent a single surrendering movement.[24]

Moltmann sees the singularity of this movement expressed in the statement of John 14.9b, "Whoever has seen me has seen the Father." Moltmann then continues:

> The Epistle to the Hebrews expresses this by saying that Christ offered himself to God "through the eternal Spirit" (*dia pneumatos aioniou*) (9.14). The surrender through the Father and the offering of the Son take place "through the Spirit." The Holy Spirit is therefore the link in the separation. He is the link joining the bond between the Father and the Son, with their separation.[25]

Certain obscurities in this passage are removed by comparison with similar statements in other places in Moltmann's work. Thus the curious phrase "surrender through the Father" becomes clear as "the giving up by the Father"; and the last two sentences are reexpressed in one as: "[S]o the Holy Spirit is what holds them together in the separation, what forms both the bond and the separation of the Father and the Son from one another."[26] Elsewhere Moltmann does not hesitate to say that the Holy Spirit "proceeds" from the event that takes place between the Father and the Son on the cross.[27] And an intimation of his conception of the role of the Spirit thus produced is conveyed by the following words from yet another place: "In this happening God is revealed as the trinitarian God, and in the event between the surrendering Father and the forsaken Son, God becomes so "vast" in the Spirit of self-offering that there is room and life for the whole world, the living and the dead."[28]

Assessment of Moltmann's Theology

Moltmann on Paul

INITIAL PAULINE TEXTS

In engaging on an assessment of Moltmann's trinitarian theology of the cross, I point out first a certain coincidence of approach between him and me on this subject, for which the reader is referred to chapter 2 of this book, where the biblical foundations of what I have to say about the Trinity are laid down. We both see the cross as a trinitarian event, indeed as the trinitarian event par excellence. We both understand the self-surrender of Father and Son that took place there as the high point of their relationship (though for Moltmann this is conceived paradoxically or dialectically), and we both recognize this relationship as embodied in the Holy Spirit, who precisely through this event is poured out upon the Church. Within this consistency of approach, however, there are important differences. To go to the heart of the matter, my principal quarrel with Moltmann is over what remains of the penal substitution theory in his theology and the implications of this for the Trinity. A methodological error that he makes is to attribute his theology, which he discovers in the letters of Paul, to the Gospel of Mark as well. But it cannot be presumed that any two biblical authors will share the same theology; and on a subject as complex and resistant to systematization as the redemption it is only to be expected that the New Testament will offer a variety of approaches, which need to be balanced against each other.

Moltmann rightly identifies Paul's theology of redemption as a theology of the cross. Luther, Calvin, and Moltmann all interpret Paul in the sense that the cross, as Christ's ultimate self-identification with sinners, drives a wedge between the Father and Christ, a wedge that then needs somehow to be overcome. But Moltmann does not want to go as far down this path as Luther and Calvin did. He specifies and limits the alienation that takes place between the Father and Christ on the cross. Outside the designated area of alienation, therefore, he is at pains to show that the Father and Christ are one. But he cannot do this convincingly, because he is already too far down Luther and Calvin's path. So against him we must say that, while Christ can represent us and atone for our sins, the Father can do neither of these things, as he is not one of us. Paul never has the Father as our representative or as our atoner. True, Paul has the Father "reconciling" us to himself (2 Cor. 5.19), but to reconcile is not the same as to atone. Likewise, Moltmann has the wrath of God as his wounded love, but wounded love is not wrath. Even if we grant, as we should, that in Paul God's wrath is grounded in his wounded love, they are still not the same. The truth is that God's wrath, however we are to understand it, is something that distinguishes the Father from Christ. Further, in thus stretching language beyond acceptable limits, Moltmann, contrary to his intentions,[29] reduces Christ to a passive instrument in the hands of the Father. This passivity is a point in common between Moltmann and the Reformers that I shall argue against as I proceed.

Edward Schillebeeckx has remarked that, in elevating suffering to an intratrinitarian event between the Father and the Son, Moltmann has effectively "eternalized" it, investing it with "some splendor,"[30] and Bauckham also has said something similar.[31] This draws attention to a fundamental problem with Moltmann's theology, his tendency to make the being of God dependent on events of history. The view argued for here is that the only eternal reality between the Father and the Son is their mutual love, which is the Holy Spirit. Even in the human domain suffering comes to an end: the time will come when "he [God] will wipe away every tear from their eyes, and death shall be no more, neither shall there be mourning, nor crying nor pain any more, for the former things have passed away" (Rev 21.4). All that will remain will be love purified by suffering. If this is so among human beings, how much more between the Father and the Son in the eternal Trinity. The Holy Spirit existed from all eternity as the bond of love between the Father and the Son. Through the creation and the Incarnation the Father opened himself to the possibility and the actuality of suffering, and the Son suffered grievously for the sins of the world. The Father opened himself to the wounding (but not the diminishing) of his love; and if the Son learned obedience through suffering (see Heb 5.8), even more, through the same means, he learned love. But when his suffering came to an end, all that remained was the love thus brought to perfection. Thenceforth the mutual love of the Father and the Son had a human dimension, in that the Son's love for the Father was authentic human love. God, of course, continues after the death of Christ to suffer through his creation and his wayward children, but it is a suffering that, mysteriously, is already overcome in principle through the death and Resurrection of Christ, the beginning of the eschaton, and that will be totally vanquished in its consummation.

Let us move now to the area where Moltmann wants to concentrate the alienation that in his theology takes place between the Father and Christ on the cross.

The texts to which he appeals for the Father-Son relationship from the side of the Father are Romans 8.32, 2 Corinthians 5.21, and Galatians 3.13, and, from outside the Pauline corpus, Hebrews 2.9. Let us deal with the last-mentioned first. Moltmann acknowledges that there is a dispute over whether the reading should be that Jesus tasted death for us all *choris theou* ("apart from God," that is, far from God, or without God) or *chariti theou* ("by the grace of God"), but says that the former "has textual preference."[32] This is not correct. Indeed the reading is poorly attested, and this is reflected in the fact that all the major English-language versions opt for the alternative (to name a few, the Revised Standard Version, the New Oxford Annotated Bible, the New Jerusalem Bible, the Revised English Bible, and the New American Bible). Also, the alternative fits in easily with the context ("of God's initiative in Jesus' saving work"),[33] which the first does not. Again, the first reading is hardly consistent with the later statement of Hebrews (at 12.2) that Jesus "for the joy that was set before him endured the cross." However, it is just possible that Moltmann is right: the second reading *may* represent an amendment of a *lectio difficilior* (a more difficult, in the sense of a more problematical, original reading).[34] But if this is so, it is still wrong to import theology from one source into another. More likely, the text would in this case reflect a historical memory of the cry of Jesus on the cross that is recorded in Mark (and I reserve till later the question of what that cry actually meant).[35] As Myles Bourke puts it, the text would then express "Jesus' feeling of abandonment in death,"[36] which is not disputed and which is an altogether different matter from actual abandonment by God. Moltmann too readily equates feeling with actuality.

If we take our starting point in Paul from the paradidonai of Jesus in Galatians 2.20, we see that there it expresses the redemption in terms of the sacrificial self-surrender of Jesus to his death for the sake of sinners, the context being that of justification by faith in Christ (as opposed to the pharisaic justification through the works of the Law). But Jesus would not have been in a position to give himself up at all had not the Father in the first place taken the initiative and sent him for this purpose. Knowing what lay in store for Jesus, the Father in sending him truly "did not spare" him but "gave him up" to his fate, as the paradidonai of Romans 8.32 asserts. The first paradidonai expresses directly Jesus' love for us, and only indirectly his love for the Father, insofar as he conforms his will to that of the Father even though this means for him suffering and death. This is to be seen also from the events at Gethsemane and particularly from the statement, "Not what I will, but what you will" (Mk 14.36). Likewise, the second paradidonai expresses only indirectly the love of the Father for the Son; directly it speaks of his love for us. The double paradidonai, then, expresses directly the unity of will of the Father and the Son, but only in regard to something external to themselves, insofar as the Son conforms himself to the Father's will for the redemption of the human race. Only indirectly does it express the bond of love that exists between them.

The Father's paradidonai is sacrificial, but in a different sense from that of Jesus. It can be compared with the statement of John 3.16 that God "gave" his only Son (except that here there is an overtone of preexistence that is lacking in Paul). But in neither case is there any ground for construing this action as though the Father thereby "parted from" Jesus, a notion that lends itself to tendentious expansion into abandonment. It merely means that the Father did nothing to impede the disastrous turn that through no fault of either himself or Jesus the latter's course had taken. This was not because he was indifferent to Jesus, still less because he derived pleasure from his suffering; rather it was because he no less ardently than Jesus willed the ultimate outcome of this course, the reconciliation of sinners. In this connection it is important to note what both texts say about the Father's love. The text from John says that he acted out of his love for the sinful "world." In the context of the Romans text (v. 39) the Father's love for "us" sinners manifested in the love (v. 35) and action of Christ is extolled, the last-mentioned being Christ's present intercession for us (v. 34), which is the end point (the intermediate points also being recounted, his raising-up and his installation at God's right hand) of the Father's initial action in giving him up "for us all" (back to v. 32).

Both texts allude to the Father's love for Jesus, which, however, is taken for granted. It is invoked indirectly, and only for the sake of lending force to the argument of the Father's love for us. Nevertheless, what is said is significant. The Father did not sacrifice for us something or someone of little or no value in his eyes (there is in fact no such thing or person), but he gave precisely his "Son." The very word, conjuring up the story of Abraham and Isaac (Gen 22), speaks eloquently of the Father's love for Jesus. It is used in both texts, John reinforcing it by "only-begotten" ("beloved" is used in the Septuagint account of Genesis 22, at vv. 2, 12, and 16), and Paul underscoring it by use of the words "spare" and "own": "he did not spare his own Son." There is no suggestion in all this that the love of the Father for his Son wavered even for an instant; indeed quite the opposite. It wavered no more than did the love of Abraham for Isaac. Moltmann's invocation of the Father's *paradidonai* to justify his claim that the relationship of the Father and the Son "breaks off" on the cross is therefore without foundation.

Naturally, I am not attacking or even querying the mutual surrender of the Father and the Son in love, especially as this comes to its definitive expression on the cross; clearly, my own theology of the Trinity, as expounded in chapter 2, fully depends on it. My concern has been to show 1) that the double *paradidonai* is at best a weak argument in regard to the relationship of the Father and the Son, and 2) that it cannot legitimately be invoked to support a real separation of the Father from the Son on the cross.

BACKGROUND: THE SUFFERING SERVANT

To what extent, then, does Paul advocate a theory of this type? Undoubtedly, one of the Old Testament themes underlying his theology of the cross is that of the Suffering Servant of Deutero-Isaiah, especially as presented in the Fourth Song, Isaiah 52.13–53.12. The reason for this is partly that the Song was perceived as a suitable explanation of the cross in terms of redemption, and partly that the identification of Jesus with the Servant goes back at least to the form in which Paul received the primitive creed (see I Cor 15.3)[37] and quite likely even to Jesus himself.[38]

The suitability of the Song as an explanation of the cross is evident in that it makes sense of the suffering of an innocent person in terms of the expiation of the sins of others. Also it takes explicitly into account an essential feature of Jesus' ministry that is often only implicit in other explanations, that in his love he turned to sinners, sought them out, identified with them in his life (without condoning their sins), healing and forgiving them and having table fellowship with them (as an offer of reconciliation and salvation), and finally identified with them in his death by undergoing the death of a sinner under the Law. That sin brought with it punishment from God in this life and even his curse was a commonplace of Old Testament theology, to be seen in such texts as Leviticus 26.14–39, Deuteronomy 28.15–46, and Jeremiah 26.4–6. Naturally, those punished were the guilty, though the early corporate sense of responsibility was later revised in favor of an individual sense, expounded in texts such as Ezekiel 14.12–23 and 18.1–32. The opening verses of the latter text (1–4) deserve to be quoted, as they show how deliberate a revision it was:

> The word of the Lord came to me: What do you mean by repeating this proverb concerning the land of Israel, "The parents have eaten sour grapes, and the children's teeth are set on edge"? As I live, says the Lord God, this proverb shall be no more used by you in Israel. Know that all lives are mine; the life of the parent as well as the life of the child is mine; it is only the person who sins that shall die.

Unusual suffering that was apparently unjust, for example, in the life of an innocent person, was therefore a great puzzle, which remained unsolved (see the Book of Job and Psalm 22) until the Fourth Servant Song of Deutero-Isaiah answered it in the wholly novel terms of vicarious atonement. By the time of Jesus this answer was established in general currency.[39] It is exemplified in such texts as 2 Maccabees 7.37–38 and 4 Maccabees 6.26–29 and 17.20–22. It was not invalidated by the insight of the last of the Old Testament books, the Book of Wisdom, which drawing on Alexandrian resources was able to say that ultimately divine retribution takes place beyond the grave (cf. 2.22–23; 3.1–12).

The text of the Fourth Servant Song does not provide the justification for their respective soteriologies that either the Reformers or Moltmann claimed from it. However, there is a biblical sense of substitution, even penal substitution, that clearly is present in the Song. This is a sense somewhat akin to that advocated by Karl Lehmann for Paul, though certainly not identical with it (for one thing, the Pauline substitution was not penal in Lehmann's understanding).[40] In the Pauline expression "for us" Lehmann recognizes a fundamental formulation of the mystery of redemption:

> [O]ne may see in a brief biblical formula of faith the (at least implicit) synthesis of all the principal aspects (of redemption), that is, the pre-Pauline and Pauline "for us" (cf. 1 Cor 15.3; 2 Cor 5.14; Rom 8.32; Gal 1.4; 2.20; Rom 5.6; 14.15, inclusive, therefore, of all the variants: for us, for all, for sins, for the brother, for me, for the Godless).[41]

But how is this "for us" to be understood?

> [A]ccording to general agreement the "for us" (inclusive of the different prepositions, *hyper, dia, peri, anti*) means literally not only "for our sake," "for our benefit," but no less "in our place," "in substitution for us." By this is meant not only that we cannot bring about salvation for ourselves, but that in the sense of Rom 3.24 it is

given to us without our contribution. The idea of Jesus' surrender *for . . .* is not sufficiently explained in terms of a strict correspondence between *servitium* (service) and *sacrificium* (sacrifice), in the sense that Jesus has offered his life *for his mission.* Is the New Testament really saying nothing more "than that Jesus in dying stepped into the gap between God and us" (Käsemann)?[42]

The verse referred to, Romans 3.24, with verse 23, says that "since all have sinned and fall short of the glory of God, they are justified by his grace as a gift, through the redemption which is in Christ Jesus." What Lehmann is saying here is undoubtedly correct. It should be noted that his positive assessment does not extend to a recognition of *penal* substitution in Paul (though it does in the Fourth Servant Song): "Gal 3.13 and 2 Cor 5.21, for example, do not speak of a substitutionary punitive suffering of Christ."[43]

Finally, as was noted earlier, the idea of substitution has come to be associated with passivity on the part of the substitute. This is because in penal substitution the substitute simply has a passive role, to undergo the wrath and punishment of God. Luther's soteriology, though not as systematic as this, provides the point of departure for it, as Luther himself stressed both the passivity of Christ on the cross and the penal character of his suffering.[44] Moltmann's "representative" is also passive, in simply "bearing" the sins of the world. In a theology of representation, however, the representative is *active* (under God) in bringing about the work of redemption. It is clear from Lehmann's presentation that the substitute also is conceived of as active. What distinguishes the substitute (thus understood) from the representative is that where the latter is conceived primarily in terms of his possession of sufficient commonality with the group so as to be able to represent it (even though he may end up doing something they are unable to do), the former is conceived primarily in terms of precisely this last-named function, of being able to achieve for the group something it could not achieve for itself, something, therefore, it can only receive as pure gift. In Lehmann's sense of substitute, then, the two terms are compatible, and, in the case of Christ, complementary: "representative" emphasizes the basic requirement of the perfect mediator (who in fact is Christ), commonality (with the group), while "substitute" emphasizes the ultimate requirement, capacity (over against the incapacity of the group). This is not at all the way in which these terms have been compared and contrasted in the past.

My treatment thus far has led, then, to the distinction of four senses of substitution. The first three are predicated of Christ in the redemption, while the fourth is predicated of the Servant in the Fourth Song of Isaiah. The first is a penal substitution, in which God not only rejects the passive substitute but punishes him; the second, Moltmann's sense, is a nonpenal substitution in which God simply rejects the passive substitute; the third, Lehmann's sense, is a nonpenal substitution in which the active, cooperating substitute achieves for the group what it cannot achieve for itself and must therefore receive as pure gift; and the fourth is a penal substitution in which God punishes, but does not reject, the active, cooperating substitute, who thus achieves for the group what it cannot achieve for itself.

There can be no doubt that God's action in the Servant's regard is penal. But there is not a word to suggest that God rejects, abandons, or curses his Servant.

Certainly, he was "despised and rejected" (53.3), but this was by human beings, not by God. Certainly, he undergoes sufferings that must be understood as punishment for sin, but how wrong "we" (the unidentified group of speakers) were shown to be! "We" took it for granted that he was being punished for his own sins: "[W]e accounted him stricken, struck down by God, and afflicted" (53.4b). And all the time he was completely "righteous" (53.11), the dedicated possessor and practitioner of true "knowledge", that is, God 's law.[45] What can this mystery mean? Only that the sins he was punished for were ours, not his own (53.4a, 5, 6), a fact that *he* understood all along. This explains his meek and uncomplaining acceptance of his lot (53.7), an attitude that really was something more than passive acceptance, namely, an active, knowing, and willing embracing of his lot: "[H]e poured himself out to death, . . . bore the sins of many, and made intercession for the transgressors" (53.12c, e, f). The text of 53.10b is uncertain: it is not clear whether it should read "when you (God) make," or "when he (the Servant) makes," "his life an offering for sin." But even if the former reading is correct, the active compliance of the Servant is affirmed, implicitly. And in the other reading it is explicit.

This active spiritual stance of the Servant gives the lie to the idea of the Servant as substitute in the sense of either the Reformers or Moltmann, as passivity on the part of the substitute is of the essence of their conceptions, even if in different ways.[46] (For the Reformers, though not for Moltmann, passivity also characterizes the beneficiaries of the substitute's sufferings.)[47] It is true that in a physical sense there is an element of passivity in the Servant: sin must be punished. But spiritually there is no passivity in the sense of undergoing godforsakenness. The only passivity there is consists in a humble acceptance of the will of God. But in undergoing punishment as he does, the Servant, the righteous one suffering for the unrighteous, wins redemption for all. If the Servant, the righteous one, makes many actually righteous (see 53.11c), this is because, in the words of Carroll Stuhlmueller, he "is suffusing within them his own spirit of sorrow and hope."[48] The active self-sacrifice of the Servant, complementing his passive submission, stands as intermediary between the objective forgiveness of God and the active, subjective contrition of the beneficiaries without which there is no actual personal forgiveness. But if the Servant is not a substitute in the sense of either the Reformers or Moltmann, that he is a substitute in some sense is beyond dispute. This is evident in the fact that only he as the righteous one can accomplish redemption for the unrighteous. They, therefore, receive it as a pure gift.

In all this it cannot be denied that the Song contains an unresolved theological problem: God inflicts punishment on the Servant, but at the same time continues to recognize his innocence and to love him, and through his punishing action accomplishes the good work of the justification of the sinful many. But how can God be so arbitrary and inconsistent? On this the Song is silent. The problem arises out of the fact that in the Old Testament everything that happens, evil included, was thought to occur by the direct will of God. Unusual suffering, as we have seen, was normally interpreted as punishment for sin. In the New Testament, however, we find that for John, in the case of the man born blind (Jn 9), the suffering is understood not in this way but as an occasion for the manifestation of God's power and mercy

(vv. 2–4), though even here the assumption holds that the man's blindness was directly caused by God.

Paul, in Romans 9.14–24, wrestles with the problem of the sovereignty of God and apparently espouses a doctrine of double predestination. But only apparently. In saying that God "has mercy on whomever he chooses and hardens the heart of whomever he chooses" (v. 18) Paul is invoking the authority of Scripture (the Book of Exodus) to emphasize the divine sovereignty. While, objectively speaking, Pharaoh, whose case he has been considering, resisted God's will in trying to prevent the saving event of the exodus from taking place, he was not consciously committing sin. When Paul speaks of real sinners, as he does in Romans 2.3–4, there is no suggestion that God is responsible. Indeed, God is said (v. 4) to tolerate them with kindness, forbearance, and patience in the hope that such treatment will bring them to repentance. Hence, when in Romans 9.22 Paul says that God, "desiring to show his wrath and make known his power, has endured with much patience the objects of wrath prepared for destruction," "desiring" is best understood concessively rather than causally (hence "*though* he desired, etc.),[49] and "prepared" (*katertismena*) is best understood as being in middle rather than passive voice (hence "having prepared themselves," therefore "ready" or "ripe").[50] The verse, therefore, is best translated, "What if God, though desiring to show his wrath and make known his power, has endured with much patience the objects of wrath ripe for destruction?"

In this pericope, therefore, as in the text from Romans 2, Paul foreshadows the later distinction of the permissive and the direct will of God, a distinction not available in any form to the author of the Song. The latter therefore was in no position to say that the Servant's sufferings were merely permitted, not caused, by God. Of course, had he been in such a position, the Song would bear a significantly different cast from that which it actually has. As it is, it labors under two internal difficulties, which can be expressed in question form: How could God punish an innocent person without thereby violating his own justice, and how could he truly be said to love the person whom he was treating thus? Admission of the permissive will by the author would have obviated both problems. But this much at least is clear from the Song: while because of its limitations it has God punishing the innocent Servant, it offers no support to either the Reformers or Moltmann's theology of the cross as allegedly discovered in Paul or elsewhere in the New Testament.

REMAINING PAULINE TEXTS

It remains critically to examine the two outstanding Pauline texts used by Moltmann: 2 Corinthians 5.21 and Galatians 3.13. Let us take the Corinthians text first: "For our sake he [God] made him [Jesus] to be sin who knew no sin, so that in him we might become the righteousness of God." The startling identification of Jesus with "sin" and of ourselves with "righteousness" is not merely literary; as we shall see, it has to do with the intended objectivity of what is thus said. The literary form, as C. K. Barrett points out, is that of chiasmus (inversion of word order), though it is imperfect.[51] With Barrett we recognize that allusion to the Fourth Servant Song is not "clear," in the sense of being spelt out, and that "sin" here is not "sin offering" as in the Song.[52] Nonetheless, with Oscar Cullmann we hold that the figure of the Servant lies behind this Pauline utterance.[53] The reasons are as follows.

First, it is scarcely conceivable that Paul could have formulated this thought except out of the background of the Servant theology. From where else could he have drawn the idea of Jesus representing sinful humanity because identified with their sin? Second, there is the parallel of God's initiative. In the context (vv. 18–20) of the text, it is *God* who reconciles us to himself, with Jesus playing only an instrumental role. In this way Paul sets up his conclusion, an appeal (in v. 20) to be reconciled to *God*. So it is that in verse 21 the idea of a sin offering is excluded: it is *God* who makes Jesus, the sinless one, to be sin (rather than Jesus offering himself for sin), *God* who brings him into that external relation to himself which normally is the result of sin.[54] In the Song also the initiative is on the side of God. There is no doubt that it is God who inflicts punishment on the Servant for the sins of others. The attitude of the Servant is mentioned and given its due place: he submits meekly to God's will and even offers himself as a sin offering. But its place is secondary; it is response to, compliance with, the initiative of God. A nicety such as this would have been out of place, no more than a complicating distraction, in the Pauline aphorism. The remaining parallels, apart from that mentioned below, are the sinlessness of the Servant and of Christ, and the fact that the outcome of God's action in each case is the righteousness of the many.

We come now to a feature of both passages that is not just a parallel but a key, perhaps *the* key, to the meaning of the Pauline text, their objectivity. When we said above that the Servant stands between the objectivity of God's forgiveness and the subjectivity of the contrition of the people, the intention was to ascribe objectivity also to the Servant, to his person and his role. Some such scheme is necessary to overcome a purely personal (subjective) relationship of individuals with God in favor of a personal relationship that is mediated socially. A religious transaction takes place between God and the Servant, and that becomes the instrument by which henceforth transactions take place between God and individuals. This instrumentality, which retains its objective character, becomes an essential component around which social religion is thenceforward organized. Punishment as the effect of sin is taken out on the Servant, who remains a servant, meek and compliant, throughout the ordeal; but the Servant himself is totally sinless; therefore the sin that is expunged is that of those who really are guilty; but their personal sins are not forgiven until they repent. The case is similar (though not identical) with the Pauline passage. On the cross a transaction takes place between God and Jesus; this is God's reconciling of the world to himself in Christ (v. 19a); thus Paul is constituted Christ's ambassador (v. 20a), entrusted with the message of reconciliation (v. 19c); those who respond to it positively become a new creation (v. 17), justified by faith. Therefore, God's reconciliation, insofar as it is accomplished in the person of Jesus, is, like that of the Servant, objective (Barrett prefers to say "forensic").[55] It is thus that the words "not counting their trespasses against them" are to be interpreted. This objectivity is seen, first, in the external relation of alienation that obtains between God and Jesus (God "made him to be sin") despite Jesus' subjective sinlessness and devotion, and second, in the fact that the righteousness that we "become" is "the righteousness of God," which does not become our subjective righteousness until we are justified by faith.[56]

It is noteworthy that at this objective level Paul sees only an exchange: Christ was made *sin that* we might become *God's righteousness.*[57] Though the figure of the Servant is in the background, Paul says nothing about the process by which Jesus became sin. There is no word about punishment of Jesus. Indeed, nowhere does Paul say that Jesus was punished by God. It seems that he has deliberately laid aside this theme from the Servant theology, where it played an essential role in explaining the relation between the Servant's sufferings and the justification of the sinful many, and has satisfied himself with the assertion of a simple exchange, a device that is both literary and theological. In this procedure the role of Jesus as substitute in Lehmann's sense, as the winner of a benefit that comes to its recipients as pure gift, is evident. In so acting, Paul has adroitly sidestepped the formidable twofold problem contained in the Servant theology to which I referred earlier. In this respect he appears to be influenced by, or at least subjected to a common influence with, the Maccabees texts already referred to, 2 Maccabees 7.37–38 and 4 Maccabees 6.26–29 and 17.20–22, which were roughly contemporaneous with his writings. In these texts the idea of the divine *punishment* of an innocent person has completely disappeared; what is now said is only that the *suffering* of an innocent person can atone for the sins of a guilty multitude.[58] In these texts the operative ideas are innocent blood as purification, an exchange, the paying of a ransom, and expiation. Paul appears to agree partly with this school of thought. I say "partly" because his deliberate association of Jesus with objective sin shows that despite his criticism his thinking remains more firmly anchored in the Servant theology than is that of the school just mentioned. This demonstrates that he can be as little claimed as the inspirer of the theory of vicarious satisfaction as of that of penal substitution.

The last text, Galatians 3.13–14 reads: "Christ redeemed us from the curse of the Law by becoming a curse for us—for it is written, 'Cursed is everyone who hangs on a tree'—in order that in Christ Jesus the blessing of Abraham might come to the gentiles, so that we might receive the promise of the Spirit through faith."

The Old Testament text referred to is the Septuagint version of Deuteronomy 21.23c, which I now quote in its context of verses 22 and 22a and b: "And if there be sin in anyone, and the judgment of death be upon him, and he be put to death, and you hang him on a tree: his body shall not remain all night upon the tree, but you shall by all means bury it on that day, for cursed by God is everyone who hangs on a tree."

Though reference to the Suffering Servant is weaker here in our Galatians text than in the former text, the statement that Christ became a curse for us is identical in content to the assertion of that text that for our sake God made him to be sin, except that here the initiative for redemption is seen as taken by Christ rather than by God. Even Christ's sinlessness, stated explicitly in the former text, is hinted at here, for the curse incurred by Christ is said to be of a different kind from ours. While we incur the Law's curse because of our sins, he does so only because of a technicality, that his body "hangs on a tree." The implication is that he was sinless. There is also the idea of an exchange, as in the former text: here a curse is exchanged for a blessing, the curse of Christ for the blessing of the gentiles. This exchange is said to be redemptive. Most important, the same objectivity that we discovered in the previous text is verified here also. Christ is brought only into an external relation of alienation from God, not an internal one, and we, far from receiving the blessing automatically, receive it only through our faith, as is explicitly stated.

It is tendentious to claim on the basis of this text that Paul considered Jesus to have been cursed by God on the cross. Numerous commentators have pointed out that, whereas both the original and the Septuagint version of the Deuteronomy text have the person whose body hangs on a tree "cursed *by God*," Paul has omitted the words "by God." This can only mean that he is deliberately *not* saying that Christ was cursed by God. Positively, he can only be wanting to assert Christ's embrace of sinners in his love and his identification with them in his death on their behalf, his substitution for them in the nonpenal sense. The idea that Jesus was cursed by God could only be paralleled from the Old Testament by reference to the scapegoat of Leviticus 16.20–28; but, as Bruce Vawter says, the New Testament never relates Jesus to this image. Vawter also points out that the unholy condition of the scapegoat precluded its being in any sense a sacrifice, and indeed that the customs connected with it were pagan rituals barely assimilated by Jewish religion.[59] Finally, there is no suggestion in this text either, that Jesus was punished by God.

Romans 2.5–11 leaves us in no doubt that Paul accepted the traditional belief that God punishes the wicked:

> [B]y your hard and impenitent heart you are storing up wrath for yourself on the day of wrath when God's righteous judgment will be revealed. For he will repay according to each one's deeds: to those who by patiently doing good seek for glory and honor and immortality, he will give eternal life; while for those who are self-seeking and who do not obey the truth but wickedness, there will be wrath and fury. There will be anguish and distress for everyone who does evil, the Jew first and also the Greek, but glory and honor and peace for everyone who does good, the Jew first and also the Greek. For God shows no partiality.

But he never says that God punishes Christ, for he knows and says that Christ was innocent. However, this does not stop him from saying, indeed it makes it possible for him to say, that the circumstances of Christ's death brought him into an objective condition of alienation from God, the alienation, namely, of sin, that allowed God to make the exchange of the objective sin of Christ for the objective righteousness of the human race, which righteousness could then be rendered subjective and personal through its appropriation by faith. Christ, therefore, was a substitute for sinners only in the nonpenal sense. Far from cursing or abandoning him, God never ceased to love and support him. Since, therefore, Christ's function on the cross was not understood by Paul in terms either of punishment or actual abandonment, we have no hesitation in concluding that neither the Reformers nor Moltmann can rightly lay claim to his support for their respective theologies of the cross.

On the question of divine punishment in general, 1 Peter 2.18–25, a pericope devoted to the conduct of Christian slaves, is of interest. Verses 19–20 contemplate the cases of two slaves, one who is punished unjustly and one who is punished justly. In each case the punishment is human, being meted out by the master. Patient submission to just punishment earns no praise; it is only what is expected of a slave. But patient submission to unjust punishment is commended, because it wins God's approval. The point is demonstrated in verses 21–25 by reference to Christ, who is spoken of in the language of the Fourth Servant Song and who is said to be an "example" for them. The clear implication is that Christ too was punished and that his punishment was unjust, but that it came from human beings, not from God. Indeed, it is said, in verse 23, that in undergoing punishment "he trusted to him who judges justly," to God, in contradistinction to human beings, who sometimes judge unjustly. What is interesting here is that the author, while clearly understanding Christ in terms of the Servant and being prepared to portray his sufferings as punishment, like Paul draws the line at having him punished by God, and so sets aside the principal difficulty bequeathed by the theology of the Song.

It seems to be against neither Scripture nor the teaching of the Church[60] to suggest that the proposition that God punishes sin not directly, by a positive act (as human authority punishes wrongdoing), but permissively (which is the sense in which he can be said to be the cause of sin itself), is a legitimate application of the later distinction of the direct and the permissive will of God. This would mean only that God does not prevent or hinder the negative effects, of alienation and separation from himself and fellow human beings (with all that this entails), in both this life and the next, which inevitably and by an intrinsic connection flow from sin. Just as God determines no one to sin and predestines no one to damnation, so too, when someone *has* sinned, he does not punish them in this life by any new, juridical act, but simply allows the effects of that free sinful decision to unfold; and, if the person dies in that state, again he does not by any juridical decree condemn them to eternal punishment, but simply allows their freely willed separation from himself and others to realize itself in eternity.[61] If we can define "vindictive" punishment as a sentence (together with its execution) part of whose object is the infliction of suffering (whether physical, mental, or both) on the wrongdoer on account of, and in proportion to, the wrong done, with the further object of their reformation or the deterrence of the wrongdoer and others (the immediate object in this view being justified by the ultimate object),[62] we need not buy into the contentious issue of whether vindictive punishment is ever justified in human communities. We can say immediately that the whole concept is misplaced with regard to God's direct will. For the most that could be said with certainty about such suffering in this life would be that it occurs by God's permissive will, while for the afterlife, seeing that there the questions of reformation and deterrence do not and cannot arise, its only possible interpretation would be revenge, which in the case of God would have to be ruled out on ethical grounds.[63]

These considerations, supported by some of the texts already examined (Jn 3.16; Rom 2.4, 8.32; 2 Cor 5.21), help us to see that the penal substitution theory errs in setting Jesus and the Father at odds over the question of sin. If Jesus placed himself in solidarity with sinners, this was only because the Father was already in solidarity with them and Jesus was doing no more than acting as his obedient revealer and minister in the world. Jesus' mode of action in lovingly identifying with sinners was neither more nor less than the revelation and embodiment of the Father's own outreach to them in mercy and grace. The three parables of Luke 15, the lost sheep, the lost drachma, and the lost son, all convey this teaching. To suggest that because Jesus identified with sinners he alienated himself from God or drew upon himself God's wrath and punishment is to falsify the teaching about the nature of God that lay at the heart of the message of Jesus and distinguished it from that of John the Baptist.[64] As we have seen, Moltmann himself has Jesus and the Father at one in their turning to sinners, and yet paradoxically, and perhaps even illogically, he has their relationship breaking down on the cross.

It follows that the redemption should be understood in wholly positive terms, of the obedience of a life offered to God in the face of great suffering, physical, emotional, and spiritual. But the suffering was not external to the obedience; it entered into its constitution and brought Jesus to perfection in its own crucible. As the Letter to the Hebrews says, "Although he was Son, he learned obedience through what he suffered; and being made perfect he became the source of eternal salvation to all who obey him, being designated by God high priest according to the order of Melchizedek" (5.8–10). In the Fourth Servant Song too the obedience of the Servant is evident, both in the very title "servant" and in the attitude taken by the Servant to God's will for him, about which I spoke earlier.

The theme of Jesus' obedience is strongly present also in Paul. Paul does not normally concern himself with Jesus' life, since the only experience he had of Jesus was of him as the glorified Lord on the road to Damascus. Even so, he speaks of the obedience of Jesus' life right up to his death when he makes his own the hymn of Philippians 2: "And being found in human form he humbled himself and became obedient unto death" (v. 8), to which he significantly adds his own words, "even death on a cross" (RSV),[65] thus portraying the death of Jesus as his supreme and culminating act of obedience to God. In Romans 5 he presents this same obedience as redemptive by again invoking the idea of an exchange: "For as by one man's [Adam's] disobedience many were made sinners, so by one man's obedience many will be made righteous" (v. 19) (RSV).

In Catholic teaching and theology this emphasis on the obedience of Christ does not detract from the sovereignty of God, who accomplishes the work of redemption as his own from start to finish. This is because human effort under grace is seen as in some mysterious way included within God's sovereign act. Hence God and human beings are not seen as competitors or rivals. This does not mean that Catholic theology claims to be able positively to explain their relationship, though it was not always so modest. In the past, Banezianism and Molinism each made precisely this claim, though in sharply constrasting ways. But in more recent times all effort to comprehend God's interaction with human beings within some human scheme has wisely been abandoned.[66]

The Pauline texts that I examined earlier bring home for the death of Jesus the identification of him with sinners that was also an essential element of his ministry ("I came not to call the righteous, but sinners" [Mk 2.17]). This they do by portraying his death on the cross as that of a sinner under the Law. In this way the theological character of his death as redemption from *sin* is made manifest. It might be thought that texts that stress the obedience of Jesus in his life and death are deficient in this respect, and that therefore the two series of texts need to be considered together for the sake of a balanced picture. Certainly it is important to integrate the differing emphases of the texts. But the "obedience" texts that I have assembled are themselves the key to this integration, which is why I said earlier that the redemption should be understood in wholly positive terms. It is no accident, therefore, that the texts from Romans 5 and Hebrews 5 link Jesus' obedience with justification and salvation, respectively, both concepts expressing the overcoming of sin.

The key is identified in the *intrinsic* nature of the link between the suffering of Jesus and his obedience, mentioned above. This is what makes it possible for Jesus to be the substitute for sinners in the nonpenal sense. While there is a certain ambiguity about suffering, such that not all suffering can be related, even indirectly, to sin, there is much suffering that can be directly related, either to one's own sins, to the sins of others, or to "social" sin; and there is no doubt that the suffering of the innocent Jesus, which like the Servant he embraced in meekness and love, was of this latter kind, a consequence of the personal sins of those immediately responsible for his death and of the social sin in which they participated, namely, a shared pride that issued defensively in an unqualified rejection of him and all he stood for because he was perceived as a threat to their understanding of religion and hence to their self-interest. Paul was right in seeing this somewhat limited objective meaning of Jesus' suffering and death as standing for a death for sinners of all times and places, since there was no psychological or spiritual limit to Jesus' outreach to sinners. Jesus' eucharistic words at the Last Supper should be interpreted along these lines.[67] This judgment was endorsed by the apostolic Church when it made its decision to turn to the gentiles, and was confirmed by the action of the Spirit in their regard. The point is that the obedience of Jesus was not enacted in a vacuum; it was formed in the face of a suffering that had precisely this meaning, the totality of sin. Because he stood before God as the representative of, and substitute for, those guilty of the totality of sin, the whole human race, Jesus was able to replace their rejection of God and disobedience with his own love and obedience and thus make it possible for the grace of God, through him, to reach even to them, convert them, and gather their newly found love and obedience up into his own. The divine exchange of which Paul speaks in several places (e.g., in 2 Corinthians 5.21, of sin for God's righteousness) is rendered possible by the obedience of Jesus, which in its execution, however, is nothing other than the revelation of God's own solidarity with sinners. And so the obedience of Jesus is related intrinsically, not extrinsically, to his identification with sinners and thus to his redemptive death. (The reader's attention is drawn to the statement made in note 63 that as the work of God the redemption is the revelation not of God's justice alone, nor of his mercy alone, but of both, so that, while it possesses a rational structure it retains the unpredictable character of gratuitous grace.)

This obedience, directed to the Father, is that of Jesus as Servant of God. But, while he was this, he was more; he was the only-begotten Son of God, who lived out his Sonship not only in perfect obedience but in perfect love of the Father. Never was this more evident than in laying down his life rather than depart to even the least degree from fidelity to the mission with which he had been entrusted, the announcing and ushering in of the Kingdom of God. Because this was an act of love, which is inseparably love of God and love of neighbor, it was also the laying down of his life "for his friends," as we are told in John 15.13. As was explained in chapter 2, this is how best to understand the self-offering of Jesus to the Father "through eternal Spirit" (Heb 9.14) *and* the Pentecostal sending by Christ of the Spirit upon the Church, or, in Johannine perspective (where the link is even clearer), the simultaneous handing over of the Spirit on the cross to the Father and to the Church (see my treatment of John 19.30). The Holy Spirit is the absolutely constant mutual love of the Father and the Son; as Spirit of God, Spirit of Sonship, he is the love of the Father for the Son, and as Spirit of Christ he is the love of Christ both for the Father and for his brothers and sisters in the Church. It is thus that men and women get caught up, passing from sinners to sons and daughters "in the Son," in the bond of love that unites the Father and the Son. Contrast this picture with that drawn by Moltmann. There the Holy Spirit does not constitute the relationship, the bond, between the Father and the Son; he enters upon it only subsequently. Rather than being the bond, he is merely the link between the bond and the separation, and therefore is external to the bond itself. As Bauckham has written, summarizing Moltmann:

> [T]he cross is a *dialectical* trinitarian event in which God identifies with what contradicts him—in the Son's alienation from the Father—so that the divine love—the Spirit of mutual surrender in which Father and Son are united—may suffer the contradiction and overcome it. The Spirit resolves the dialectic, reconciling the god-forsaken to God.[68]

But as was shown earlier, there *was* no separation in any case, and the whole idea of a simultaneous bond and separation, Moltmann's "dialectic," is sheer mystification. Further, Moltmann has no valid way, comparable to that outlined above, of joining Christian men and women to the Spirit who attains his full effectiveness for us on the cross and who is revealed there and is sent from there (not who "proceeds" there); he can only offer the rather lame explanation that on the cross the Spirit becomes so "vast" that "there is room and life for the whole world."[69]

Moltmann on the Cry on the Cross

I move on now to consider the cry of Jesus on the cross recorded in the Gospel of Mark: "My God, my God, why have you forsaken me?" (15.34), which is a quotation from the opening of Psalm 22. As we saw, as reported in Mark and interpreted in terms of a real abandonment it forms an integral part of Moltmann's theology of the cross. Before proceeding, however, I need to address the question of the historicity of the actual words of the cry. The objections against historicity are formidable.[70] In the light of these, Moltmann does not claim that the words are historical, but only that they render faithfully the meaning of the cry.[71] It seems, however, that despite the difficulties the words are historical. This is argued partly from their shocking character (Matthew preserved them [27.46], but Luke and John did not), partly from the fact that they are given first in Jesus' own language, Aramaic, a point not destroyed by the fact that they would have had to be recorded in Hebrew if the confusion about Jesus calling on Elijah (v. 35) were to be made intelligible.[72] In any case, as expressive of his mental state in the face of death on the cross they are fully consistent with the desolation he had exhibited only a short time before in the garden of Gethsemane (cf. Mk 14.32–42), a desolation in which the only available consolation was that which came from a trusting inner submission to God's will ("Not what I will, but what you will" [14.36]).

Consulting the commentaries, one notes that, generally speaking, Protestant exegetes favor Moltmann's kind of interpretation of the cry of Jesus. I argue here for a different interpretation. What, then, is the meaning of Jesus' cry?[73] It is unthinkable that Mark, whose principal thesis is that Jesus is the Son of God (see 1.1 and 15.39), would have recorded as his last words a statement that effectively annulled this thesis, that he died rejected by God. Shocking though they were, these words must have been patient of a meaning consistent with the rest of the Gospel and its purpose. As has often been argued, the sought-after meaning emerges in the light of the fact that the words are a quotation. The psalm of which they form the opening begins with a confession of a feeling of desolation in extreme need but ends with a ringing testimony to hope in the saving power of God (particularly vv. 19–26). Therefore, while Jesus' words on the cross express with stark honesty exactly how he felt (which was how he felt also at Gethsemane), they simultaneously convey his unshakable trust in the God who even in this terrible hour does not cease to be *his* God ("My God, my God . . .") (which was also his fundamental attitude at Gethsemane only a short time before). Dennis Nineham assures us: "Taken as a whole, this Psalm is anything but a cry of despair; it is the prayer of a righteous sufferer who yet trusts fully in the love and protection of God, and is confident of being vindicated by him."[74]

He continues: "There is some evidence that among the ancient Jews the opening words of this Psalm were interpreted in the light of the rest of it and were recognized as an effective form of prayer for help in time of trouble."[75]
A similar point is made by John Meier in his commentary on the parallel passage in Matthew:

Ps 22 is typical of those psalms of lament in the OT which begin on a note of desperation and end on a note of joy and thanksgiving. The psalmist dares to protest so vehemently to God precisely because he trusts his basic relationship with God; the psalms end with a vindication of that trust. Ps 22 would be especially well known to pious Jews and would readily come to their lips in moments of great distress. Knowing as they would the way the psalm ends, they would not mistake its initial cry for the despair of an atheist. On the other hand, we should not think of Jesus as disinterestedly saying the breviary on the cross. His pain and anguish are real, and his use of the psalm is heartfelt. It is by holding fast to the mysterious will of his Father even in the midst of such terrible suffering that he proves his sonship.[76]

Dillistone attempts the impossible task of reconciling the two interpretations here discussed. But for him the position for which I argue here prevails, for a reason already given earlier:

The darkness, the pain, the sense of desertion by all earthly friends, were symbolic of something deeper—that here the Divine reaction against every form of human sinfulness had come to its ultimate expression. Yet the One Who bears on His own spirit the crushing load of this Divine reaction, Who faces the threat of final annihilation, still cries "My God, my God." The question of how much of the rest of the psalm was uttered can never be resolved. But in the words *My God,* cried out in face of all that symbolized the withdrawal of the grace and favour of God, the crucial act of atonement is expressed.[77]

An extra dimension is added by Karl Rahner in his fascinating study of death.[78] Approaching the matter in his characteristic way, systematically and philosophically, he arrives at a position that coincides remarkably with the one argued here from exegetical considerations, even to the point of linking, in a positive way, the death of Christ with the sins of human beings. First, he distinguishes between death as it would have been experienced even in Paradise and death as experienced now after the Fall.[79] In the former case it would have been "a pure active self-affirmation" free of any "violent dissolution" of the bodily constitution "through a power from without."[80] Now, however, it is characterized by its own proper "darkness," which results from its dialectical nature, where the dialectic is one of "act and fate, of end and fulfillment, of being willed and being suffered, a fullness that is, at the same time, an emptiness."[81] Then, against this background he is able to say of the death of Christ:

> It is precisely in its darkness that the death of Christ becomes the expression and the incarnation of his loving obedience, the free offering of his entire created existence to God. What had been, therefore, the manifestation of sin thus becomes, without its darkness being lifted, the contradiction of sin, the manifestation of a "yes" to the will of the Father.[82]

It is from precisely this darkness that Jesus recoils in desolation and it is precisely this loving self-offering for sinners that he is thereby enabled to express, when he gives utterance to the mysterious words recorded by Mark.

This presentation of Rahner needs to be completed by a statement, at least in summary form, of his soteriology.[83] This is an unfolding of the implications of the assertion that in Christ humankind encounters God's definitive "word and offer" to itself. He argues that this word and offer can only truly be definitive if it is accepted "at least and in the first instance in this man." Moreover, this acceptance needs to take place in the entire life of the man, which will include, and reach fulfillment in, his death. This acceptance in turn needs to be accepted by God and made manifest historically in the resurrection of the man. Here we have, I suggest, a brilliant application of one of Rahner's basic theological categories, the "self-communication of God." As well as providing a fully orthodox soteriology free of the objections that plague the dominant Western models, it throws welcome light on the sinlessness, obedience, and love of Christ. And it illustrates very well the point made earlier that Catholic theology recognizes no conflict between the sovereign action of God and the free response of human beings.

Let Sandra Schneiders have the last word:

> It is important for us, no matter how difficult we find it to do so, to realize that Jesus underwent the experience of death as every human being must. We tend to imagine that he had read the script ahead of time and knew that as soon as the curtain went down on the Calvary act he could "un-die." This is not what the Gospel tells us. Jesus was terrified of death, begged to be spared, and experienced the absolute abandonment by God that the human experience of separation from life entails (cf. Mk 15:34). Every person who faces death stands at a crossroads. One road is marked with the sign of human wisdom which tells us that death is the enemy that will finally win; that death is the descent into nothingness, the end of

all our loves and all our works. The other road is marked with the sign of faith. Faith defines death as the final passage from this world to God, the moment of total loving surrender of ourselves into the hands of the God whom we do not see but in whom we believe. Jesus stood at this crossroads at the moment of his own death. All those around him, and his own inner experience of abandonment, urged him down the road of human wisdom toward the death of ultimate despair. Jesus chose the road of radical faith. He transformed his death from defeat at the hands of finitude and evil into the ultimate act of self-gift, thereby changing forever the significance of death itself.[84]

I conclude against Moltmann that his theory of the real abandonment of Jesus on the cross finds no justification in the Gospel of Mark. Nor can it be justified from any other part of the New Testament. Certainly, the cry of Jesus on the cross in no way signifies an actual abandonment of him by the Father.

Remaining Points from Moltmann

It is appropriate now to comment, very briefly, on two theses of Moltmann announced at the beginning of this treatment. The first is that the doctrine of the Trinity is necessary because the older theism, monotheism, inevitably provokes the protest of atheism, since it postulates a God who is immutable and therefore unable to love. The Trinity is held to avoid this problem because it allows mutability in God, the mutability being grounded in the distinction of persons. In chapter 5 I have already dealt with the basic issue at stake here, change in God, but in a way that puts me at odds with Moltmann. The question of change, suffering, love, in God is one that has to be faced at the level of the *unity* of God, the divine nature that is common to the three persons, and cannot be postponed to the level of the Trinity. As I have shown, it *can* be faced at the level of the divine unity, and without adopting the positions of Process theology. There is a certain mutability in God (in relation to creatures), but it is grounded not in the distinction of persons but in the dynamism of the divine being (which also grounds the distinction of persons). The question of change is as much a question for Judaism as for Christianity, and equally a problem that Judaism in principle should be able to solve.[85] Therefore, to see the Trinity as coming to the rescue of the doctrine of God is to view the question in a false and misleading perspective.

The second thesis of Moltmann is that the doctrine of the Trinity is necessary to discredit the system of monarchy, whether political or clerical, that takes its cue from unqualified monotheism. In a rapid sketch (which owes much to Erik Peterson) he outlines how the Christian apologists were among the first to make a case for "political monotheism" in their zeal to show that, far from being the enemy of the state, the Christian Church was its most solid support, in that it alone could provide the foundation for universal peace. If the one true God of Christianity were allowed to vanquish the competing deities of the warring nations, peace could at last reign in the world. Against a background of support from Arianism, other Christian writers extolled the dignity and authority of the emperor as the supreme representative of the one God on earth. Moltmann recognizes that historically the last instance of political monotheism was the European absolutism of the Enlightenment period.

And he admits that, though knowledge of the Trinity was possessed from earliest Christian times, it never exerted a moderating influence on the doctrine of political monotheism.

It is clear, then, that the doctrine of the Trinity, with its emphasis on community, interpersonal relations, love, and service, can and should contradict the regrettable theoretical support given in the past by some Christian writers to despotic regimes. This kind of testimony is in fact being given at present in South America and elsewhere as part of the apostolate of liberation theology.[86] However, in many countries today, certainly in the West, the Christian Church is unable directly to influence political systems. It would be better advised in these circumstances to concentrate on its own structures to ensure that they embody trinitarian values, and to be content with influencing political systems only indirectly, by example and evangelical witness. It should be pointed out also that there is no *necessary* connection between monotheism and monarchy. Historically, the situation could have been otherwise: it could be argued, for instance, that the one transcendent God of Christianity relativizes *all* human beings, revealing their fundamental equality before God. The political form the emergence of which would be encouraged in that case would be democracy.

When he addresses the intra-Church question, which he calls "clerical monotheism," Moltmann reveals some surprising misunderstandings of Catholicism. For example, the "monarchical episcopate" (which many theologians prefer to call the "monoepiscopate") is assumed, quite arbitrarily, to be of its nature an abusive, authoritarian system. But the authority that it in principle embodies is *Christian* authority, which is a *ministry* in the community, a necessary ministry, and one that can be properly exercised only in love. Abuses, of course, will occur, and the community needs to learn to protect itself against them.[87] But it is clear that Moltmann's problem is not just with authoritarianism but with pastoral authority itself.[88] His perception is very different from that of the Lima Statement of the Faith and Order Commission of the World Council of Churches, which recognizes that there should be at both the local and the regional level of the Church an ordained minister exercising a "service of unity," and suggests that for the sake of clearly signifying participation in the apostolic succession churches that have lost the episcopacy may need to recover it.[89] Of the papal, or Petrine, ministry Moltmann shows even less understanding. This ministry is not meant to be monarchical at all; the Second Vatican Council taught that it is a "collegial" office, in that the pope presides over the college of bishops in a way analogous to that in which Peter presided over the other apostles.[90] By analogy with the local bishop, the pope may be said to render a service of unity to the universal Church.

Moltmann sees a contradiction between an authoritative pastoral ministry and the communion model of Church implied by the Trinity; but in fact the two are so intimately connected that the ministry is the *sacrament* of trinitarian communion. Christ in his person is the paradigm of trinitarian communion: throughout his life and now for all eternity he remains in communion with the Father through the bond of the Holy Spirit whom he receives in all fullness from the Father and whom he returns to him. Ordained ministers continue the authoritative ministry of Christ (spreading the Kingdom of God that he embodied in his person) in and to the world.

Through their instrumentality believers are admitted to solidarity with Christ (becoming "sons and daughters of the Kingdom" [Mt 13.38]) and *thus* are admitted to trinitarian communion, which is the object of Christian life.

Moltmann's Philosophy

Finally, I consider briefly the philosophy underlying Moltmann's work. This is a philosophy of dialectic rather than analogy. As John O'Donnell points out, Moltmann does not reject analogy altogether: if all were well with the world, it could raise our minds to a knowledge of God; however, through the sins of human beings it is in a chaotic state and in no position to lead us to God.[91] This moves Moltmann to choose revelation over philosophy, and there he finds the very opposite to analogy, which operates on the principle that "like is known only by like": "God is only revealed as 'God' in his opposite: godlessness and abandonment by God. In concrete terms, God is revealed in the cross of Christ who was abandoned by God."[92]

This position of Moltmann's is reminiscent of, and doubtless dependent on, that of Luther, though it is not as extreme.[93] Luther too espoused what he called the *theologia crucis* (the theology of the cross), according to which the truth of God is revealed *sub contrario* (under its opposite), but he rejected the alternative, the *theologia gloriae* (the theology of glory), the theology guided by the principles of philosophy and particularly by analogy, far more radically than Moltmann does. Both reject for the believer any integration of natural knowledge and faith: Moltmann discards analogy (and therefore natural knowledge) in favor of faith because of the present sinful state of humanity, while Luther rejected analogy altogether because he saw a contradiction between it and faith. In the words of Gerhard Ebeling, for Luther "there is no question of the additional raising up and perfecting of the natural knowledge of God to the supernatural level through revelation. Rather, faith is opposed to the wishful thinking of reason, for the rational knowledge of God is a challenge to seeking God in the darkness."[94]

In presenting analogy and dialectic as strict alternatives, Moltmann fails to take into account the fact that analogy itself contains an element of dialectic.[95] This is so even with knowledge of the world, but, as can be seen from my treatment of this matter in chapter 5, it is more clearly so with knowledge of God. The adage "like is known only by like" does not exhaust the reality of analogy. As well as an affirmation of similarity, it includes an affirmation of dissimilarity, and hence of dialectic. In the case of God the dialectic is resolved at the level of transcendence in a way unknown to us. To repeat the example given earlier: God is good; God is not good (in the way creatures are); God is good (in an eminent way that we do not know).

Further, the rejection of any integration of natural knowledge and faith on the part of Moltmann and Luther is based on a propositional view of revelation and faith that is now outmoded. The simple fact is that in practice no one knows the existence and nature of God who does not already believe in him.[96] This becomes all the more obvious once it is realized that, while saving faith ideally includes a confession of the existence of God and his providence for us in Christ, it is possible for it to exist in essence as self-dedication (of course under grace, the offer of which is never lacking) to the transcendent (however conceived) *without* the attainment of so high a degree of explicitness. Because it took into account not only such texts as Hebrews 11.6 and Acts 4.12 but also 1 Timothy 2.3–4, the Second Vatican Council was able to affirm this position: "[I]n ways known to himself God can lead those who, through no fault of their own, are ignorant of the Gospel to that faith without which it is impossible to please him (Heb 11:6)."[97] Faith gives shape to and orientates knowledge. Within faith, therefore, according to its degree of explicitness, there is contained natural knowledge, knowledge that can be, and is, justified on rational grounds; without faith (at least in the broad sense just described) such knowledge is in practice never found. Analogy cannot simply be disconnected from faith. In a fundamental sense it pertains to the very structure of the human mind. As Jörg Splett and Lourencino Bruno Puntel write,

> In the exercise of its freedom and knowledge, the human spirit stands in the light of what is unconditional, yet attains the plenitude of this latter only in and through the finite. By its very nature, therefore, it is subject to the law of analogy. Hence analogy is decisively located in the ontological relation between God and finite being and in the cognitive relation between the finite mind and each of these.[98]

Hence, unless analogy were operating, no acceptance could be given to the verbal revelation of the Gospel when it occurred, nor could any sense be made of it. As Bauckham, has observed, "The expression that love is revealed only in hate cannot mean that hate is a revelation of the love of God. It must mean that love is revealed in the *context* of hate."[99]

God's love, therefore, is revealed, analogically, in an act that takes place within our world, an act that despite some appearances is rightly identified by the believer as an act of love on God's part.

In practice, therefore, there is no natural knowledge of God apart from faith (in technical language, it is physically possible but morally impossible), and in the believer there will always be an integration of these two components. Verbal revelation when it occurs will correct, modify, direct, and integrate the natural knowledge attained with the help of grace. This position is compatible with, and even indicated by, both Scripture and the statements of the First Vatican Council.

On the inspiration of Moltmann's philosophy O'Donnell says:

> Moltmann writes, "In concrete terms, God is revealed in the cross of Christ who was abandoned by God." This theology then attempts to be a biblically-grounded theology in so far as it brings no independent philosophical presuppositions or ontological preconceptions to interpret the biblical revelation. It attempts to let the biblical revelation create its own ontology.[100]

This would be a risky enough procedure at the best of times, but if one's theology happens to be seriously flawed, as Moltmann's is at this critical point, the outcome for one's philosophy is disastrous. At least Moltmann maintains a consistency between his theology and his philosophy. The problem is that both are gravely defective. This is a great pity, since, as has been frequently noted, his work presents many valuable positive aspects, to which all would do well to attend.

7

Recent Theology

Jüngel, Mühlen, and von Balthasar

In this chapter I complete what I began in the last, the consideration of four selected "Paschal Mystery" theologians of the Trinity. In the last chapter I considered Jürgen Moltmann; in this I shall consider Eberhard Jüngel, Heribert Mühlen, and Hans Urs von Balthasar, and I shall conclude with a brief summary of my own conclusions in regard to a trinitarian theology of the cross.

Eberhard Jüngel

I begin with Jüngel, and turn immediately to his *God as the Mystery of the World.*[1] This is a long, complex and difficult book, and here I shall do no more than present in summary form, and assess, a single one of its several accomplishments, its theology of the Trinity. This theology's point of departure is the death of Jesus on the cross as the *event* in which the Trinity is enacted. This does not mean that the being of God is conceived as absorbed into the economy, for God is understood as the one who "comes" to the human scene in the event of the cross. But it does tell of the historicity of God's immanent being, of the fact that in this being he is already *our* God.

Jüngel analyzes the death of Jesus in terms of the self-differentiation of God: God identifies himself with the dead Jesus and thus differentiates himself, in the sense not of self-destruction but of definition "from outside," that is, the dead Jesus defines the being of God. At the same time Jesus is defined as the Son of God. But through the Resurrection the Holy Spirit relates anew those who have thus been differentiated. And the whole process of differentiation and relationship is to be seen as the operation of love:

> It is solely the Spirit of God as the relation of the relations [of fatherhood and sonship] who constitutes the being of love as an event. This love as event is what makes up the essence of deity, so that the full identity of the divine essence and divine existence has been thought in these three divine relations: the Father, who

131

loves himself; the Son, who has always been loved and has loved; and the constantly new event of love between the Father and the Son which is the Spirit.[2]

The differentiation of Father and Son, which Jüngel always sees as a *self-differentiation* of God, is enlarged, by reference to Heribert Mühlen (whose theology I shall examine next), into a differentiation "than which nothing greater can be imagined" through his interpretation of the death of Jesus along similar lines to Moltmann. In this regard Jüngel avails himself of the same biblical texts as Moltmann and interprets them in the same way. Strangely, the nature and function of the Holy Spirit are argued not from scriptural but from rational considerations, indeed one might say rationalistic considerations, reminiscent of, if not identical with, those of Richard of St. Victor: the statement "God is love" requires within God a lover, a beloved, and a bond of love. Further, the Holy Spirit is not only the bond but "the *gift* in which and as which God relates himself to humankind in such a way that humanity is drawn effectively into the event of divine love."[3] Thus God comes to humanity *from* God (the Father) *to* God (the Son) *as* God (the Holy Spirit). Finally, Jüngel claims that his construction corrects the classical doctrine of God and at the same time does away with three of its traditional axioms, those, namely, of the absoluteness, the apathy, and the immutability of God.

There is with Jüngel a far more extensive coincidence with my own theology than there is in the case of Moltmann. With the latter, Jüngel places the principal emphasis on the cross, or rather (and better) on "the crucified one," as he states in the subtitle of his book. But while I hold that the death and Resurrection of Jesus are the principal *locus* of the divine revelation and self-communication, he has them as the *event* of the Trinity itself, a claim that is questionable, both because it appears to situate the historicality of God in the inner depth of his nature rather than in his relationality (to the world) where it belongs, and because it raises the specter of adoptionism. Most impressive is the fact that Jüngel has the Holy Spirit as the mutual love of the Father and the Son, even though he does not base this position, as I do, on Scripture. He even has human beings involved in the trinitarian life through being drawn into this bond of love. Here, though, I would claim to be more precise than he, in doing this through an appeal to the unity (in difference) of love of God and love of neighbor on the part of Christ.

The chief problem with Jüngel's theology of Trinity is that at times he fails to distinguish between God as absolute person and God as the three relative persons, with the result that he can give the impression that God was somehow divided and then reconciled in himself, in a single person, as though he had suffered from a split personality now happily healed. This impression is conveyed in the following paragraph:

> [T]he God who identifies himself with the dead Jesus encounters himself in the death of Jesus in such a way that he participates in Jesus' God-forsakenness. But that is a meaningful assertion only if it is possible to make a real differentiation between God and God. In that God differentiates himself and *thus*, in unity with the crucified Jesus, suffers as God the Son being forsaken by God the Father, he is God the Reconciler. God reconciles the world with himself in that in the death of Jesus he encounters himself as *God the Father* and *God the Son* without becoming disunited in himself. On the contrary, in the encounter of God and God, of Father

and Son, God reveals himself as the one who he is. He is God the Spirit, who lets Father and Son be one in the death of Jesus, in true distinction, in this encounter. The "chain of love" (*vinculum caritatis*) emphasizes God's eternal being in the death of Jesus. Thus God is differentiated in a threefold way in his unity: in the encounter of Father and Son, related to each other as Spirit. But in the fatal encounter, God remains *one* God. For he remains as Father and Son in the Spirit the one "event God."[4]

A more fundamental problem is that, because he has judged the traditional metaphysics of God irredeemable, Jüngel has abandoned it in favor of what may be called a metaphysics of love. While such a metaphysics has much to commend it and demonstrably can produce some good results, the abandonment of the philosophical tradition, and with it the intellectual discipline it imposes, permits him to make statements like those noted in the paragraph quoted, which he thinks serve well the theology of the Trinity but which in reality are profoundly at odds with it. Thus the three relative persons in God do not simply *compose* the absolute person, as Jüngel has it. The absolute person relates as such ad extra (to the outside); ad intra (to the inside), each of the three relative persons is identical with the absolute person, inasmuch as the absolute person is the subsistent divine nature, and each person is, as I have said, only virtually or formally distinct from the latter. This means that in regard to the divine will all three are strictly one, a fact borne out in the case of Jesus (i.e., in his humanity) by the testimony of the New Testament to his unswerving devotion to the will of the Father revealed in both his sinlessness and his dedication to his mission. What Jüngel proposes, a rupture between the Father and Jesus on the cross, apart from its lack of proper foundation in the New Testament, is simply impossible. To put it another way, in itself it is destructive of the doctrine of the Trinity, because in putting the Father at odds with the Son it destroys the unity of the divine will and with it the unity of the divine nature. And it completely neglects the distinction of the direct and the permissive divine will in regard to evil. It is no answer for Jüngel to say, "[T]he wrath of God is only for the sake of his love which is present in the distinction between God and God, even when it is concealed, as it 'surrenders itself to lovelessness in all its malformities, without retreating one step' " (Kähler).[5] The point is that in Jüngel's construction the Father bears toward the Son an attitude of wrath, however concealed, which the Son does not reciprocate (if he did, the theological situation would be even worse). Further, the Father's wrath, as directed against Jesus, is unreasonable and unjust, unworthy of a human being let alone God.

Jüngel's presupposition that the relative persons compose the absolute person shows that he thinks of absolute person and relative person as operating on the same plane. This is the thinking that allows him to say that God encounters himself as God the Father and as God the Son, or that there is a differentiation between God and God, or that God comes from God to God. In speaking so deliberately of "God," Jüngel should be indicating as subject simply God, absolute subject, not a God undergoing the trauma of split personality. As we saw in chapter 3 with the help of Lonergan (who is not mentioned in Jüngel's book), Father, Son, and Holy Spirit are three distinct, relative subjects (though they share the one subjectivity). The concepts of absolute and relative person do not operate on the same plane, and considerable confusion and error result from deploying them as though they do. Thus, to adjust Jüngel's statements one by one, it is only the Father who encounters himself as God the Father, and only the Son who encounters himself as God the Son; and though the self-differentiation of God is a legitimate concept, the differentiation that actually takes place is between the Father and the Son; and, finally, it is the Father who comes, and the one he comes to is the Son.

In conclusion, it seems that, though Jüngel has achieved much in his original attempt to rethink the doctrine of the Trinity, his abandonment of the traditional metaphysics has left him exposed on several important fronts. In my opinion it is better to do what I have at least attempted in this book, to undertake a reworking of the traditional metaphysics with a view to surmounting its difficulties, a daunting task, in which, however, the theologian does not stand alone but receives valuable, indeed essential, help from contemporary philosophers, Christian and other. Also, Jüngel's adherence to a soteriology based on the divine abandonment must be counted no small drawback to his trinitarian theology, as I argued in the case of Moltmann.

Heribert Mühlen

We pass on now to consider the trinitarian theology of Heribert Mühlen. This was presented first in his 1963 book, *Der Heilige Geist als Person* (The Holy Spirit as Person),[6] and then again, as a theology of the cross, in a pamphlet (lecture) entitled *Die Veränderlichkeit Gottes als Horizont einer zukünftigen Christologie* (The Mutability of God as Horizon of a Future Christology) in 1969.[7] In his earlier work Mühlen presents for the immanent Trinity a theology of "proper pronominalization" (my term), in which the Father is "I," the Son "Thou," and the Holy Spirit in some sense "We."[8]

Mühlen characterizes the Holy Spirit as the "subsistent We-act between Father and Son," the "We-act in person," the " 'We' in person," the "We-relation," or "one person in two persons."[9] In so doing, he overlooks the following fundamental point of John Cowburn's, to which I have referred several times already in earlier chapters:

> We have shown that human ecstatic love—whether it produces immanent terms or not—must be objectivized: the loving persons must produce something or someone to embody their relationship and make it real. Moreover, we have shown that they do not so much love each other and then objectivize their love, as love each other in objectivizing it. The analogy with the spiration of the Holy Ghost is direct: the Father and the Son, we maintain, love each other as persons in "producing" the Holy Ghost, who is the realization of their oneness as persons.[10]

In other words, the Holy Spirit is not the "We" of any of the above-mentioned constructions, but the one who stands *over against* the "We" (therefore in a relationship of opposition to it [them]), as the *objectivization* of its (their) notional (i.e., person-producing) activity. That activity, as I have shown, is, ultimately, their mutual love. If at times I have resorted, and do resort, to shorthand and refer to the Holy Spirit simply as "the mutual love" of the Father and the Son, the usage is legitimated by the fact that this expression already objectivizes to some extent the activity of the two divine persons in question (in that their mutual love is not just the sum of their individual loves but something over above and beyond them though inclusive of them); but the fuller and more exact expression would have to be that the Holy Spirit is the objectivization, or hypostasization, or personalization, of this mutual love, and hence in this sense its product or outcome.[11] However, objectivization is completely absent from Mühlen's expressions, even from the two containing the words "in person" (since these two words are not used in an objectivizing sense in the expressions). Mühlen subsumes his theology of proper pronominalization unchanged into his second work. We note that this theology suffers from the serious shortcoming that it cannot be carried through consistently in the case of all three persons. While the Father may perhaps be designated "I," and the Son "Thou," the Holy Spirit is in no sense "We," nor does there exist any other pronoun by which he may be properly designated.

To Mühlen's second work I now turn, since it has exercised considerable influence in German theology both Catholic and Protestant, and has significant features in common with Moltmann and Jüngel. I shall comment now only on what is specifically new in it in relation to the first work, but I ask the reader to bear in mind my critique of the latter. Mühlen takes his point of departure from a sentence of Felix Malmberg, "The 'divine being,' the divine nature, insofar as it expresses the mutual unity in love of the three different divine persons, is the Holy Spirit *in person*."[12] The Holy Spirit is "the *homoousion* of Father and Son in the personal mode of existence." Within the traditional horizon of being the divine nature is apprehended first as a *suppositum indistinctum*, a nondistinct supposit, of which it is later said that it subsists in three persons. With this approach is to be contrasted the personal horizon, within which the divine nature appears first as the *perichoresis*, the circuminsession (*Ineinandersein*) of the divine persons, so that the divine beingness must be characterized as "the *we-natured* (*wirhaft*) divine beingness that reveals itself in salvation history":

> The Father as the trinitarian "I" releases from himself his corresponding opposite number as the thou-natured mode of existence of the one divine beingness, and then the Spirit himself proceeds from the Father and the Son as the we-natured mode of existence of the divine beingness. He is as it were the divine beingness itself in person. This beingness has always as it were taken shape from the opposition of relation between I and Thou itself and mediated itself to itself in the operation and procession of the Spirit, so that the latter as person is the mediatedness of Father and Son itself.

Mühlen continues his argument in dependence on Letter 38 of Basil the Great (which he recognizes probably had as its true author Gregory of Nyssa).[13] In this letter is worked out for the first time the distinction of *ousia* and *hupostasis*, nature and person. The divine indivisibility, previously conceived materialistically, is now understood as the undividedness of the divine persons. The commonality of the nature is sharply distinguished from the exclusive properties of the persons, and so strongly is the propriety of each person stressed that it is said of the Son in this respect that "he has nothing in common with the Father or the Holy Spirit." This leads Mühlen to formulate his "basic law": "The difference of the divine persons *insofar* as they are persons (i.e., in regard to their respective modes of existence) is so great that it could not be conceived as greater, while their unity (i.e., their mutual circuminsession) is so intensive that it could not be conceived as more intensive."[14]

This brings us to Mühlen's theology of the Trinity as a theology of the cross. Here, like Moltmann and Jüngel, and by appeal to the same scriptural texts and at times even to the same theological sources (e.g., Popkes), he embraces a soteriology of divine abandonment, in, however, a distinctive way enabled by his preparatory work:

> The whole scandal of the cross first becomes clear when it is realized that for us the Father has made his coequal divine Thou "sin" and "curse." The Son, therefore, has become not just other than him, namely, a creature, but has been made totally alien to him, sin; and here is revealed in all clarity that the Father and the Son, insofar as they are persons, have absolutely nothing in common.[15]

Hence Jesus' cry of abandonment on the cross reveals that "the Father's delivery [of the Son] to sin gives the Son over in salvation history to a difference so great that it cannot be conceived as greater, namely, to total godforsakenness." However, "*in* this absolute difference is revealed the absolute *closeness* of Father and Son, which likewise is so great that it cannot be conceived as greater."

By this means the Holy Spirit is introduced into the theology of the cross. He is, in his person, the positive member of the dialectic just enunciated:

> The love with which the Father delivered his Son "for us" is nothing other than that love with which the Son delivers himself "for us." Now insofar as the Holy Spirit is this love itself (as person), which is strictly identical in the Father and the Son, he is (as person) the absolute closeness and identity in the difference between Father and Son itself.[16]

Mühlen then summarizes his position in the following words:

> The essence of the essence of God is, in the perspective of salvation history, delivery, that is to say, self-delivery. Here truly the divine *einai* [to be] is revealed as *agape* [love]. The *trinitarian* structure of the event appears in the following facts: the Father is the one who delivers up his Son, the Son is the one who delivers up himself, and the Spirit is the *process* of delivery itself, strictly identical in the Father and the Son. One could therefore even say that the event of the cross is the procession of the Holy Spirit in salvation history, the so-called *spiratio activa* [active spiration] *as* an event of salvation history, which then primordially makes possible and releases every delivery of word, office and sacrament in the Church. According to the wonderfully ambiguous word of John 19.30, *paredoken to pneuma* ["he delivered up the spirit"], Jesus on the cross not only gave up his human spirit, as in Luke 23.46, but precisely in and on the basis of his extreme godforsakenness delivered up to the Church his divine Spirit, his equality-of-being with the Father. . . . Hence the event of the cross is the temporal dimension of the procession of divine love as the divine beingness as such, accomplished by the Father and the Son in strict identity; it is as it were the process in which the a priori we-natured divine beingness or love "concretizes" itself into the third divine mode of existence and therewith releases the Church out of itself. While the incarnation of the Son is the temporal dimension of the divine Thou, insofar as the man Jesus is taken up into the Thou-relation of the Son to the Father, the event of the cross is the temporal dimension of the divine "We."[17]

I embark now on an assessment of the second stage of Mühlen's trinitarian theology, that is, as a theology of the cross, confining myself to matters of moment (and so passing over matters of detail). Its weakest point is its dependence on a soteriology of divine abandonment, which I have claimed and I hope shown, both to be exegetically incorrect and to convey a false conception of God. In his preparatory work Mühlen has carefully laid the ground for the reconciliation of Father and Son that is needed to overcome the alienation declared to have occurred on the cross. What appears in salvation history as a resolution formed through successive stages, reconciliation following upon alienation, is justified in the immanent Trinity by the dialectic, there remaining by contrast unresolved, of, respectively, the unity and the difference of the persons.

Taking his cue from Basil the Great (or Gregory of Nyssa), Mühlen has rhetorically dramatized this dialectic in his "basic law": the difference of the persons from each other "could not be conceived as greater," and their unity "could not be conceived as more intensive" (a point that, as we saw, also impressed Jüngel). We shall see to what purpose this step was taken. But let us not forget that, minus the dramatization, all that the dialectic actually says is that *three distinct* persons are given in the *one* divine nature (in the sense of each being identical with it). The point of the dramatization is soon made clear: it is to allow the Son not only to become a creature but to be alienated from the Father as "sin" and "curse." No such exercise is undertaken in the case of the Holy Spirit. But does not he in turn have to be different, by a difference that "could not be conceived as greater," from both the Father and the Son? And by what title is he identified with just one member of the dialectic, the positive one, when the Father and the Son are each identified with both members, the positive and the negative? Here we have an object lesson in the danger of confusing rhetoric with literal truth.[18]

The next weakness in Mühlen's theology is his failure to appreciate that it is the mutual love of the Father and the Son that is productive of the Holy Spirit. Admittedly, in this he is only following the traditional Thomistic line, which he does in direct dependence on T. L. Penido, for whom the formal principle of the spiration is the essential divine love, not the mutual love of Father and Son. He quotes Penido, "In a word, Saint Thomas brings back the reciprocity from the notional plane to the essential plane,"[19] the exact opposite of the methodology for which I argue.[20] For Mühlen, in both works considered, the notional act of the Father and the Son is, consistently, a common act, not a mutual one. The example he gives in *Der Heilige Geist als Person* is sexual intercourse as a common act of two persons, productive of a third, though naturally he is at pains to exclude from the analogy its specifically sexual and biological aspects.[21] As an example of a common physical act, the analogy is a good one. But the notional act productive of the Holy Spirit must also be spiritual. Mühlen has no difficulty with this: he accepts the Western tradition on this point and agrees that it is an act of love. In the passages I have quoted from *Die Veränderlichkeit Gottes* one can also see how insistent he is that also as an act of love it is a common act. In one quotation he even identifies the Holy Spirit with the common act of love by which the Father and the Son love *us*. (But note, I am not suggesting that he hereby identifies this act with the notional act productive of the Holy Spirit. He must, however, envisage an inner-trinitarian act to which it corresponds, probably the common act by which Father and Son together love the divine nature.)[22] But as a spiritual act precisely of love by which parents produce a child, the act is their mutual love, not a common love by which they love someone or something else.[23] While it may be common as a physical act (though even here one might argue that it is mutual), it is certainly mutual as a spiritual act. Hence Mühlen's analogy, and with it his theology, fails at this vital point. This failure is a likely explanation, at least in part, of his inability to do anything like justice to the relationship between Jesus and the Father on the cross.

As we saw, for Mühlen in *Die Veränderlichkeit Gottes* "the event of the cross is the procession of the Holy Spirit in salvation history," insofar as the Spirit is there delivered up by the Father and Christ to the Church. Hence the missions of the Son and the Holy Spirit are presented as taking place at the Incarnation and in the event of the cross, respectively. Yet in *Der Heilige Geist als Person* Mühlen has the Holy Spirit entering salvation history in person by anointing the humanity of Christ at the first moment of the Incarnation, insofar as he is the ointment poured out on the sacred humanity by the Father and the Word, from whom he proceeds, as the Word unites himself hypostatically to that humanity.[24] Further, this is for Mühlen the beginning of the mission of the Holy Spirit, which at the time is hidden but is revealed at the baptism. One could understand how Mühlen in a later revision might come to see the cross as the final and definitive revelation of this mission. But how in the later work he can so dissociate Christ's personal reception of the Spirit from his bestowal of it on the Church as to characterize the latter absolutely as "the procession of the Holy Spirit in salvation history," as the mission of the Holy Spirit, is not so easily understood. In any case, in my theology, depending as it does on the mutual love theory and the identity-in-distinction of love of God and love of neighbor, the two missions, though distinct, are inseparably united, in that it is the radical bestowal on Jesus of the Holy Spirit by the Father that brings about the Incarnation of the Son, and Jesus throughout his life loves his neighbor with the same love, namely, the Holy Spirit, received from the Father but now his own, as that with which he loves the Father. Further, it is not just a matter of a progressive revelation of a reality once and for all perfectly constituted, but rather of a progressive realization of divine Sonship in Jesus in the course of his life through the development, physical, psychological, and spiritual, of his humanity, whereby it is rendered an ever more apt medium for the expression of divinity, and with this realization a progressive appropriation of the Holy Spirit, so that at his death the realization and the appropriation are complete. It is this definitive condition of Jesus' appropriation of the Holy Spirit that enables him to pour out the Spirit upon the Church from the cross as the final and all-embracing stage of his love of neighbor, corresponding to his love of God. Therefore, rather than speak simply of revelation, it is better to speak of a growing "sacramentalization" of the humanity of Christ, that is, both the revelation *and* the self-communication of the Father, whereby Jesus in his death and Resurrection is constituted by the Father as the perfect sacrament of divine grace, the Gift of the Holy Spirit.

Finally, I direct attention to the sharp and essentially false contrasts Mühlen draws between the "traditional horizon of being" and the "personal horizon," between a metaphysics that takes its point of departure from beings in general and one whose point of departure is persons. Preferable is a personal metaphysics that *transcends* general metaphysics, incorporating the latter within itself. So, for example, rather than embrace the concept of God as the circuminsession of the three persons (personal), replacing the more primitive idea of a nondistinct supposit subsisting in three persons (traditional), it is better to see him as *both* absolute person *and* relative persons, both concepts being at the same time personal and traditional. (Simply to identify the circuminsession with the divine nature, as Mühlen does, is an error of logic, the confusion of an attribute with its possessor.) In this matter the words of Wolfhart Pannenberg should be heeded:

> In "genuine ontology" (Stammler) or in a comprehensive ontological anthropology such as is being worked out today on various fronts the personalistic distinction of person and being would have to be overcome. In this it will be the task of theology to understand human beings in the unity of the relations formed in life towards things (openness to the world) with relatedness to God and fellow-humans.[25]

Hans Urs von Balthasar

We pass now to consider the trinitarian theology of the Swiss Catholic theologian Hans Urs von Balthasar, who died in 1988. Over a long life he produced a prodigious body of work, which drew on an astonishingly deep erudition and broad culture, and centered on a fifteen-volume theological trilogy, *Herrlichkeit*, *Theodramatik*, and *Theologik*, which is now being translated into English under the titles *Glory of the Lord*, *Theo-Drama*, and *Theo-Logic*.[26] Here I draw mainly on his contribution to volume 3, part 2 of the German dogmatic theology series *Mysterium Salutis*, titled *Mysterium Paschale*,[27] and published separately in English under the same title.[28] It is to this translation that I shall, in general, refer. A further source will be the collection of translated excerpts from his various writings called *The von Balthasar Reader*.[29] In his vast output von Balthasar returns again and again to the same trinitarian themes. Clearly, then, there is virtue in my adhering closely to one source and complementing it from others only when this is necessary or especially helpful. In classical style, von Balthasar moves from the immanent to the economic Trinity. He understands the former in terms of a separation between the Father and the Son that is as great as possible but nevertheless is bridged over by the Holy Spirit. Thus,

> That God (as Father) can so give away his divinity that God (as Son) does not just receive it as something borrowed but possesses it as an "equal by essence" implies a "separation" of God from himself so inconceivable and unsurpassable that every separation made possible (through it!), be it ever so dark and bitter, can take place only *within* it.[30]

And

> [I]t must be said that with the "emptying" of the paternal heart by the generation of the Son every possible drama between God and a world is already included and surpassed, as a world can have its place only within the difference of Father and Son that is both held open and bridged over by the Holy Spirit.[31]

The Holy Spirit, bond of the Father and the Son, is also the product of their mutual love, and as such is its objectivization:

[T]he Spirit . . . gives up an aspect of its divine form: to be the superabundant product of the love between Father and Son. . . . [T]he never-ending surprise that mutual love conceals more in itself than in the lover would have been able to surmise the experience that love is beyond comprehension, even though it is the nature of comprehension to be perfected in the "letting be" of the other, so that what is breathed out by the lovers does not appear again as something strange (a "bottled spirit"), but what is commonly "really meant" by both together, what is "bestowed" on them in their union: both the representation of the form of this mutuality and its testimony.[32]

And

[T]he Spirit has a twofold face from all eternity: he is breathed forth from the one love of Father and Son as the expression of their united freedom—he is, as it were, the objective form of their subjectivity; but, at the same time, he is the objective witness to their difference-in-unity or unity-in-difference.[33]

The latter quotation shows especially clearly that what I have distinguished as two different but complementary models of the Trinity, the procession model and the return model, von Balthasar sees merely as different aspects of the one model (though it is to his credit that he does as much as this). Admittedly, I have argued here for something similar to this, that is, the legitimacy of integrating the procession model into the return model, the latter being viewed, as it can be, as comprehensive. But note that where von Balthasar simply has the one model, the procession model, with two different aspects, I have two different models, the one presupposing and including the other.

Coming to the economic Trinity, we see that von Balthasar, like the other theologians we have been considering, embraces a theology of the cross. Unlike them, however, he subscribes to a soteriology of penal substitution, though probably he is not directly influenced by Luther or Calvin. Both the substitutionary (though not yet the penal) character of his soteriology and his ambivalence toward Luther are to be seen in the following passage:

More fateful is something different: the interpretation of the Pauline *pro me* (Gal 2.20) in—at least in its tendency—an anthropocentric sense ("how can *I* find a gracious God?"). This has worked itself out fatefully in Protestant theology down to the present day. The whole existential seriousness of the *pro me* is maintained undiminished only when the opening-up of the trinitarian love for the sinner, there visible, is answered by the latter with a radical *pro te*, and when, furthermore, he understands that in the *pro me* of Christ's self-surrender he is already taken over by this love and surrendered, so that his faith is not his own "work" but the ratification of what God has already done and hence the transference of himself into the triune love.[34]

The only point perhaps requiring clarification here is the identification of the *te* in the expression *pro te*. But from the context it emerges that it is the triune God; and so the expression is meant to echo the verse preceding the one referred to here, Galatians 2.19: "For I through the Law died to the Law, that I might live to God." This "living to God" (the radical pro te) lies at the heart of the "faith" of which von

Balthasar here speaks. What comes through with sharp clarity in this text is the thoroughly substitutionary sense assigned to the Pauline *pro me*, its designation as "in my stead," as distinct from the "anthropocentric" sense, "on my behalf," which is here asserted to be favored by Luther against the general drift of his soteriology. In what appears to be an implicit criticism of Rahner, von Balthasar says of this latter sense:

> The anthropocentric tendency will never be able to keep within view the Trinitarian background of the Cross, since in the last analysis it is concerned with the inter-pretation of individual "existence," in a kind of theological transcendentalism, whereas the movement opposed to it is able to make manifest, and to interpret, all that is christological and soteriological by rooting it in the mystery of the Trinity.[35]

Elsewhere von Balthasar criticizes Rahner explicitly (though admittedly in a rather veiled manner), for his "extrinsicism" in the handling of the redemption, that is, for not identifying Jesus closely enough with sin and sinners, and thus for opting for a possibly "minimalist interpretation" of the Pauline texts.[36] Further, he does not hes-itate to speak of Jesus as a "scapegoat," appealing for support to Hebrews 13.11–13, though, as we have seen, the text cannot in fact bear this interpretation.[37] And finally, he declares that through Jesus the Father "wishes to conquer sin *from within*" (my emphasis).[38]

This expression betrays on the part of von Balthasar a literal identification of Jesus with sin. Other examples include his reference to "the sin he (Jesus) has within him" and his characterization of Jesus as "the embodiment of sin,"[39] so that it is impossible for God to have anything to do with him: "As the embodiment of sin he can no longer find any support in God; he has identified himself with that which God must eternally turn away from himself."[40] Hence Jesus' literal "godforsakenness" on the cross,[41] and the theological, as distinct from merely psychological, basis for his cry of abandonment.[42] It is one short step from this to say that God actually punished Jesus on the cross (and, as we shall see, in hell itself) for the weight of sin that he bore, and indeed von Balthasar does say it. He quotes approvingly Nicholas of Cusa in saying that "Christ's suffering, the greatest one could conceive, was like that of the damned who cannot be damned any more. That is, his suffering went to the length of infernal punishment."[43] And he also says it in his own right: "And in the turning point [the cross as the turning-point from the 'old' to the 'new'], in the crucified, these coincide: God's wrath which will not come to terms with sin but can only reject it and burn it out, and God's love which begins to disclose itself precisely at the point of this inexorability."[44]

Under the influence of his friend and associate the visionary Adrienne von Speyr, von Balthasar develops a theology of "Holy Saturday," a theology of the dead Jesus in terms of his "descent into hell."[45] Of Jesus' death he writes:

> [F]or the death of Christ to be inclusive, it must be simultaneously exclusive and unique in its expiatory value. This aspect of Christ's death . . . can be developed in three directions: as experience of the "second death" (where for the first time the New Testament concept of Hell makes its appearance); as experience of sin as such (which allows us to give its proper place to the theme of "*descensus* as triumph");

and lastly as Trinitarian event, since each and every saving situation in the life, death and resurrection of Jesus Christ can only be interpreted, ultimately, in a Trinitarian way.[46]

Von Balthasar builds up his theology of the death of Christ in successive stages. He notes that Luther admitted the experience of hell not only for Jesus on the cross but also for the dead Jesus, though he (Luther) understood the latter experience precisely as Jesus' triumph over hell, and in this was followed in a one-sided way by Melanchthon and later Lutheranism.[47] Calvin took a similar line, laying, however, more stress on the suffering of Jesus in hell, and he in turn was followed in this by the Heidelberg Catechism.[48] Nicholas of Cusa, however, whom von Balthasar quotes at length and whom he affirms to be "fundamentally right," far from seeing the descent into hell as a triumph of any kind, saw it as the extreme of Jesus' suffering and separation from God, triumph being reserved solely for the Resurrection.[49] It is precisely this extreme of godforsakenness that von Balthasar sees as constituting hell in the New Testament sense as distinct from the Hades of the Old Testament. In line with Nicholas, it seems that the "proper place" for the "*descensus* as triumph" is precisely Jesus' delivery from hell by the Father (and hence, strictly speaking, no longer his descent) in what must be seen as the beginning of the Resurrection. In hell Jesus undergoes "the experience of sin as such":

> The object of this *visio mortis* (the vision of death) cannot be a populated Hell, for then it would be the contemplation of a defeat; nor an inhabited Purgatory, for theologically there could be no such Purgatory "before" Christ . . . ; nor a populated "Pre-Hell," which is rightly represented symbolically as depopulated by the "descent of Christ." The object of the *visio mortis* can only be the pure substantiality of "Hell" which is "sin in itself."[50]

Finally, the death of Christ represents "the utmost pitch of obedience" of Jesus to the Father, the "obedience of a corpse" (von Balthasar here borrows a phrase from St. Francis of Assisi).[51] Involving the Father as well as the Son (strangely, the Holy Spirit is not mentioned at this point), the death of the Son is revealed not as something exclusive to himself but as a trinitarian event.

It thus becomes clear that von Balthasar's theology of the cross is a theology not just of substitution but of penal substitution.[52] In a long note in *Mysterium Paschale* he essays a sketch of its background in a way meant to reveal its embeddedness in German theology, reaching back to Johann Tauler and the Rhenish mystics of the fourteenth century.[53] Gérard Rossé, however, thinks somewhat differently.[54] His view, based on the text of Tauler's sermon on "spiritual winter," is that Tauler only intended to speak of Jesus' cry of abandonment in the sense of what St. John of the Cross later called the "night of the spirit." In speaking of the divine *punishment* of Jesus, Luther, according to Rossé, crossed a threshold that the Rhenish mystics never crossed. However, as we have seen, Nicholas of Cusa crossed this very threshold in the fifteenth century. It is small wonder, then, that it was taken up so naturally by Luther and especially Calvin, or that even today it survives in German theology, Catholic as well as Protestant, as well as non-German theology directly under the influence of the Reformation. Is it too much to suggest that it is an idea that not only arose in Germany but is profoundly congenial to the German psyche? It is based on an interpretation of the Pauline texts that not only takes literally the identification there made of Jesus with sin and sinners but also sees him as subject to God's punishment.

In quotations given here I have broached in the economic Trinity the dialectic of separation and unity, of the Son and the Father that von Balthasar has already set in place in the immanent Trinity. There the separation of Father and Son, which is as great as it could be, is bridged over by the Holy Spirit. Such is the case in the economic Trinity too. On the cross, though abandoned by the Father,

> still he [Jesus] is the Son who can proceed and live only from the source of the Father, hence his infinite thirst for the inaccessible God. It is a thirst that burns in him like eternal fire, bodily, psychically, spiritually. The Holy Spirit which accompanied him through his whole life as the Spirit of the Father, is now just the enkindler of this thirst: the Spirit unites Father and Son while stretching their mutual love to the point of unbearability.[55]

In the Resurrection the separation of Father and Son in salvation history, which had reached its furthest point in the descent into hell, is finally overcome through this dynamism of the power of the Holy Spirit. Accordingly, there now takes place,

> after a perfectly fulfilled mission (Jn 19.30), the reunion with the Father, of the Son gone into the world and to the cross—speculatively one could say the reunion of Father and Son (in his human nature!) into a single (economic) principle of spiration—as the presupposition for the (economic) egress of the Spirit into the Church and the redeemed world.[56].

Jesus' giving up of the spirit on the cross (see John 19.30) is to be understood in the light of the *end* of the process there begun, the reunion of Father and Son in the Resurrection:

> If Jesus on the cross breathes out his *pneuma* (spirit), so doubtless he breathes out also the missionary Spirit (*pneuma aionion*, Heb 9.14) "bestowed without measure," whom the Father in raising him gives back to him as in the highest way personally his own, but henceforth as the manifestly divine Spirit identical with *dunamis* (power) and *doxa* (glory) (see Rom 1.4).[57]

Finally, von Balthasar points, as I also have done, to an "inversion" witnessed to by Scripture in certain of its statements about the economy, an inversion, that is, of the order of the second and third persons of the Trinity.[58] Thus, while on the one hand the Holy Spirit derives from the Father and the Son and in that sense follows upon the Son, on the other hand the same Spirit mediates the Incarnation of the Son and in that sense precedes him. This moves von Balthasar to take up the question of a possible disruption of the correspondence between the economic and the immanent Trinity.

Von Balthasar notes, as I also did in my book on grace,[59] that St. Thomas, and, following him, Mühlen, insist on the immutable order Son—Spirit in the economic as in the immanent Trinity.[60] He also notes that Walter Kasper, invoking "a wealth of scriptural references," attacks this view; and he quotes from him a sentence that is typical of what I have been saying in this book: "The sanctification of Jesus by the Spirit is . . . not merely an adventitious consequence of the sanctification by the *Logos* through the hypostatic union but its presupposition."[61] With this view of Kasper von Balthasar aligns himself, but, as was pointed out earlier, in so doing he shows no appreciation of the fact that the new order (or *taxis*) in the economic Trinity calls for a new trinitarian model. He therefore falls back, with an explanation that (to me) is totally unconvincing, on the only model of the Trinity he recognizes, the one that I have called the procession model (in distinction from the return model):

> The infinite vitality of the relations between the divine Persons is so rich in aspects that one such aspect can precipitate the Son's Incarnation, and the "inversion" we have described, without requiring any change in the internal divine order. All that is required is that the Son, in his eternal origin from the Father, should go back to a point where he can receive the power of (participating in) breathing forth the Spirit. Thus, in "economic" terms, his reception of this power corresponds to the first *status* of the Incarnate Son [the "state of emptying"], whereas the actual breathing-forth of the Spirit (in conjunction with the Father) corresponds to the second [the "state of exaltation"].[62]

Finally, I draw attention, very briefly, to the fact that von Balthasar invokes precisely the "event" of the Trinity to demonstrate *reciprocal* relations between God on the one hand and the world and human beings on the other, on the basis of 1) nature, that is, creation, and 2) grace, that is, the Incarnation and the cross. This is a subject that has been studied in detail by Gerard O'Hanlon.[63] He presents von Balthasar's thought in the following words: "[M]ost of all the trinitarian event as presupposition of creation allows one to give to creation—and in particular to humankind—an identity which is capable of interaction with God. This is so because it is of the essence of God, who is absolute and thus dependent on nothing outside himself, to be triune."[64] O'Hanlon continues:

> The way forward—with the help of one of the Fathers, Hilary, and the Russian theologian Bulgakov—is through the hypothesis on an intra-trinitarian "event" at the heart of God. This event involves the disinterested self-giving of the divine persons as pure relations within the intra-trinitarian life of love. It means that God is not first and foremost "absolute power" (or "absolute Being"), but rather "absolute love," and so that God's sovereignty may manifest itself in the self-emptying characteristic of love. This trinitarian event of tri-personal self-giving is, then, the condition of possibility of God's externalization in kenotic events such as the incarnation and the cross.[65]

In assessing von Balthasar's theology of the Trinity I shall in general follow the order of presentation that I have adopted here. As in the case of Mühlen, I note the use of freewheeling rhetoric in his statements about the immanent Trinity so that his subsequent theology of penal substitution and the descent into hell can be accommodated. On any other construction such expressions as an "inconceivable and unsurpassable separation of God from himself" would be unintelligible. At the same time I note with approval that, unlike Mühlen, he accepts and uses the mutual-love theory, even to the extent of having the Holy Spirit as the objectivization of the mutual love of the Father and the Son.[66] However, he is unable to capitalize on this gain, as he fails to realize that he is dealing with a different trinitarian model. Clearly, he thinks that his theology of the immanent Trinity (what I have called the procession model) can deal adequately with both the Incarnation and the inversion of order under discussion, as the quotation from *Theo-Drama* III, p. 190 (see note 62) shows. Yet the second sentence of this quotation, which is meant to be the explanatory key to this problem, in fact explains nothing, as it contains a confusion at its essential point. Von Balthasar rightly says that the Son is receptive in regard to the Father and active in regard to the Holy Spirit. According to the active aspect, the taxis is the traditional one, Father—Son—Holy Spirit. The receptive aspect is the one that is supposed to handle the inversion, Father—Holy Spirit—Son. Von Balthasar thinks it does, because the Son receives at the hands of the Father the power to breathe forth the Holy Spirit, the *vis spirativa*. But this power is not identical with the Holy Spirit. On the contrary, it is identical with the Father and the Son (together), and is not even possessed by the Holy Spirit. Only the mutual love theory truly has the Holy Spirit mediating between the Father and the Son. Von Balthasar has tried to set up a comprehensive trinitarian model based on the procession model. But, as I have shown, the true comprehensive model of the Trinity is not the procession model but the return model, the mutual love theory.

Von Balthasar's theology of the economic Trinity depends on the penal substitution theory of the redemption and the descent into hell, both highly questionable concepts. I shall not repeat here my objections to the penal substitution theory, but I ask the reader to bring them to bear on von Balthasar's theology at this point. What I shall do now is take up the two objections against Rahner, and treat them in the inverse of my order of presentation. First, there is the charge of "extrinsicism" in regard to Rahner's soteriology. The point needs to be made that *any* orthodox soteriology will be extrinsicist. The only way a soteriology can become truly "intrinsicist" (to coin a word) is by having Christ actually a sinner, but clearly von Balthasar does not want to say that. In fact he is careful to say the opposite.[67] Extrinsicism, then, is a matter of degree as well as of simple fact. This point taken, and given the facts that Jesus identified himself with sinners during his life and that he even died the death of a sinner, the challenge to theologians is to construct a soteriology that is as little extrinsicist as possible, one that genuinely respects these facts but at the same time remains within the bounds set by the teaching of the whole Bible, especially the New Testament doctrine of God, and by enlightened exegesis of particular texts. Von Balthasar claims that his soteriology does remain within these bounds,[68] but, as will be clear from our earlier treatment, Rahner's does, and his does not.

The second objection, arising from von Balthasar's well-known negative stance against Rahner's fundamental philosophical and theological method, is that of "transcendentalism." The alternative, espoused by von Balthasar, is a Christology (and soteriology) that is rooted in the Trinity rather than in "individual existence" or the "subject." Inasmuch as it unconsciously objectifies the subject, this statement reveals a poor grasp, on the part of von Balthasar, of the nature of transcendental philosophy and theology. Rahner would want to ground Christology in the Trinity as its objective pole just as much as von Balthasar does, and indeed does so, but transcendental theology, having overcome the "naively objectivating metaphysics" that previously obtained,[69] never allowed him to forget that the person performing this task was a believing subject, who necessarily acted out of the a priori conditions that constituted them both as a subject and as a believer and inevitably affected the knowledge they achieved. In other words, once the essential point of transcendental theology is grasped, it is also grasped that there is simply no alternative to it. It will be clear from this (and also from what was said in the last chapter) that von Balthasar's implicit criticism of Rahner for his advocacy of an "anthropocentric" as opposed to a substitutionary sense of the Pauline pro me is misplaced. As we saw, these two senses should be complementary rather than opposed. It is *because* Jesus can act as my substitute that he can be a savior on my account. The substitutionary sense does not rule out the anthropocentric sense: it implies it. Perhaps Rahner is open to criticism for failing to grasp that there is a legitimate sense of substitution, but he should not be criticized for maintaining the anthropocentric sense of pro me, which is traditional in both Catholicism and Protestantism and is well founded exegetically.

Von Balthasar's theology of Jesus' descent into hell is the furthest possible extension of the penal substitution theory. I shall comment on it briefly here, since, while it is by no means held by all proponents of the latter theory, as a theology of "Holy Saturday" it is an integral part of von Balthasar's spiritual and theological thought. First we must ask what warrant there is, if any, for a literal descent of Jesus into hell. In his treatment of the descent as found in the Apostles' Creed, J. N. D. Kelly remarks that it was "a commonplace of Christian teaching from the earliest times."[70] However, the "hell" he means is the abode not of the damned but simply of the dead, the Jewish Sheol. The same is the intention of the New Testament texts that have been appealed to in this regard. Kelly lists them as follows: Matthew 12.39–40, 27.51–53, Acts 2.27–31, Romans 10.7, Colossians 1.18, Hebrews 11.39–40, 12.22–23, and finally the major references, 1 Peter 3.19 and 4.6.[71] On examination, the two Hebrews texts and the second text from Matthew reveal themselves to be not about Jesus at all. They are relevant only in that they are concerned with the fate of the dead and the difference Jesus makes to it. The first text from Matthew, that from Acts, and those from Romans and Colossians do refer to Jesus, but in thoroughly conventional Jewish style speak of the period between his death and Resurrection as passed in Sheol. Despite von Balthasar's attempt to argue the contrary,[72] the two "major" texts turn out to be completely irrelevant. The first, 1 Peter 3.19, refers to Jesus' ascension, not to his alleged descent into hell; and the second, 1 Peter 4.6, refers not to preaching by the dead Jesus to dead people, but to the ordinary Christian ministry of preaching, to people alive at the time of preaching but deceased in the meantime.[73] In other words, there is no basis in the sources for a descent into hell in a literal sense by the dead Jesus. This fact renders it superfluous for me to argue against such secondary difficulties attaching to von Balthasar's position as his literal interpretation of the interval between Jesus' death and Resurrection and his anthropological presuppositions that would allow Jesus both to act and to suffer during it. The inevitable conclusion from all this is that the proposition that Jesus descended into hell means simply that he died. (However, as it stands in the Creed today the expression can serve to remind us that in the manner of his death as of his life Jesus, in obedience to the mission of his Father, reached out to sinners and identified with them in order to reclaim them for God.)

Von Balthasar's idea that the "reunion" of the Father and the Son through the Resurrection makes possible their sending of the Holy Spirit into the Church and

the world inasmuch as Father and Son are thus constituted a single economic principle of spiration presumes in the first place that they were ever parted. It presumes
also that they did not send the Spirit prior to this "reunion." True, the sending of
the Spirit consequent upon the Resurrection was qualitatively different from any that
took place beforehand: it was a perfect, eschatological sending, and it acquired this
character through the fact that the Resurrection brought Jesus to completion in his
humanity, thus making him a perfect co-sender of the Spirit along with the Father.
But the gospels bear witness to the fact that Jesus acted in this capacity, albeit in a
humble and limited way, even during his earthly ministry. How else are his "mighty
works" and the power of his words to be understood? In any case, with von Balthasar
the notion of an economic Filioque should be upheld, though we should go beyond
him to stress its sacramental structure: the visible sending by Christ is the *sacrament*
of the invisible sending by the Father. And we should not refer to Christ as "coprin-
ciple" of the Spirit even in an economic sense, "cosender" being the limit of what is
acceptable here, as the created nature of his humanity, in which by definition he
acts, imposes this restriction.

As to von Balthasar's view that the Trinity provides the presupposition of creation, we agree that the "event" of the Trinity is the *immediate* reference point for
the act of creation and the reciprocal relations that it sets up. But, as was pointed
out at the end of chapter 5, whatever happens in the Trinity happens because the
divine being allows, indeed imposes, it. Though we cannot know of God's triunity
apart from revelation, when we do know it thus we perceive its ground in the dynamism of the divine being. This same dynamism allows, though it does not impose, creation. If, then, the Trinity is the immediate reference point for creation,
the dynamism of the divine being in its unity is its ultimate reference point. On its
own, therefore, it is able to account perfectly well for creation along with all its
implications. It does not need to invoke its further specification in the Trinity. In
principle, then, Judaism and Islam, both of which have a doctrine of creation,
would be able to ground this doctrine in the unity of the divine being just as well
as Christianity does. Also, the word "kenotic" should not be reserved for God's actions in grace alone. As I also pointed out in chapter 5, it applies to God in the act
of creation as well, even if in an analogous sense. Finally, full recognition should
be given to the importance of von Balthasar's insight that, as verified in the Trinity
in the case of the Son and the Holy Spirit, receptivity in God, far from being an
imperfection, is a positive perfection. We can go even further and indicate receptivity also in *the Father*, inasmuch as he receives the Holy Spirit, that is, as bestowed on him by the Son (it is this that allows us as Christians to relate to the
Father as a person, as Jesus himself did). However, I insist that as found in the
persons of the Trinity receptivity is only an indicator of the receptivity that belongs to the divine nature as such, where it is grounded in the dynamism of the
divine being, which then acquires "superreal" relations to creatures, to beings
freely called into existence by God, and hence acquires also receptivity in regard to
them.

A more differentiated stance must be adopted when it comes to a consideration of God's actions in grace. In principle, if the dynamism of the divine being
can account for the fact of creation, it can also account for God's actions in grace.

But when on the basis of revelation we consider what these actions actually are, the Incarnation of the Son and the gift of the Holy Spirit, we realize that it is precisely these actions that give rise to our knowledge of the Trinity in the first place. These precise forms of kenosis, then, are possible only on the premise that God is triune in himself. But a kenosis in the domain of grace does not of itself require that God be triune—at least we cannot see that it does.

Conclusion

Allow me by way of conclusion to bring together the positive elements that have emerged from my dialogue with the Paschal Mystery theologians in this and the last chapter and integrate them with other findings of this book and my previous work, and so present a synthesis of my trinitarian theology as it culminates in the cross and resurrection of Jesus. My previous work on the Trinity began with the patristic theme of the Incarnation as the anointing of Jesus at his conception by the Father with the Holy Spirit, the Spirit of God, the Spirit of Sonship.[74] This theology I developed to the point of being able to say that by this anointing, the Holy Spirit, love of the Father for the Son in the immanent Trinity, in the one act created the humanity of Jesus from nothing, radically sanctified it in the fullness of grace, and united it hypostatically to the preexistent divine Son.[75] By this act there began together, in coordination, though in a way awaiting progressive revelation, the respective missions of the Son and the Holy Spirit. The Holy Spirit, now seen as the answering love of the Son for the Father, was appropriated by Jesus as his own Spirit, the Spirit of Christ, "incarnated" as his human love for the Father, the power in which he accomplished his mission in obedience and love, and returned to the Father through his life and death. The double mission stood fully revealed and effective, "sacramentalized," in Jesus' resurrection from the dead. This theology is an economic application of St. Augustine's understanding of the Holy Spirit as the mutual love of the Father and the Son, the bond of love in the Trinity.

Authentic human love is necessarily at the same time love of God and love of neighbor. Jesus' love of the men and women to whom he was sent is therefore one with his love of the Father and identical with the Holy Spirit as Spirit of Christ. The Spirit that he pours out on humankind from the cross, the Spirit by which he is present and active for the rest of time in the Church thus brought into existence, is the same as the Spirit that on the cross he returns definitively to the Father. This Spirit, active in the Church's ministry of word and sacrament, draws those who respond into union with Christ, and thus into the ambit of activity of the same Spirit as Spirit of God, Spirit of the Father, Spirit of sonship and daughterhood, whereby they are re-created, forgiven, and sanctified by grace, and drawn into stable union with the Son, thus becoming "sons (and daughters) in the Son." The one Spirit is simultaneously Spirit of God and Spirit of Christ. His visible action in the world as the Spirit of Christ is the "sacrament" of his invisible action as the Spirit of God.

The reader will doubtless be struck by the difference between this theology and that of the four Paschal Mystery theologians discussed in this and the previous chapter. My theology comes to the cross as the climax of the life and ministry of Jesus, whereas theirs concentrates on the cross exclusively. Mine sees Jesus' path to the cross in terms of his sinlessness, and therefore as an undeviating and un- wavering return to the Father in obedience and love, in which their mutual rela- tionship goes from strength only to strength. It was this devotion on Jesus' side that enabled him fully to actualize his divine Sonship and so to appropriate fully the Spirit bestowed on him at conception. Theirs, on the other hand, understands the cross in terms of dialectic. For them the relation of Father and Son is there strained to the limit, and is bridged over only by the Holy Spirit, reconciler of op- posites. The reader must judge for themselves who has the better case from the standpoint of Scripture. We are all agreed, however, that access to the doctrine of the Trinity is had via the trinitarian structure of salvation in Christ. For Catholics another way had long been customary, namely, to elaborate with ever-growing so- phistication the psychological analogy of St. Augustine. However, while this cer- tainly has a continuing place in spirituality, it is not where we should look for God's revelation of himself as Trinity.

The Paschal Mystery theologians have taught us to take with much greater se- riousness the word of Jesus, "I came not to call the righteous, but sinners" (Mk 2.17). As was said in chapter 6, in his ministry Jesus turned to sinners, sought them out, consorted with them (without condoning their sins), had table fellow- ship with them as an offer of reconciliation and salvation, healed and forgave them on behalf of God, and finally identified with them by undergoing the death of a sinner under the Law. His eucharistic words at the Last Supper gave precisely this interpretation to his approaching death. The reader will recall that in the same chapter the view was expressed that God does not punish sin by any new juridical act. Rather, from the nature of things sin carries with it its own "penalty" of alien- ation from God. In assuming the sins of the world Jesus also assumed this alien- ation. Thus are we to understand the strange expressions of Paul that God "made him to be sin" (2 Cor. 5.21) and that he was made "a curse for us" (Gal 3.13). And so he "paid the price" of our sins. But Jesus was sinless, as Paul reminds us in the very verse in which he says that he was made to be sin. The alienation that he experienced was the apparent failure of his mission, the absence of God as a consoling presence, the torment of the legal judgment that had been passed on him as a sinner under the Law, the darkness that death assumes as a consequence of sin, all of which came to expression in the cry from the cross. But this aliena- tion remained for him at the level of psychological and spiritual experience, not at the level of actual reality. For him it was the supreme trial and test of his faith, hope, and love, a test that he passed triumphantly and that therefore brought the relationship of mutual love between the Father and himself to completion. For in identifying with sinners as he did, Jesus, ever one with the Father, was only acting out the Father's own outreach to them in reclaiming love. Together with his Res- urrection and sending of the Spirit, the death of Jesus brings to its climax the the- ology of the Trinity that I have striven to present as a theology dependent on the relation of mutual love between Jesus and the Father that was realized in the course of Jesus' life and ministry. The Paschal Mystery theologians are right in holding that the triune God revealed in the Mystery of Christ is an involved God, a God who himself suffers in bringing remedy to the human tragedy. The relation of mutual love that obtains between the Father and the Son in the immanent Trinity is translated into the economy only with difficulty, only with unimaginable suffering on the part of both. Only thus does it issue in full reality and effectiveness as the salvation of humankind in the Holy Spirit.

Conclusion

This chapter will begin with a brief chapter-by-chapter summary of the contents of the book, then proceed to some summary observations about the working of the return model of the Trinity, and end with some remarks on the Filioque question. I start, then, with the chapter summaries.

In chapter 1 I "set the scene" by arguing, on the basis of the functional concept of God in the Bible, that the patristic trinitarian theology should be grasped as a transition from the biblical to the immanent Trinity, a transition that then required a return to the biblical data to affirm them in the light of the new understanding, the outcome being the economic Trinity. This was not a procedure confined to the patristic age; of necessity it has been maintained to the present and is destined to continue as long as Christians reflect on the question of God. I found a rational explanation of this procedure in the epistemology of Bernard Lonergan, whereby the mind proceeds from the apprehension of data to their understanding and thence to a return to the data for their affirmation in the light of this understanding. This meant that I could no longer totally accept Karl Rahner's dictum of the simple identity of the economic and the immanent Trinity or Piet Schoonenberg and Walter Kasper's methodology of proceeding only from the economic to the immanent Trinity (and not vice versa). True, I proceed from the biblical to the immanent Trinity, but then the direction of thought is from the immanent to the economic Trinity. And while I can affirm the identity of the economic with the immanent Trinity, the transcendence of God over the creation prevents my affirming the converse. To this extent at least, I must agree with Karl Barth. Finally, I found it necessary to reject the agnosticism of Roger Haight and others about the actual existence of the immanent Trinity. Though for the sake of the relevance of the doctrine of the Trinity I endorse the modern emphasis on the economic Trinity, the immanent Trinity remains necessary as both a concept and a reality, if the existence of the economic Trinity itself is to be upheld.

Then, in chapter 2, I took up a point from the first chapter, that the traditional understanding of the Trinity came about from reflection on the Fourth Gospel to the exclusion of the Synoptics. The official models of the Trinity that arose in East and West, Monopatrism and Filioquism, respectively, are simply variants of the Johannine descending scheme. This theology I have called the "procession" model because its concern is with the outgoing movement of the Son and the Holy Spirit from the Father. The synoptic theology, given a new lease of life through the recent ascendancy of Christology "from below," presents a rather different picture. There the Father's radical bestowal of the Holy Spirit on Jesus at the moment of his conception brings about his divine Sonship, and in the power of this Spirit Jesus returns to the Father in his life and death. This I have called the "return" model. But these models, far from being contradictory, are complementary, in that the return model presupposes and includes the procession model. The procession model, in either Eastern or Western form, is thereby shown to be partial, and the return model comprehensive. Extrapolated from Scripture, the return model is revealed to be identical with the "mutual love" theory of St. Augustine, the theory whereby the Holy Spirit is grasped as the mutual love of the Father and the Son. Further, a correct methodology requires descending New Testament data to be integrated with the procession model, and ascending data with the return model. Also, our return to God is correctly understood in trinitarian terms not simply by inverting the procession model as has consistently been done, but by deploying the return model.

In chapter 3 I considered at some length the relationship between the procession and return models in the immanent Trinity and developed our understanding of the return model, defending it against its critics, especially Rahner and Yves Congar. It was necessary in this connection to examine the nature of "spirativity," the power by which the Father and the Son "breathe forth" the Holy Spirit, and my suggestion was that it is based in the "likeness" existing between Father and Son by virtue of the generation of the latter from the former. I noted the teaching of St. Thomas that "likeness is the principle of loving," and suggested that on the basis of this personal likeness (not shared by the Holy Spirit, who is not generated, and of whom Scripture never affirms, as it does of Christ, that he is the "image of God") arises their mutual love, from which emerges the person of the Holy Spirit. I concluded the chapter with a revision, in the light of our reflections, of Rahner's key concept, the "self-communication of God," and was able to show that while the Son comes from the self-communication of the Father, the Holy Spirit comes from the self-communication of the Father and the Son (to each other). This enabled me to characterize the divine persons in the following way: the Father is the Giver, the Son the Receiver, and the Holy Spirit the Gift, of the self-communication of God.

In chapter 4 the question of the propriety of calling the Father, the Son, and the Holy Spirit "persons" is addressed. Though St. Augustine, Barth, and Rahner all had reservations about this concept as applied to the Trinity, I have argued here positively for its retention. While acknowledging the danger of tritheism if it be used in a sense too close to univocality with our modern psychological understanding, I maintain that by invoking the concept of analogy we can successfully avoid this pitfall, and can reason that if human beings are persons in the modern sense then the divine entities are "superpersons." This step I have accomplished through recourse to the Thomistic concept of subsistent relation, the crucial point here being to establish that, theologically, human beings themselves are subsistent relations. However, in this chapter I resist the temptation to situate the personhood of God precisely in the divine triunity. Before that, in his simple unity, God is already person in the absolute sense recognized by St. Thomas, a sense that I have shown to imply an actual but nonnecessary relation to creatures. Its nonnecessity is grounded in the divine being's necessary dynamism, which, given the free act of creation, becomes relation in that circumstance. In all this I have taken due account of contemporary preoccupations concerning person, particularly that of relation. In this respect I have gone beyond Norris Clarke, as unlike him I acknowledge a precedence of relation (in the sense just explained) over substance, a precedence that I claim to be manifest already in the structure of the phrase "subsistent relation."

In regard to the question of change in God, I accept in chapter 5 the challenge, though not the substance, of Process philosophy and theology. With due acknowledgment of the work of William Hill, I confidently claim that a renewed philosophy of being (of substance in this sense) can handle the objections raised by Process theology against the immutable God of traditional theology. This will be a philosophy based on the dynamism of the divine being. It allows God to be at the same time immutable in himself and mutable, and therefore personal, in his relations with creatures. (Here the traditional terminology of essence and energies, though not the philosophy, of Palamas merits wider recognition and acceptance.) And, as Clarke has pointed out, receptivity should be admitted as a perfection, not an imperfection, of persons. Here again the temptation to locate these qualities precisely in the triunity of God should not be succumbed to. He possesses them already in his unity as absolute person. Hence in principle my suggested solution is as much accessible to Judaism and Islam as to Christianity.

From this it will be evident why a correct theological understanding of the death of Christ is decisive for a theology of the Trinity. Hence my concentration on this question in chapters 6 and 7. I shall not repeat here my reasons for rejecting the soteriologies of penal substitution or real divine abandonment to the degree that I met them in the writings of both Catholics and Protestants, specifically Jürgen Moltmann, Eberhard Jüngel, Heribert Mühlen, and Hans Urs von Balthasar. Nor do I attempt to establish in their place the vicarious satisfaction theory so long associated with Catholicism. The latter is too legalistic, too extrinsic (detaching the sin from the sinner), too anthropomorphic, too human (laying the whole stress on the death of Jesus as an action winning redemption from God) to deserve to be seriously entertained today, whatever the contribution it might have made in the past. These theories should now be laid to rest, as others have been in the history of soteriology, for example, the quaint patristic "ransom" theory (according to which the life of Jesus was paid as a ransom to the devil for fallen humanity, the devil being tricked in this transaction as he failed to perceive the victorious divinity concealed in Jesus' humanity). Good points, however, can be salvaged from both the penal substitution theory and the vicarious satisfaction theory. From the former can be learned how seriously we should take Jesus' identification with sinners for their salvation; and from the latter we can learn in the death of Jesus to value human action cooperating however humbly with the all-powerful action of God in grace. This said, however, we need to approach the redemption afresh from the New Testament. We noted the emergence of a promising approach in the soteriology of Rahner combined with his theology of death.

Regarding penal substitution, two points of special interest emerged from my study of the "Paschal Mystery" theologians. The first, for which I am indebted to Karl Lehmann, is that substitution, though not penal substitution, is undeniably Paul's way of conceiving the redemption. This is a concept, however, in which substitution and representation, instead of being opposed to each other as traditionally they have been (Protestant versus Catholic), emerge as reconciled and complementary. The second, which I owe to von Balthasar, is an insight into the Germanness of the penal substitution theory, despite the fact that it was given systematic form by Calvin, a Frenchman. Luther did not invent it; he found it already in the German Catholic tradition that preceded him. Perhaps this explains the survival of the theory today in attenuated form (usually) among Protestants of whatever nationality and some (a few) German-language Catholics. In any case, the construction of an alternative to these two theories allowed me to grasp the death of Jesus qua redemption as the climax of a journey of undeviating love and obedience on his part, a journey in which he drew ever closer to the Father, becoming fully one with him (in a precise sense explained in the book) in his Resurrection, the obverse side of his death on the cross. Every action of Jesus performed as it was in the Spirit, including his identification with sinners, was a revelation of the true mind and heart of the Father. And the Father himself remained undeviatingly constant in love for his loving and obedient Son, whose faith was sorely tested through the actions of sinful human beings. The whole life of Jesus, therefore, climaxing in his death, emerges as nothing other than a progressive revelation of the saving mystery of the Trinity.

I proceed now to my remarks on the working of the return model of the Trinity. In this perspective the earthly life of Jesus and especially the mysteries associated with it (the conception, the baptism, the Transfiguration, the death and Resurrection, the Ascension and the sending of the Spirit) are of the highest importance for the acquisition of a theology of the Trinity. These mysteries progressively reveal the divine Sonship of Jesus as in the course of his life he returns to the Father in the power of the Holy Spirit. In this way they reveal the Trinity. Also very important is to see this return as a journey of love on the part of Jesus, primarily love of the Father, whose will he fulfills at all times, but, because of the unity (in distinction) of love of God and love of neighbor, also a love of the neighbor, that is, of those to whom he is sent and ultimately of his brothers and sisters in the Church. This love is identical with the Holy Spirit, received by Jesus from the Father at the moment of conception (indeed the very power by which he is conceived), but progressively appropriated in the course of his life so as to become the Spirit of Christ himself. The process of appropriation reaches its climax with the death of Jesus on the cross, when he definitively returns the Spirit as his own to the Father and at the same time pours it out upon the Church thus brought into existence. When we in our own Damascus road or Pentecost experience receive the Spirit in the Church (beginning with our baptism), we do so in structured, mediated, sacramental divine acts, in which the action of the Spirit as Spirit of Christ is the sacrament of the action of the same Spirit as Spirit of God, making us sons and daughters (of God the Father) "in the Son" and thereby forgiving us our sins and bringing us God's salvation. Because the Spirit as we receive him from Christ is the same as the Spirit in which Christ returns to the Father (because of the unity-in-distinction of love of neighbor and love of God), insofar as we receive the Spirit as Spirit of Christ we are caught up in and share Christ's personal relationship with the Father. Hence in our one act we experience the Spirit as Spirit of Christ and Spirit of God.

I end with a word on the Filioque, the major outstanding ecumenical problem between East and West. In the book I have taken the view that the Eastern and Western positions of Monopatrism and Filioquism, respectively, are reconciled in that the Son himself proceeds from the Father, provided the monopatrist position be interpreted in the sense that the Holy Spirit proceeds *ultimately* from the Father alone. What is needed from the East is a recognition that the Son plays a positive role, subordinate to that of the Father, in the spiration of the Holy Spirit (and not just in the latter's economic manifestation), and this without prejudice to the fact that the Father and the Son constitute a single principle of spiration. The West in turn could recognize more openly that there is an important sense in which the Holy Spirit must be acknowledged to proceed from the Father alone. While the unqualified Filioque represents an extreme (if correct) position of the West, Monopatrism represents an extreme (and also correct) position of the East. The original formula of the Nicene-Constantinopolitan Creed, that the Holy Spirit "proceeds from the Father," because of its silence on the role of the Son, represents a one-sided, though not extreme, Eastern position, which is explained by the fact that the First Council of Constantinople was an exclusively Eastern event recognized only subsequently in the West as ecumenical. Though the restoration of the original formula has valid supportive arguments, the best solution in an ecumenical age would undoubtedly be a negotiated compromise that in a short and simple statement gave better expression to the full tradition of the Church, a formula that permitted, without actually stating, the more extreme positions of both sides. Such, I suggest, is "The Holy Spirit proceeds from the Father and receives from the Son," which is well attested in Scripture and tradition. My argument in this book is that the mutual love theory best accommodates the various true, though at times apparently contradictory statements of both sides, and alone explains exactly what it is that the Holy Spirit receives from the Son, namely, the quality of being the Son's love of the Father, which, completing that of the Father for the Son, constitutes in its objectivization the person of the Holy Spirit.

This, however, is a higher viewpoint that needs to be recommended to both sides. The West for its part should be able to recognize it embedded in its own tradition, particularly in Augustine and Aquinas, and overcome the superficial objections raised against it in recent times. The East, not so open to this idea of the Holy Spirit, should observe, however, that it is not just the despised psychological analogy under a new guise, and, for all its unfamiliarity, should be able to recognize that their own beloved Palamas came quite close to it in his writing, while since then other Eastern writers have evinced a promising openness to it.

Notes

Sources

The documents of Vatican II are published in *Sacrosanctum oecumenicum concilium Vaticanum II—constitutiones decreta declarationes* (Rome: Secretaria generalis concilii oecumenici Vaticani II, 1966), and in English translation in *The Documents of Vatican II*, ed. Austin Flannery (New York: Pillar Books, 1975).

Unless it is otherwise noted, quotations from St. Thomas Aquinas are from the Leonine edition, Rome, 1882 ff.

Unless it is otherwise noted, quotations from the Bible are from the New Revised Standard Version of the Bible. The exceptions are from the Revised Standard Version of the Bible (RSV).

Abbreviations

DS H. Denzinger and A. Schönmetzer (eds.), *Enchyridion symbolorum definitionum et declarationum de rebus fidei et morum*, 36th edn. (Freiburg, Germany: Herder, 1976)
PG *Patrologiae cursus completus*, ed. J. P. Migne, series latina (Paris: Garnier-Migne, 1844–1855)
PL *Patrologiae cursus completus*, ed. J. P. Migne, series graeca (Paris: Garnier-Migne, 1857–1866)

Introduction

1. Ralph Del Colle, *Christ and the Spirit: Spirit Christology in Trinitarian Perspective* (New York: Oxford University Press, 1994).

2. See Richard of St. Victor, *De trinitate*, book 3 (Migne: PL 196), 915–930.

3. See Casey Miller and Kate Smith, "Who's in Charge of the English Language?" a talk reprinted in *The Norton Reader*, 8th ed. (New York: Norton, 1992), 367.

4. G. Clarke Chapman, "What God Can Help? Trinity and Pop Religions of Crisis," *Cross Currents* (Fall 1994): 326. See my review of Anthony Kelly's *The Trinity of Love* in *Pacifica* 4, no. 2 (1991): 230.

5. That Jesus is called Word in the Prologue of the Fourth Gospel and in Revelation 19.13, a total of five occurrences, is not sufficient to render the appellation privileged.

6. However, because of the strict unity of person effected by the Incarnation, it is preferable that there be the same name for the second person in both the economic and the immanent Trinity, and that this name consist of a single word or concept, to anticipate and prevent division of the person along the lines of the two natures. Given the maleness of Jesus, this name would have to be masculine. In the light of these considerations, "Son" is the obvious choice.

7. This exercise is undertaken by Elizabeth Johnson in *She Who Is—The Mystery of God in Feminist Theological Discourse* (New York: Crossroad, 1994), not only for the second person of the Trinity (Jesus-Sophia) but for the first (Mother-Sophia) and the third (Spirit-Sophia). With regard to the second person it is particularly problematical. See note 4.

8. See note 4.

9. John Macquarrie, review of Robert W. Jenson's *The Triune Identity*, in *Scottish Journal of Theology* 36, no. 3 (1983): 388.

One. Setting the Scene

1. See Vatican II, Dogmatic Constitution on the Church, *Lumen Gentium*, art. 16.

2. Aloys Grillmeier, *Commentary on the Documents of Vatican Two*, ed. H. Vorgrimler, vol. 1 (London: Burns & Oates, 1967), 183.

3. From the text of the Nicene Creed of the International Committee on English Translation used in the Roman Missal of 1974.

4. St. Anselm of Canterbury, *Cur Deus Homo*, books 1 and 2 (Migne: *PL* 158).

5. See The New Jerusalem Bible (London: Darton, Longman, & Todd, 1985), 157, note a, to Leviticus 17.1.

6. "Spirit of God" is the regular expression of the Old Testament, "Holy Spirit" being late and occurring only three times in the Hebrew Bible, in Psalm 51.11 and Isaiah 63.10, 11, and twice more in a deutero-canonical book, in Wisdom 1.5; 9.17.

7. See James D. G. Dunn, *Jesus and the Spirit* (London: SCM Press, 1975), 318–326, 350–357.

8. See Norman Tanner, ed., *Decrees of the Ecumenical Councils* 1 (Washington, DC: Georgetown University Press, 1990), 21, 28.

9. See David Coffey, "The Holy Spirit as the Mutual Love of the Father and the Son," *Theological Studies* 51 (1990): 201–205.

10. For a more detailed presentation of this view see my article, "The Pre-existent and Incarnate Word," *Faith and Culture: Contemporary Questions*, ed., Margaret Press (Sydney: Catholic Institute of Sydney, 1983), 62–76.

11. Pierre Benoit, "Préexistence et Incarnation," *Revue Biblique* 77 (1970): 5–29.

12. Ibid., 18.

13. See Francis Moloney, *The Johannine Son of Man* (Rome: Libreria Ateneo Salesiano, 1976), 213.

14. James D. G. Dunn, *Christology in the Making* (London: SCM Press, 1980), 259. For Philippians 2.6–11 see Jerome Murphy-O'Connor, "Christological Anthropology in Phil.2.6–11," *Revue Biblique* 83 (1976): 25–50.

15. Dunn, *Christology in the Making*, 241.

16. Ibid., 248.

17. Ibid., 347, note 105. Dunn appears to consider that New Testament statements that Jesus was "born," taken in conjunction with assertions of his preexistence (if such indeed are made), would clinch an argument for metaphysical incarnation in the New Testament. See *Christology in the Making*, 42, and note 165, p. 285. But not so. Such statements would only underline the necessity of Jesus' being born, rather than just appearing in the world, if he

were truly to change his condition and identify with the human lot. After all, he could hardly die without having first been born. The conjunction to which Dunn refers could only serve to establish a functional incarnation, not a metaphysical one.

18. See Vatican II, Dogmatic Constitution on the Church, *Dei Verbum*, art. 9.

19. See Robert Hamerton-Kelly, *Pre-existence, Wisdom, and the Son of Man* (Cambridge: Cambridge University Press, 1973), 209.

20. Other early contenders for this honor might be Ignatius, in *Ephesians*, 7.2, and Aristides, in *Apology*, 15.1; but on examination these texts turn out to be inconclusive.

21. I therefore disagree with the general thesis of *The Myth of God Incarnate*, ed. John Hicks (London: SCM Press, 1977), while accepting its New Testament premises.

22. Karl Rahner, *The Trinity* (London: Burns & Oates, 1970), 22.

23. Vatican I, Dogmatic Constitution on the Catholic Faith, *Dei Filius*, ch. 2 (DS 3005).

24. See Yves Congar, *I Believe in the Holy Spirit*, vol. 3 (New York: Seabury Press, 1983), 83.

25. See Jacques Maritain, "The Immanent Dialectic of the First Act of Reason," *The Range of Reason* (London: Geoffrey Bles, 1953), 66–85.

26. Walter Kasper, *Jesus the Christ* (London: Burns & Oates, 1976), 180.

27. Bernard Lonergan, *Insight* (San Francisco: Harper & Row, 1958), 357.

28. Anthony Kelly, *The Trinity of Love—A Theology of the Christian God* (Wilmington, DE: Michael Glazier, 1989), 146–147.

29. This is an appropriate place to comment briefly on Catherine LaCugna's recent book *God for Us: The Trinity and Christian Life* (San Francisco: HarperSanFrancisco, 1991), in which she abandons the language of economic and immanent Trinity in favor of that of oikonomia and theologia. While recognizing the serious problem that she identifies, the breach that has occurred between the theology of God in himself and that of God as involved in the economy of salvation, the reason I do not follow her example is that I believe the former terminology actually to be a philosophically and theologically more sophisticated form of the latter, and to have nothing to do with the breach in question. Her main reason for preferring the oikonomia/theologia framework is the same as mine for *not* preferring it: "[I]t is not contingent on substance metaphysics" (see her contribution to a review symposium on her book in *Horizons* 20, no.1 [Spring 1993]: 137). My comment is that it all depends what sort of substance metaphysics one has in mind. This should be clear already from the earlier text, in which a Lonerganian substance metaphysics is embraced, and I hope it will become clearer still as the book progresses. See also Thomas Weinandy's very critical observations in his extended review of LaCugna, "The Immanent and the Economic Trinity," *The Thomist* 57 (1993): 655–666, and more of the same from Earl Muller in "The Science of Theology—A Review of Catherine LaCugna's *God for Us*" (*Gregorianum* 75, no. 2 [1994]: 311–41).

30. It was her failure to do precisely this in *God for Us* that drew on Catherine LaCugna the sharp criticism from Thomas Weinandy and Earl Muller mentioned in the preceding note.

31. See Karl Barth, *Church Dogmatics* 2, pt. 1 (Edinburgh: T. and T. Clark, 1957), 303.

32. Timothy Bradshaw, "Karl Barth and the Trinity: A Family Resemblance," *Scottish Journal of Theology* 39 (1986): 162.

33. See Barth, *Church Dogmatics* 2, pt. 1, 301–302.

34. See Paul Molnar, "The Function of the Immanent Trinity in the Theology of Karl Barth: Implications for Today," *Scottish Journal of Theology* 42 (1989): 369.

35. See Barth, *Church Dogmatics* 1, pt. 2 (1956): 135; 258–259.

36. DS 71.

37. Leonardo Boff, *Trinity and Society* (Maryknoll, NY: Orbis, 1988).

38. Ibid., 236.

39. Roger Haight, "The Point of Trinitarian Theology," *Toronto Journal of Theology* 4, no. 2 (1988): 191–204.

40. Ibid., 200.

41. Ibid., 202.

42. Ibid.

43. Ibid., 203.

44. Ibid., 198.

45. See ibid.

46. See ibid.

47. See DS 125, 126.

48. See Haight, "The Point of Trinitarian Theology," 199.

49. See ibid., note 14, p. 204.

50. Ibid., 201, 202.

51. See ibid., 204, note 12.

52. See Rahner, *The Trinity*, 37–38.

53. Ibid., 38.

54. Haight, "The Point of Trinitarian Theology," 203.

55. Ibid., 192.

56. Ibid.

57. Ibid.

58. See Vatican II, Decree on Ecumenism, *Unitatis redintegratio*, art. 11.

59. Bernard Lonergan, *Method in Theology* (London: Darton, Longman, & Todd, 1972), 338.

60. See Michel René Barnes, "De Régnon Reconsidered," *Augustinian Studies* 26, no. 2 (1995): 51–79. See Théodore de Régnon, *Études de théologie positive sur la Sainte Trinité*, 3 vols. (4 bound as 3) (Paris: Retaux, 1892–1898).

61. See John Meyendorff, *A Study of Gregory Palamas* (London: Faith Press, 1964); David Coffey, "The Palamite Doctrine of God: A New Perspective," *St. Vladimir's Theological Quarterly* 32 (1988): 329–358.

62. Rahner makes a similar observation in regard to calling the distinction between each divine person and the divine nature a "virtual" distinction (in the Thomistic system widely regarded as being equivalent to the Scotistic "formal" distinction): "[I]t is not enough to point out that in God the relations are 'virtually' distinct from the essence and that this suffices to make them not identical *with each other*, although they are really identical with the essence. . . . The virtual distinction of essence and person in God may contribute to solving the basic difficulty only if we emphasize at once the fact that, in the case of this virtual distinction, we do not have a distinction between two absolute realities, but a virtual distinction between an absolute and a relative reality" (*The Trinity*, 70).

63. See *Summa theologiae*, I, q. 13, a. 7, and q. 45, a. 3 ad 1.

64. For an able defense of St. Thomas on this point see Thomas Weinandy, *Does God Change? The Word's Becoming in the Incarnation* (Still River, MA: St. Bede's Publications, 1985).

65. See Rowan Williams, "The Philosophical Structures of Palamism," *Eastern Churches Review* 9, nos. 1–2 (1977): 32.

66. Ibid.

67. Ibid.

68. "It should be noted that for God to be the logical term of the relationship does not mean that he is not closely related to the creature. Just as was seen above that to say that creation does not mean change, does not imply a lack of dynamism, but rather something more dynamic than any change or movement, so now to say that God is logically related to creatures demands a closeness to creatures which is far greater than any mutually real relation.

If in creation God creates by no other act than the pure act that he is, and if the creature only exists by being related to the very act that God is, then God is present in the creature by his very essence, by the pure act that he is. For Aquinas 'God is said to be in all things by essence, not indeed of the things themselves, as if he were their essence, but by his own essence; because his substance is present to all things as the very cause of their being' (*Summa theologiae*, I, 8, 3, ad 1). Even pantheism falls short of such a close relationship, for in pantheism God is never fully present as he is in himself." Ibid., 92–93.

69. Vlamdimir Lossky, *The Mystical Theology of the Eastern Church* (London: James Clarke, 1957), 80.

70. Ibid., 85.

71. E.g., Walter Kasper, *The God of Jesus Christ* (New York: Crossroad, 1986), 220, to name just one such theologian.

72. Raymond Brown, *The Gospel According to John (XIII–XXI)* (Garden City, NY: Double-day, 1970), 689.

73. Lossky, *Mystical Theology*, 70.

74. St. Basil of Caesaria, *On the Holy Spirit*, chapter 18.46 (Migne: *PG* 32, 152).

75. St. Gregory of Nyssa, *Catechetical Oration*, chapter 2 (Migne: *PG* 45, 17). On this matter see Brian Gaybba, *The Spirit of Love* (London: Geoffrey Chapman, 1987), 56–57.

76. See St. Augustine, *De trinitate*, book 15, chapters 17 and 19 (Migne: *PL* 42, 1079–1082, 1083–1087).

77. Second Council of Lyons, Constitution on the Supreme Trinity and the Catholic Faith (DS 850).

78. *Summa theologiae*, I, q. 36, a. 4, ad 1.

79. See ibid., I, q. 37, a. 1 ad 3.

80. See ibid., I, q. 27, a. 3.

81. Ibid., I, q. 27, a. 2.

82. Ibid.

83. Ibid., I, q. 27, a. 4.

84. See Kelly, *Trinity of Love*, chapter 6 (pp. 139–173).

85. *Summa theologiae*, I, q. 36, a. 2.

86. Lossky, *Mystical Theology*, 55.

87. By contrast, the terminology of Father and Son in the Trinity is analogical rather than metaphorical. See Francis Martin, *The Feminist Question: Feminist Theology in the Light of Christian Tradition* (Grand Rapids, Michigan: Eerdmans, 1994), 228–229, 287. Even an Eastern Orthodox theologian like Lossky is willing to acknowledge a secondary status for the term "Word" in regard to the Son: "The very name of the Word—*logos*—attributed to the Son is itself primarily a designation of the 'economic' order, proper to the second hypostasis as manifesting the nature of the Father" (*Mystical Theology*, 83).

88. Rahner is prepared to award it only the status of a "hypothesis." See *The Trinity*, 118.

89. Peter Carnley, *The Structure of Resurrection Belief* (Oxford: Clarendon Press, 1987), 331.

90. St. Augustine, *De trinitate*, book 15, Chapter 17 (Migne: *PL* 42, 1080).

91. See Vatican II, Dogmatic Constitution on Divine Revelation, *Dei Verbum*, art. 9. Joseph Ratzinger draws attention to the helpful formula of Geiselmann, "totum in sacra scriptura—totum in traditione" ("everything in Sacred Scripture, everything in Tradition"), intended to replace "partim in sacra scriptura, partim in traditione" ("partly in Sacred Scripture, partly in Tradition"), a formula encapsulating the highly inadequate "two-source" theory. See Herbert Vorgrimler (ed.), *Commentary on the Documents of Vatican II*, vol. 3. (London: Burns & Oates, 1969), 191.

92. See David Coffey, "The Teaching of the Constantinopolitan Creed on the Holy Spirit," *Faith and Culture: Issues for the Australian Church* (Sydney: Catholic Institute of Sydney, 1982), 65–75.

93. See Second Council of Lyons, DS 850, and the Council of Florence, Decree for the Greeks, DS 1300.

Two. From the Biblical to the Immanent Trinity

1. The Creed actually says *propter nos homines et propter nostram salutem*, "on account of us human beings and on account of our salvation," but a few lines later uses the more succinct Pauline phrase *pro nobis.*

2. See David Coffey, "The Holy Spirit as the Mutual Love of the Father and the Son," *Theological Studies* 51 (1990): 213–214.

3. In speaking of Christ's acts as human, I do not wish to convey the impression that he is *merely* human. As I explained in my book *Grace: The Gift of the Holy Spirit* (Sydney: Faith and Culture, 1979), 174, the activity of Christ, corresponding to his being, is most properly called "theandric," divine-human, which means that it is human at base and therefore "categorial," the opposite of "transcendental," taking place in the parameters of the world. The theological anthropology at work here is that of Karl Rahner, according to which the divinity of Christ is the supreme actualization of humanity under grace, of his individual human nature under the unique grace of the Incarnation. See his "On the Theology of the Incarnation," *Theological Investigations*, vol. 4 (Baltimore: Helicon, 1966), 105–120.

4. See M.-E. Boismard, *Le Prologue de Saint Jean*, Lectio divina 11 (Paris: Éditions du Cerf, 1953), 108, 129, 179.

5. See Coffey, *Grace*, 166, and Robert Koch, "Spirit," *Encyclopedia of Biblical Theology*, ed. J. B. Bauer, vol. 3. (New York: Herder and Herder, 1970), 885. In the *Theological Dictionary of the New Testament*, ed. Gerhard Kittel, vol. 6 (Grand Rapids, MI: Eerdmans, 1968), Rudolf Bultmann (p. 219–20) and to a lesser extent Eduard Schweizer (p. 426) present a view of faith that precludes seeing it as in any way inspired by the Holy Spirit, though Bultmann notes that St. Augustine is not with him on this point. It is true that, apart from Galatians 5.22 (where *pistis* probably denotes fidelity rather than initial faith), St. Paul does not speak of faith in this way, but the reason is more likely to be that Paul did not care, or even think, to pursue the question of the operation of the Spirit prior to the Christian life, than that he wanted to place between faith and works the absolute dichotomy asserted by Bultmann in line with Reformation theology. It seems more reasonable to understand that the Spirit as power of God, received in identifiable fashion by "hearing with faith" (Gal 3.2), must have been already at work in a hidden way to dispose the person to the faith by which they receive God's salvation.

6. See Matthias Scheeben, *Die Mysterien des Christentums*, Gesammelte Schriften, vol. 2 (Freiburg, Germany: Herder, 1958), 123.

7. Readers who desire a more detailed presentation are referred to my book *Grace*, chapter 8 (pp. 120–144) and chapter 7 (pp. 91–119); and my article "The Holy Spirit as the Mutual Love of the Father and the Son," *Theological Studies* 51 (1990): 193–229.

8. "[W]here Luke and John seem happy to attribute the gift of the Spirit equally to God and to the exalted Christ, Paul thinks only to attribute it to God." James D. G. Dunn, *Christology in the Making* (London: SCM Press, 1980), 143.

9. See Karl Rahner, "Reflections on the Unity of the Love of Neighbour and the Love of God," *Theological Investigations*, vol. 6 (Baltimore: Helicon, 1969), 231–249.

10. Ibid., 234.

11. See David Coffey, "The 'Incarnation' of the Holy Spirit in Christ," *Theological Studies* 45 (1984): 466–480.

12. See Raymond Brown, *The Gospel According to John, XIII–XXI* (Garden City, NY: Doubleday, 1970), 931.

13. F.F. Bruce, *Commentary on the Epistle to the Hebrews* (London: Marshall, Morgan, & Scott, 1964), 205.

14. For a detailed presentation see my article "A Proper Mission of the Holy Spirit," *Theological Studies* 47 (1986): 227–250.

15. See Vatican II, Dogmatic Constitution on the Church, *Lumen Gentium*, art. 48.

16. See Edward Kilmartin, "The Active Role of Christ and the Holy Spirit in the Sanctification of the Eucharistic Elements," *Theological Studies* 45 (1984): 241.

17. From this it can be seen that it is essential that the mission of the Holy Spirit be grasped as proper to himself, a point on which Catholic theology has historically been highly inadequate. See my article, "A Proper Mission of the Holy Spirit."

18. See Coffey, "The Holy Spirit as the Mutual Love of the Father and the Son."

19. A distinction rejected, for no good reason, by Edward Schillebeeckx. See his *Christ: The Experience of Jesus as Lord* (New York: Seabury Press, 1980), 432. For an exposition of these terms see Edward Krasevac, " 'Christology from Above' and 'Christology from Below,' " *The Thomist* 51 (1987): 299–306. Krasevac distinguishes these terms, which apply to theological method, from "high" and "low" Christology, which characterize particular Christologies.

Three. Models of the Immanent Trinity

1. See William Hill, *The Three Personed God—The Trinity as a Mystery of Salvation* (Washington, DC: Catholic University of America Press, 1982), 214.

2. See Mary Ann Fatula, "A Problematic Western Formula," *One in Christ* 17 (1981): 324–34, specifically 324–326.

3. See Karl Rahner, "Theos in the New Testament," *Theological Investigations*, vol. 1 (London: Darton, Longman, & Todd, 1961), 79–148.

4. Cf. Jean-Miguel Garrigues, "A Roman Catholic View of the Position Now Reached in the Question of the Filioque," *Spirit of God, Spirit of Christ—Ecumenical Reflections on the Filioque Controversy*, ed. Lukas Vischer, Faith and Order Paper No. 103 (London: SPCK/Geneva: World Council of Churches, 1981), 157, where a similar distinction is made, between the perception of the generation of the Son as, respectively, a negative condition and a positive condition, of the procession of the Holy Spirit.

5. See St. Augustine, *De trinitate*, book 15, chapters 26 and 17 (Migne: *PL* 42, 1095, 1081).

6. See John Cowburn, *Love and the Person* (London: Geoffrey Chapman, 1967), 295.

7. This is the ultimate ground of the fact that of the three divine persons only the Son can be incarnate. It is appropriate here to comment on Thomas Weinandy's *The Father's Spirit of Sonship: Reconceiving the Trinity* (Edinburgh: T. and T. Clark, 1995). As he tells us in the opening sentences, Weinandy has in the writing of this book "one simple objective." This is "to argue that within the Trinity the Father begets the Son in or by the Holy Spirit, who proceeds then from the Father as the one in whom the Son is begotten." Weinandy feels impelled to this conclusion by his examination of the biblical evidence and by the need to uphold the correspondence of the immanent and the economic Trinity. Several times he remarks on how close in my own writings I come to this thesis. However, as he notes, in the immanent Trinity I adhere to the traditional order or taxis, Father, Son, Holy Spirit. His main complaint about this is that it assigns to the Holy Spirit a passivity that is hardly compatible with his being a person.

At one time I seriously considered the thesis that Weinandy proposes, but in the end rejected it. The main problem with it is that it runs counter to tradition. The *taxis* of the immanent Trinity, along with the origins of the divine persons of which it is a sign, pertains to the developed faith of the Church in both East and West, and hence must be regarded as a theological datum, even if one secondary to Scripture. Second, this thesis does not account for all the scriptural evidence. Its inadequacy is shown up by material bearing on the divine missions. As several theologians, e.g., Kasper and von Balthasar as well as me (see chapter 7), have observed, the total scriptural data yield *two taxeis*, apparently opposed to each other, namely, Father—Son—Holy Spirit and Father—Holy Spirit—Son. It is the task of the theologian to account for this fact in a way that is reconcilable with official dogmatic formulations.

This is what led me to deduce *two* models of the immanent Trinity from the scriptural material, the outgoing model, which I have called the procession model, and the return model. It is important to note that each of these has the traditional taxis, Father, Son, Holy Spirit. Further, these two models are to be seen not as opposed, but as essentially compatible, with the second, in comprehensive style, including the first. It is when we apply these models to the economic order that we meet the difference of taxis noted above, with the mission model dealing with the traditional taxis in the descending mode, and the return model with the variant one in the ascending mode. In the return model the difference in *taxis* between the immanent and the economic Trinity is accounted for by the fact that the Spirit who rests on the Son in the immanent Trinity draws into union with him in the economic Trinity (see earlier discussion in text). In the light of this it can be noted that the tradition has hitherto concerned itself only with the first set of biblical data and so only with the procession model. Hence what is needed is that the tradition be expanded, a far less drastic procedure than that advocated by Weinandy, which requires its radical revision.

It is true that traditionally the personal property of the Holy Spirit, as acquired through the procession model, is expressed only passively, as "originated" or "spirated." But this in no way contradicts the activity of the Holy Spirit in the economy as attested by Scripture, for even in the immanent Trinity the passive property of the Holy Spirit does not prevent his being, according to the more comprehensive return model, the dynamic bond between the Father and the Son, mediating them to each other, which is an active, not a passive, role.

8. See Dumitru Staniloae, "The Procession of the Holy Spirit from the Father and His Relation to the Son, as the Basis of our Deification and Adoption," *Spirit of God, Spirit of Christ*, 179.

9. St. Gregory Palamas, *Physica, theologica, moralia et practica capita CL*, chapter 36 (Migne: *PG* 150, 1144–1145), my own translation, with assistance of the late Rev. Dr. Patrick Ryan.

10. *Summa theologiae*, I–II, q. 28, a. 6.

11. DS 850, 1300.

12. Jürgen Moltmann, "Theological Proposals towards the Resolution of the *Filioque* Controversy," *Spirit of God, Spirit of Christ*, 169.

13. Ibid.

14. See St. Gregory of Nyssa, *De Spiritu sancto adversus Pneumatomachos Macedonianos*, no. 10 (Migne: *PG* 45, 1313).

15. St. Augustine, *De trinitate*, Book 15, chapter 26 (Migne: *PL* 42, 1094).

16. See *In I sententiarum*, 10, 1, 2.

17. Gary Badcock writes, in "The Anointing of Christ and the *Filioque* Doctrine," *Irish Theological Quarterly* 60 (1994): 242, "[T]he suggestion of [the] Faith and Order [Commission of the World Council of Churches] is that the cause of theological reconciliation might be best served, not by a re-examination of the two ancient and divergent traditions, but by an advance to a new standpoint which somehow comprehends the concerns of both." This is exactly what

I have claimed to do earlier. The Faith and Order Memorandum is printed in *Spirit of God, Spirit of Christ*, pp. 3–18.

18. See David Coffey, "The Teaching of the Constantinopolitan Creed on the Holy Spirit," *Faith and Culture Issues for the Australian Church* (Sydney: Faith and Culture, 1982): 65–75.

19. This is an appropriate place to take note of the "clarification" of the Filioque question, titled "The Greek and Latin Traditions Regarding the Procession of the Holy Spirit," by the Vatican's Pontifical Council for Promoting Christian Unity, for which see the English-language weekly edition of *L'Osservatore Romano*, no. 38 (20 September 1995) 3, 6. This document works through the material according to four unmarked divisions: 1) the Eastern position of the Monarchy of the Father; 2) the Eastern position of the *per Filium*; 3) the Eastern Filioque, that is, the Alexandrian version; and 4) the Western Filioque. As a summary the document constitutes a helpful contribution to the ecumenical discussion. It is only with section 4 that points of difference are met head-on, and there the document is content to quote the new *Catechism of the Catholic Church*, n. 248, which points out that while the East stresses the Monarchy of the Father, the West by the Filioque stresses the consubstantiality of the Father and the Son, and goes on to state that "this legitimate complementarity, provided it does not become rigid, does not affect the identity of faith in the reality of the same mystery confessed." While this is largely true (not, however, in regard to a positive role for the Son in the procession), considerably more is needed before East and West can be brought to peace on this issue.

20. Karl Rahner, "Der dreifaltige Gott als transzendenter Urgrund der Heilsgeschichte," chapter 5, *Mysterium Salutis—Grundriss heilsgeschichtlicher Dogmatik*, vol. 2 (Einsiedeln: Benziger Verlag, 1967), 387. This is my own translation of the passage that appears on p. 106 of the English, *The Trinity* (London: Burns & Oates, 1970).

21. See St. Thomas Aquinas, *Contra Gentiles* 4, 23.

22. For St. Thomas, "notional" acts are "those that designate the origin of divine persons by procession of person from person or persons" (see David Coffey, *Grace: The Gift of the Holy Spirit* [Sydney: Faith and Culture, 1979], 17). While the meaning of this term is not immediately clear, I have no choice but to adopt it, since the term that would naturally suggest itself, "personal," while it applies to the first procession, does not apply to the second, since it is two persons acting together that constitute the principle of the Holy Spirit.

23. See St. Anselm, *Monologium*, chapters 53 and 54 (Migne: *PL* 158, 202).

24. See John Bessarion, *De Spiritus Sancti processione ad Alexium Lascarin Philanthropinum*, ed. Emmanuel Candal (Rome: Pontificium Institutum Orientalium Studiorum, 1961), nos. 84, 96, 100, 101.

25. See *1 sent.*, d. 29, q. 1, a. 4, ad 2. (*Scriptum super libros sententiarum*, vol. 1, ed. P. Mandonnet [Paris: Sumptibus P. Lethielleux, 1929], 696). Here St. Thomas uses the expression *suppositum indistinctum* ("nondistinct supposit") in regard to the divine essence as Creator of the world; he forbears to use it of the Father and the Son as spirating the Holy Spirit because at this stage, when he makes no material distinction of the noun *spirator* ("Spirator") from the adjectival participle *spirans* ("breathing"), he is not prepared to admit that the Father and the Son, being distinct persons, constitute a single Spirator of the Holy Spirit. In the *Summa*, however, where he makes precisely this distinction (I, q. 36, a. 4, ad 7), and so is able to endorse the formula "*duo spirantes, unus spirator*," he can be presumed to have withdrawn this refusal. Billot, therefore, is true to St. Thomas's thought when he changes *suppositum indistinctum* into *subsistens indistinctum*.

26. See Louis Billot, *De Deo uno et trino*, 5th ed. (Prato: Giachetti, 1910), 532.

27. In the next chapter I shall be modifying this position in a way that is important but nevertheless does not affect the conclusion reached here, that the Father and the Son constitute

subsistent spirativity without thereby becoming a fourth person. The modification will affect the argument insofar as the latter will then depend on nondistinctness alone, not at all on communicability, to establish the nonpersonshood of subsistent spirativity.

28. Thus in his *Refutatio photiani libri de Spiritu Sancto* (PG 141, 744–745 [no. 6]) Beccos declares that the way the Father and the Son have in common that by which they produce the Holy Spirit is not the same as the way all three persons have what they have in common. In each case this commonality is the divine essence. But as productive of the Holy Spirit it constitutes a principle situated midway between person and essence, the Father and the Son considered not singly as persons but as together constituting the single principle of the Holy Spirit.

29. See text for note 23.

30. *Summa theologiae*, I, q. 27, a. 2.

31. Ibid., I, q. 27, a. 4 ad 2.

32. See St. Bonaventure, *In 1 sent.*, d. 10, a. 1, q. 3, ad 3 (*Doctoris seraphic: S. Bonaventura opera omnia*, vol. 1 [Quaracchi: Ex Typographia Collegii S. Bonaventure, 182[, 199).

33. Ibid., d. 11, a. 1, q. 2.

34. See note 25.

35. Yves Congar, *I Believe in the Holy Spirit*, vol. 1 (The Experience of the Spirit) (New York: Seabury Press, 1983), 90, quoting H. F. Dondaine, "Saint Thomas et la Procession du Saint-Esprit," *Saint Thomas d'Aquin, Somme Théologique. La Trinité*, vol 2 (Paris, 1946), 397–401.

36. Rahner, "Der dreifaltige Gott," 387, again my own translation.

37. Bernard Lonergan, *De Deo Trino*, vol. 2 (Rome: Pontificia Universitas Gregoriana, 1964), 186 (see 186–193).

38. Walter Kasper, *The God of Jesus Christ* (New York: Crossroad, 1986), 289.

39. See Karl Rahner, "Reflections on the Unity of the Love of Neighbour and the Love of God," *Theological Investigations*, vol. 6 (London: Darton, Longman, & Todd, 1969), 231–249.

40. See Richard of St. Victor, *De Trinitate*, book 6, no. 7 (Migne: PL 196, 972).

41. At the outset I refer readers to my own earlier account of this concept, in *Grace*, 37–42, which here is updated in several respects.

42. See, e.g., "Selbstmitteilung Gottes," *Lexikon für Theologie und Kirche*, vol. 9, col. 627; "God's Self-Communication" (under entry "Revelation"), *Sacramentum Mundi*, 5:353–355; "What Does the 'Self-Communication of God' Mean?" *Foundations of Christian Faith*, (London: Darton, Longman, & Todd, 1978), 117–126.

43. Rahner, "Selbstmitteilung Gottes." The statement is repeated in *Trinity*, 34–35.

44. Rahner himself uses this argument, in another context, in *Trinity*, 11, note 6.

45. John McDermott, "The Christologies of Karl Rahner," *Gregorianum* 67 (1986): 88–89.

46. I recognize that the image is not appropriate from Rahner's point of view. First, he would think of a meeting rather than a collision; and second, he would envisage complementary movements, which cannot be depicted through arrows. I have chosen the image because it suits what I want to say (rather than what he wants to say); and I mention him at this point in the text because he really does differ from me in conceiving the movements as opposed.

47. See Rahner, "Selbstmitteilung Gottes."

48. The objection that the Father is also receiver and the Son also giver is answered in the following way. As both the Father and the Son give and receive the second self-communication, they are not distinguished on that account. What distinguishes them is that the Father alone gives the first self-communication and the Son alone receives it. The Holy Spirit alone is given and received.

49. In the first procession, my emphasis on generation and on the fact that the Father acts out of self-love should be enough to mark my theology off from that of Richard of St. Victor, which despite its initial attractiveness is beset with too many difficulties to be of much service. See introduction.

50. See Wolfhart Pannenberg, *Jesus—God and Man* (London: SCM Press, 1968), 334.

51. Hence the title of the Faith and Order Paper of the World Council of Churches already referred to, *Spirit of God, Spirit of Christ*, is particularly apt. That in this structured sacramental relationship we have an economic transposition of the Filioque is clear from the unity of the Father and the Son there manifest. This unity corresponds in the economic Trinity to the *tamquam ab uno principio et unica spiratione* of the immanent Trinity.

52. On p. 35 Rahner anticipates the return model in a rudimentary way: "The Father gives himself to us too as *Father*, that is, precisely because and insofar as he himself, being essentially with *himself*, utters himself and *in this way* communicates the Son as his own, personal self-manifestation; and because and insofar as the Father and the Son (receiving from the Father), welcoming each other in love, drawn and returning to each other, communicate themselves *in this way*, as received in mutual love, that is, as Holy Spirit." But having said this, he goes on to deny, on p. 106 (p. 387 of the German text, cited in note 20 of this chapter), the possibility of a properly mutual love between the Father and the Son.

53. So, e.g., on p. 85 (both modalities), also on p. 63 (first modality) and p. 67 (second modality).

54. See David Coffey, "A Proper Mission of the Holy Spirit," *Theological Studies* 47 (1986): 227–250.

Four. Persons, Divine and Human

1. Karl Rahner and Herbert Vorgrimler, "Person," *Dictionary of Theology*, 2nd ed. (New York: Herder and Herder, 1981), 378–381; Rahner, "Person," *Sacramentum Mundi*, 4:415–419.

2. See John McDermott, "The Christologies of Karl Rahner," *Gregorianum* 67 (1986): 310–313.

3. Friedrich Jacobi, quoted by Wolfhart Pannenberg in his article "Person," *Die Religion in Geschichte und Gegenwart*, 3rd ed., vol. 5, col. 232.

4. Petro Bilaniuk, quoted by Earl Muller, " 'Person' in Christian Thought, East and West" (Report on Seminar on Trinitarian Theology), *CTSA Proceedings* 46 (1991): 172.

5. See Pannenberg, "Person," col. 230.

6. See Aloys Grillmeier, *Christ in Christian Tradition*, vol. 1, 2nd ed. (Atlanta: John Knox Press, 1975), 129–131.

7. Pannenberg, "Person," col. 231.

8. St. Gregory of Nazianzus, *Oratio* 29, 16 (Migne: PG 36, 96).

9. See Irenée Chevalier, *S. Augustin et la pense greque: Les relations trinitaires* (Fribourg, Switzerland: Collectanea Friburgensia, 1940), 141ff.; and Eugene TeSelle, *Augustine the Theologian* (London: Burns & Oates, 1970), 294–295.

10. See William Hill, *The Three-Personed God—The Trinity as a Mystery of Salvation* (Washington, DC: Catholic University of America Press, 1982), 49.

11. See John Meyendorff, *A Study of Gregory Palamas* (London: Faith Press, 1964), 214–215.

12. See TeSelle, *Augustine*, 295.

13. See Migne: PL 42, 912–913.

14. See Migne: PL 42, 913–914.

15. Migne: PL 42, 914.

16. TeSelle, therefore, is not precise when he says (*Augustine*, 298, note 24), "Augustine clearly puts forward a doctrine that is in all essentials the same as the Thomist," nor is J. N. D. Kelly in speaking of Augustine's doctrine without further ado as one of "subsistent relations" (*Early Christian Doctrines*, 5th ed. [London: Adam & Charles Black, 1977], 274). Except once and then only secondarily (in *De potentia*, q. 8, a. 3), it is not Augustine's authority that St. Thomas invokes in this matter, but that of Boethius. And Richard of St. Victor, writing only a hundred years earlier, saw the question as so open that he could argue for distinction of persons based solely on origin (see his *De trinitate*, book 4, chapter 15, Migne: PL 196, 939). (It is his opinion that Thomas selects for refutation in his treatment in the *Summa*, at 1, q. 40, a. 2.) These facts would be difficult to explain if Augustine's doctrine were as clearly "Thomist" as TeSelle and Kelly take it to be.

17. Pannenberg, "Person," col. 231.

18. Ibid., col. 232.

19. Ibid.

20. Ibid.

21. See Franciscus Diekamp, *Theologiae Dogmaticae Manuale secundum Principia S. Thomae Aquinatis*, vol. 1 (Paris: Desclee, 1949), 387–388.

22. *Summa contra gentiles*, book 4, chapter 14.

23. *De potentia*, q. 9, a. 5, ad 13 (*Quaestiones disputatae*, vol. 2 [Turin: Marietti, 1953]).

24. I draw attention to the strange doctrine of Scotus that (in the words of Friedrich Wetter) "because of the unity of nature the divine persons are not individuals" (Wetter, *Die Trinitatslehre des Johannes Duns Scotus* [Münster/Westf.: Aschendorffsche Verlagsbuchhandlung, 1967], 273). Against this it must be said that the unity of the divine nature requires only that the trinitarian persons be individuals in a different (analogous) sense from other individuals (which all belong to species), not that they not be individuals at all.

25. Hence, when with Rahner I speak of the Incarnation and grace as "self-communications of God," I refer, not to multiplications of the one God, but to assimilation and admission, by participation, to his life.

26. This is so because, as St. Thomas says (*Summa theologiae*, I, q. 40, a. 2), "[I]n God there is no difference between the abstract and the concrete."

27. It is worthwhile pointing out that, as the divine persons simply *are* the relations, they may be termed, though not defined as, "relative subsistences." They are *defined* as "subsistent relations." See also note 58.

28. *Summa theologiae*, III, q. 3, a. 3, ad 1.

29. See Etienne Gilson, *Being and Some Philosophers* (Toronto: Pontifical Institute of Mediaeval Studies, 1952), 182–185.

30. Ibid., 184.

31. Ibid.

32. Bernard Wuellner, *Dictionary of Scholastic Philosophy* (Milwaukee: Bruce, 1956), 108.

33. Gilson, *Being and Some Philosophers*, 183.

34. Ibid., 184.

35. Ibid., 183.

36. I am indebted here to W. Norris Clarke's article, "Person, Being, and St. Thomas," *Communio* 19 (1992): 601–618, especially for drawing attention to the views of Gilson. However, I disagree, for reasons stated above, with Clarke's philosophical statement that "substance is the primary mode, in that all else, including relations, depend [sic] on it as their ground" (p. 607). Also, some of his theological observations and conclusions are rather questionable. For example, in upholding the relationality of the divine being, he in fact compromises the divine transcendence by positing the creation as necessary, though he thinks he eludes this

charge by asserting that God's freedom is safeguarded by the observation that his choice of this particular universe for creation, as against other possible universes, is free (pp. 615–616). In my explanation given earlier, there is no necessity for the creation of any universe, and God's transcendence remains intact. Further, Clarke falls into a rationalism that theologians of the Trinity strive hard to avoid, by declaring that the relationality of the divine being, which can be known from philosophy, demands "*some* kind of interpersonal relation on the divine level" (p. 617), but he thinks he avoids this charge by pointing out that such philosophical knowledge would not include "just what form this would have to take or how many persons it would have to involve" (ibid.). In my explanation given earlier, the necessary dynamism of the divine being is accounted for with complete adequacy by the divine essence itself. This leaves open the possibility of internal relations, which, when revealed as fact, are revealed also as necessary, though the ground of their necessity remains hidden. For the most recent statement of Clarke's thought see his Aquinas Lecture, 1993, at Marquette University, *Person and Being* (Milwaukee, WI: Marquette University Press, 1993).

37. What I am struggling to say here, Palamas would have said with ease, by use of his formula: God is nonrelational in his essence, relational in his energies.

38. Leonardo Boff writes, "The distinction between Persons and essence cannot be *real*, or we would have a quaternity: one essence *plus* three Persons, making four. Neither is this distinction purely in the mind, or we would have modalism; there would be just one essence and three verbal or mental modes of expressing it. So there has to be some sort of distinction between the one essence and the Persons. Theologians say there is a "formal" ("virtual" in the Thomist school) distinction, which avoids fusing the Trinity into unity and at the same time maintains a differentiation within the divine identity" (*Trinity and Society* [New York: Orbis, 1988], 80–81). Rahner identifies the value of this distinction in the fact that it distinguishes not between two absolute realities, but between an absolute and a relative reality (see *The Trinity* [London: Burns & Oates, 1970], 70).

39. Pannenberg, cols. 231–232. For an attempt to achieve a similar result from the perspective of Thomistic philosophy (and, like my own effort, inspired by Thomistic trinitarian theology), see Robert Connor's "Relational *Esse* and the Person," *American Catholic Philosophical Quarterly* (Annual ACPA Proceedings) 65 (1991): 253–267. Connor's argument is that esse is not the actuality of a substance, as is commonly supposed, but an intensive act of which substantiality is a mode, where by "intensive" he means "expansive as an *agere*," such expansiveness being another mode of the same esse. In the case of a spiritual subject, this expansiveness is relational, because through *intelligere*, the power of knowing, the esse is able to become "an infinity of other beings in an immaterial, intentional way." From Josef Pieper he borrows the idea that the combination of intrinsic existence and nonaccidental relationality, that is, dwelling most intensively within oneself and being able to grasp the universe constitutes the essence of finite spirit. Person is thus esse-as-relation, of which substance is a mode. While Connor's argument does not reach as far as the Scotistic argument that I develop in this chapter, it certainly moves in the same direction and makes similar use of Gilson. Further, as a credible philosophical view of person, as non-accidental relation to the universe, it is open to transmutation into the theological understanding here argued for, viz., person as subsistent relation to God. For another attempt within Thomism see W. Norris Clarke's article, "Person, Being, and St. Thomas," and his Marquette lecture, *Person and Being*, referred to in note 36, which likewise do not reach as far as the Scotistic argument.

40. Heribert Mühlen, *Sein und Person nach Johannes Duns Scotus* (Werl/Westf.: Dietrich-Coelde-Verlag, 1954). The same thought is twice acknowledged to the same source, on pp. 296 and 341, in Pannenberg's *Jesus—God and Man* (London: SCM Press, 1968).

41. Interested readers are referred to two articles that I wrote on this subject, the second being to some extent a revision of the first: "Death as a Question of Negative Theology,"

Reflections on Faith and Culture (Sydney: Faith and Culture, 1981), 66–76; and "Christian Anthropology," *Bicentennial Reflections* (Sydney: Faith and Culture, 1988), 130–141.

42. J. F. Donceel, *Philosophical Anthropology* (New York: Sheed and Ward, 1967), 448.

43. See G. Greshake and G. Lohfink, *Nahewartung—Auferstehung—Unsterblichkeit*, 4th ed. (Freiburg, Germany: Herder, 1982).

44. Ibid., 172.

45. See Mühlen, *Sein und Person*, 122.

46. It is not necessary here to buy into the controverted question of the relation of nature and grace raised by the *nouvelle théologie* of the 1940s. Suffice it to say that I am thinking of the *existential* human situation, in which human nature is affected by grace even before the operation of free decision.

47. See Mühlen, *Sein und Person*, 124–125. The text from Scotus there quoted (reference: Ox. 1, d. 3, q. 5, n. 14; 9, 221a) reads as follows: "Dico quod aliud est relationem esse priorem cognitione causati cogniti per causam, et aliud ipsam includi in cognitione causati; licet enim prius lapis habeat respectum ad Deum quam lapis cognoscatur, et ideo non cogniscitur perfecte nisi cognito Deo, tamen lapis cogniscitur, non cognito respectu ad Deum; et ex hoc sequitur quod ille respectus non est de essentia lapidis, quia nihil perfecte cogniscitur nisi cognito eo quod est de essentia sua."

48. My treatment of this point is a revision of what I wrote in "Christian Anthropology," 139.

49. *Summa theologiae*, II–II, q. 2, a. 3.

50. It will be clear that my argument here, as a theological argument, is consistent with James O'Connor's argument as a philosophical argument (for which see note 39). What I have theologically called "God," O'Connor, writing as a philosopher, can only call the totality of being, or, to use scholastic language, *ens commune* (being in general). Further, again as a philosopher, he only considers human persons. In the light of this, his nonaccidental relation to the universe is seen to be the same as a subsistent relation to *ens commune*. Transposed into the theological arena, this becomes subsistent relation to absolute being (*ens absolutum*), or God.

51. As mentioned in note 39, Robert Connor covers this aspect of person by drawing attention to the power of *intelligere* as the ability to become "an infinity of other beings in an immaterial, intentional way." While not denying this, indeed while wholeheartedly affirming it, I consider it more adequate to the reality of person to emphasize love rather than knowledge, and have it person-directed rather than object-directed.

52. Karl Rahner, "Über die Einheit von Nächsten-und Gottesliebe," *Schriften zur Theologie*, vol. 6 (Einsiedeln: Benziger Verlag, 1965), 288 (my translation).

53. Ibid., 295.

54. Karl Rahner, *Geist in Welt* (Munich: Kösel-Verlag, 1957), *Spirit in the World* (London: Sheed and Ward, 1968).

55. See Karl Rahner, "The Unity of Spirit and Matter in the Christian Understanding of Faith," *Theological Investigations*, vol. 6 (Baltimore: Helicon, 1969), 174–175.

56. Timothy Ware, *The Orthodox Church*, Penguin Books (Pelican) (Middlesex: Harmondsworth, 1963), 222. On the subject of person in Orthodox theology, some mention should be made of the work of John Zizioulas, which has been received enthusiastically by a number of Catholic theologians. See, for example, his *Being as Communion* (Crestwood, NY: St. Vladimir's Seminary Press, 1985) and "Human Capacity and Human Incapacity: A Theological Exploration of Personhood" (*Scottish Journal of Theology* 28 [1975]: 401–448). While I recognize much of value in Zizioulas's contribution, I have difficulty with some of his basic positions. For example, while I agree with him that person is the ultimate category of existence, I would identify person in this case as the absolute person of God, not, as Zizioulas does, the

person of the Father. In saying that "the one divine substance is consequently the being of God only because it has these three modes of existence, which it owes not to the substance but to one person, the Father" (*Being as Communion*, 41), he seems to revert to a pre-Athanasian understanding of the *homoousion*. For my part, I would put the matter thus: it is of the one being of God to exist in three persons, the second two of whom draw their existence from the first, the Father. Also, Zizioulas makes a great deal out of the proposition that person is the bearer of its nature in totality (see, for example, "Human Capacity and Human Incapacity," 408). While there is a certain obvious truth in this proposition, it cannot be taken with the complete literalness that Zizioulas desires and needs for it. In a word, it seems to me that Zizioulas's work requires to be subjected to a more critical appraisal than hitherto before its lasting value can be ascertained.

57. These statements presuppose some such theology as that presented by Rahner in his essay, "Anonymous Christians" (*Theological Investigations*, vol. 6 [Baltimore: Helicon, 1969], 390–398).

58. In the definition of person as "subsistent relation" the syntactical arrangement of adjective and noun throws the emphasis on the noun, "relation," from which it is immediately known that we are in the realm of person. This is not the case with "relative subsistence." Hence this latter phrase cannot serve as a definition of person. The fundamental point, established above, is that relation is the term that specifically defines personhood (spirituality) over and above individual, subsistent, supposit or hypostasis, all of which can be used of infrapersonal beings. See note 27.

59. See *Summa theologiae*, I, q. 7, a. 1.

60. See Karl Rahner, articles on "Person" referred to in note 1, *Sacramentum Mundi*, 4: 405, and *Dictionary of Theology*, 378.

61. Francis M. Tyrrell, *Man: Believer and Unbeliever* (New York: Alba House, 1974), 152.

62. See Mühlen, *Sein und Person*, 106–121.

63. As the *Fides Damasi* (DS 71) says, "Pater Filium genuit, non voluntate, nec necessitate, sed natura" ("The Father generated the Son, not according to the will, nor according to necessity, but according to nature").

Five. Change in God

1. For a bibliography of Hartshorne's publications up to 1981, see *Process Studies* 6, no. 1 (Spring 1976): 73–93, and 11, no. 2 (Summer 1981): 108–112. His writings since then include the book *Omnipotence and Other Theological Mistakes* (Albany: State University of New York Press, 1984).

2. See David Pailin, "The Utterly Absolute and the Totally Related: Change in God," *New Blackfriars* 68, no. 805 (1987): 244.

3. Cited from Hartshorne's book *Aquinas to Whitehead: Seven Centuries of Metaphysics of Religion* (Milwaukee: Marquette University Publications, 1976), 23, by Santiago Sia, in "A Changing God?" *Word and Spirit: A Monastic Review* 8 (1986): 30, note 13.

4. See Pailin, "The Utterly Absolute," 249, where he refers to Hartshorne's *Man's Vision of God*, 346.

5. See ibid., 248.

6. See Sia, "A Changing God?" 18.

7. See Sia, "The Doctrine of God's Immutability: Introducing the Modern Debate," *New Blackfriars* 68, no. 805 (1987): 228.

8. See ibid., 229.

9. See Sia, "A Changing God?" 17.

10. Principally, *Society and Spirit: A Trinitarian Cosmology* (Selingsgrove, PA: Susquehanna University Press, 1991); *The Triune Symbol: Persons, Process and Community* (Lanham, MD: University Press of America, 1985); *What Are They Saying About the Trinity?* (New York: Paulist Press, 1979); "Process Perspectives and Trinitarian Theology," *Word and Spirit* 8 (1986): 51–64; "Subsistent Relation: Mediating Concept for a New Synthesis?" *Journal of Religion* 64 (1984): 188–204; "The Holy Trinity as a Community of Divine Persons," *Heythrop Journal* 15 (1974): 166–182, 257–270.

11. See Wolfhart Pannenberg, *Systematische Theologie*, vol. 1 (Göttingen: Vandenhoeck & Ruprecht, 1988), 414–415; English translation: *Systematic Theology*, vol. 1 (Grand Rapids, MI: Eerdmans, 1991), 382–384.

12. Bracken, *Society and Spirit*, 123.

13. Ibid., 127–128, where the reference is to *The Triune Symbol*, 45–47.

14. Ibid., 129.

15. Ibid., 130.

16. Ibid.

17. Ibid., 131.

18. See Alfred North Whitehead, *Process and Reality: An Essay in Cosmology*, edition corrected by David Ray Griffin and Donald W. Sherburne (New York: Free Press, 1978), 88 (no. 135).

19. Robert B. Mellert, *What Is Process Theology?* (New York: Paulist Press, 1975), 48–49.

20. See ibid., 49.

21. Bracken, *Society and Spirit*, 133.

22. See ibid., 133.

23. See ibid., 134.

24. Sia, "The Doctrine of God's Immutability," 221–225.

25. "One, singular, wholly simple and unchangeable spiritual substance," Vatican I, Dogmatic Constitution on the Catholic Faith, *Dei Filius*, ch. 1 (DS 3001). See also the Fourth Lateran Council, DS 800.

26. Lewis S. Ford, "Process Trinitarianism," *Journal of the American Academy of Religion* 43 (1975): 199–213.

27. William Hill, *The Three-Personed God: The Trinity as a Mystery of Salvation* (Washington, DC: Catholic University of America Press, 1982), 208.

28. One notes in this respect a certain similarity to Buddhism. In giving an account of the Buddha's thought on this matter, Walpola Rahula writes: "In order to avoid a confusion it should be mentioned that there are two kinds of truths: conventional truth and ultimate truth. When we use such expressions in our daily life as 'I,' 'you,' 'being,' 'individual,' etc., we do not lie because there is no self or being as such, but we speak a truth conforming to the convention of the world. But the ultimate truth is that there is no 'I' or 'being' in reality" (Walpula Rahula, *What the Buddha Taught*, 2nd ed. [London: Gordon Fraser, 1967], 55). The reason for this, like that claimed by Process thought, is that "everything is conditioned, relative and interdependent" (ibid., 53).

29. Henri Bouillard, *The Knowledge of God* (New York: Herder and Herder, 1968), 104–112.

30. Ibid., 106.

31. Ibid., 109.

32. Ibid., 111–112.

33. See William J. Hill, "Does God Know the Future?" *Theological Studies* 36 (1975): 4, note 5.

34. See ibid., 7.

35. Hill's references: *Summa theologia*, I, q. 14, a. 13, a. 8; cf. q. 86, a. 4; *1 Sent.*, d. 28, q. 1, a. 5; *Contra gentiles* 1, 67; *De verit.*, q. 2, a. 12; *De malo.*, q. 16, a. 7; on eternity cf. *Summa theologia*, I, q. 10.

36. Hill, "Does God Know the Future?" 7.

37. A highly anthropomorphic and inappropriate term imposed by convention.

38. Hill, "Does God Know the Future?" 13.

39. Ibid., 14. Again, shades of Palamas!

40. It is also the condition of possibility of the change that takes place in God because of the Incarnation, a situation that Rahner describes thus: "God can become something; he who in himself is immutable can *himself* be mutable *in the other*" (*Schriften zur Theologie*, vol. 4 [Einsiedeln: Benziger Verlag, 1964], 147, my own literal translation). In the accompanying note (note 3), he adds that this statement is not to be taken either as a denial of the immutability of God in himself or as simply an affirmation of a change *of* the other, of the sacred humanity. The many theologians who profess themselves mystified by this position of Rahner's need to come to terms with the following two facts: 1) The position is imposed by the faith-statement that in the Incarnation God *became* human. If the word "became" is to retain anything of its proper meaning, God, then, must have changed in *some* way. And 2) The position begins to become intelligible when based on the ground that because of the contingency and mutability of creatures (and not just of *free* creatures) God, having freely created them, changes in his relationship to them according as they themselves change, changes, however, not in his nature (which would be impossible) but in his intentionality (i.e., in his contingent knowledge and love of these creatures), as is aptly expressed by William Hill in the passage quoted in the following text. But the possibility of even this limited change is itself grounded in something more fundamental, the reality ("superreality") of God's relationship to the world. This, then, must be the ultimate, if unacknowledged, ground of Rahner's position.

41. Hill, "Does God Know the Future?" 15 and 18.

42. Ibid., 14.

43. Ibid., 7.

44. "The relation between God and creature is a primordial ontological datum not sus-ceptible of further resolution. In the fundamental transcendental experience of man's orien-tation towards God as the incomprehensible mystery, both man's independence and his der-ivation from God are simultaneously given. This experience is the most fundamental datum of the mind and even if it becomes the object of explicit reflection only later and imperfectly, it is logically prior, as the condition of the very possibility of existence as a person with intellectual knowledge and freedom. It culminates in the experience of the independent yet derivative character of freedom, and this manifests its specific nature. Consequently the rela-tion God—freedom must be taken as primordial; there is nothing "prior" to it by which it can be rendered intelligible, any more than we, having come to know God "from" the world, can then understand the world anew, with God as starting-point." Karl Rahner, "Grace and Free-dom," *Sacramentum Mundi*, 2:426b.

45. Michael Vertin, "Is God in Process?" *Religion and Culture: Essays in Honor of Bernard Lonergan, S.J.*, Ed. T. Fallon and P. Riley (Albany, NY: State University of New York Press, 1987), 45–62.

46. Ibid., 55.

47. Ibid., 51–52.

48. Ibid., 52.

49. Ibid.

50. Ibid., 53.

51. Ibid., 53–54.

52. Ibid., 54.

53. Ibid.

54. See Bernard Lonergan, *Insight* (New York: Philosophical Library, 1958), 641–677.

55. Ibid., 674.

56. Ibid., 657–669.

57. Vertin, "Is God in Process?" 54.

58. Ibid.

59. Lonergan himself took little account of Process philosophy. However, there is on record an answer he gave to a question about it after a lecture, an answer that reveals both his low estimation of it and the fact that Vertin has interpreted his mind correctly. The answer, in part, is as follows: "Now the concept of God in *Insight* is a concept of an unrestricted act of understanding, an absolute intelligibility. In Whitehead's *Process and Reality* God is the first accident. There is a radical opposition there because an accident is something that is not intelligible; it just happens." Bernard Lonergan, *Philosophy of God, and Theology* (London: Darton, Longman, & Todd, 1973), 64.

60. See W. Norris Clarke, "Person, Being, and St. Thomas," *Communio* 19 (1992): 608.

61. See John Wright, "The Method of Process Theology: An Evaluation," *Communio* 6 (1979): 52.

62. See ibid., 53–54.

63. Ibid., 53.

64. See Whitehead, *Process and Reality*, 68.

65. Ibid.

66. Ibid.

67. Ibid., 69.

68. Ibid.

69. Ibid., 283.

70. Ibid.

71. Alfred North Whitehead, *Science and the Modern World* (Cambridge: Cambridge University Press, 1932), 159.

72. Ibid., 157.

73. Ibid., 151.

74. In any case, Whitehead's opinion on this matter seems at least debatable from the scientific point of view. He himself recognizes that Einstein would probably disagree with him. See *Science and the Modern World*, 154.

75. Whitehead, *Science and the Modern World*, 149.

76. Ibid., 150.

77. Ibid., 157.

78. Ibid.

79. Ibid., 158.

80. See Lonergan, *Insight*, 388. Newman is said to have had a similar adage: "Truth defends itself and falsehood refutes itself."

81. W. Norris Clarke, *Person and Being*, The Aquinas Lecture, 1993 (Milwaukee, WI: Marquette University Press, 1993), 84.

82. Elizabeth Johnson, *She Who Is—The Mystery of God in Feminist Theological Discourse* (New York: Crossroad, 1994), 270.

83. Ibid.

84. See Catherine LaCugna, *God for Us: The Trinity and Christian Life* (San Francisco: HarperSanFrancisco, 1991), 192–197.

85. John Meyendorff, *A Study of Gregory Palamas* (London: Faith and Order Press, 1964), 225.

86. See David Coffey, "The Palamite Doctrine of God: A New Perspective," *St. Vladimir's Theological Quarterly* 32 (1988): 351.

87. See ibid., 335.

88. In Thomistic theology it is called a "virtual" distinction. See note 38, preceding chapter 4.

89. Leonardo Boff, *Trinity and Society* (Maryknoll, NY: Orbis, 1988), 81.

90. Rowan Williams, "The Philosophical Structures of Palamism," *Eastern Churches Review* 9, nos. 1–2 (1977): 27–44.

91. Williams, "The Philosophical Structures of Palamism," 38.

92. Martin Jugie, *Theologia Dogmatica Christianorum Orientalium ab Ecclesia Catholica Dissidentium*, vol. 2 (Paris: Letouzey et An, 1933), 148.

93. Williams, "The Philosophical Structures of Palamism," 40.

94. Ibid., 44.

95. See Karl Rahner, *The Trinity* (London: Burns & Oates, 1970), 70. See this whole section, pp. 68–73.

Six. Recent Theology: Moltmann

1. See Anne Hunt, *The Trinity and the Paschal Mystery—A Development in Recent Catholic Theology* (Collegeville, MN: Liturgical Press, 1997).

2. See James Empereur, "Paschal Mystery," *The New Dictionary of Theology*, ed. J. Komonchak, M. Collins, and D. Lane (Wilmington, DE: Michael Glazier, 1987), 744.

3. F. W. Dillistone, *The Christian Understanding of Atonement* (London: SCM Press, 1968), 196. It should be added, however, that in the work of redemption Calvin also allowed a role to Christ's obedience. See F. Wendel, *Calvin: Origins and Development of His Religious Thought* (London: Collins, 1963), 218–219.

4. Dillistone, 196.

5. Barth himself, though not departing from the doctrine of penal substitution, tempered it significantly by his emphasis on God's victory over sin. See R. G. Crawford, "The Atonement in Karl Barth," *Theology* 74 (1971): 355–358.

6. See Jürgen Moltmann, *The Crucified God—The Cross of Christ as the Foundation and Criticism of Christian Theology* (New York: Harper & Row, 1974), 219–227.

7. See Moltmann, *The Trinity and the Kingdom of God—The Doctrine of God* (London: SCM Press, 1981), 192–200 (political monotheism) and 200–202 (clerical monotheism, episcopal and papal).

8. See John O'Donnell's discussion of this point in his *Trinity and Temporality—The Christian Doctrine of God in the Light of Process Theology and the Theology of Hope* (Oxford: Oxford University Press, 1983), 147–149.

9. Moltmann, "The Theology of the Cross Today," *The Future of Creation* (Philadelphia: Fortress Press, 1979), 76.

10. Ibid., 74.

11. See Richard Bauckham, *Moltmann—Messianic Theology in the Making* (Basingstoke, Hants: Marshall Pickering, 1987), 108, 109, 111.

12. See Moltmann, *The Crucified God*, 240–247; *The Church in the Power of the Spirit—A Contribution to Messianic Ecclesiology* (London: SCM Press, 1977), 93–98; *The Future of Creation*, 71–77; *The Trinity and the Kingdom*, 75–83; *History and the Triune God: Contributions to Trinitarian Theology* (London: SCM Press, 1991), 44–56; "The Cross of Christ: The Pain of the Love of God," essay in a book written jointly with Elisabeth Moltmann-Wendel, *God—His and Hers* (New York: Crossroad, 1991), 63–76; *The Way of Jesus Christ—Christology in Messianic Dimensions* (San Francisco: HarperSanFrancisco, 1990), 151–181.

13. See Moltmann, *The Trinity and the Kingdom*, 77. Wolfhart Pannenberg, interpreting Luther, says: "One must see Jesus in his relatedness to the rest of humanity whose guilt he took on himself in such a way that he bore it as his own guilt and thus suffered for us the

punishment of the cross as though he deserved it: 'Ipse fuisse passum pavorem horroremque conscientiae perturbatae et iram aeternam gustantis' (*WA* 5, pp. 603f.)." (*Jesus—God and Man* (London: SCM Press, 1968), 278). He goes on to say that "Luther was probably the first since Paul and his school to have seen with full clarity that Jesus' death in its genuine sense is to be understood as vicarious penal suffering" (ibid., 279).

14. Moltmann, "Justice for Victims and Perpetrators," *History and the Triune God*, 51.

15. See also ibid., "Only God can represent us and bear us with our guilt."

16. See ibid., 50.

17. See ibid, 44 and 50.

18. See ibid., 47, 50–51.

19. Ibid., 51–52.

20. Moltmann, *The Crucified God*, 263.

21. Ibid.

22. Moltmann, ibid. It is an indirect quotation. But see also Luther's commentary on Galatians 3.13 in Jaroslav Pelikan (ed.), *Lectures on Galatians, 1535, Chapters 1–4, Luther's Works*, vol. 26 (Saint Louis, MO: Concordia, 1963), 276–291.

23. See Moltmann, *The Crucified God*, 241; *The Future of Creation*, 73.

24. Moltmann, *The Trinity and the Kingdom*, 82.

25. Ibid.

26. Moltmann, *History and the Triune God*, "The Cross of Christ," 69.

27. See Moltmann, *The Crucified God*, 244; *The Future of Creation*, 74.

28. Moltmann, *The Church in the Power of the Spirit*, 96.

29. See Moltmann, *The Way of Jesus Christ*, 176.

30. See Edward Schillebeeckx, *Christ—The Experience of Jesus as Lord* (New York: Crossroad, 1980), 728.

31. "This conclusion results from the temptation, which Moltmann from *The Crucified God* onwards seems unable to resist, to see the cross as the key to the doctrine of God, not only in the sense that it reveals God as the kind of love which is willing to suffer, but in the sense that the actual sufferings of the cross are essential to who God is. This attempt to take God's temporal experience as seriously as possible oddly ends by eternalising it." Bauckham, *Moltmann*, 109.

32. See Moltmann, *The Trinity and the Kingdom*, 233, note 27.

33. See Myles Bourke, "The Epistle to the Hebrews," *The New Jerome Biblical Commentary*, ed. R. Brown, J. Fitzmyer, and R. Murphy (Englewood Cliffs, NJ: Prentice Hall, 1990), 924b.

34. Ibid.

35. It is not likely that the same event is being referred to as in Hebrews 5.7, which speaks of Jesus' "loud cries and tears." This in all probability refers to Gethsemane rather than Golgotha. See Oscar Cullmann, *The Christology of the New Testament*, New Testament Library (London: SCM Press, 1963), 95–96.

36. Bourke, "The Epistle to the Hebrews," 924b.

37. See Bruce Vawter, *This Man Jesus—An Essay Toward a New Testament Christology* (London: Geoffrey Chapman, 1973), 75.

38. "It is historically certain that the soteriological interpretation of the death of Jesus is to be understood as early post-Easter knowledge. Its reduction to Jesus himself is burdened with uncertainties and is therefore controversial: against sceptical reserve (e.g., the words of Jesus at the last supper cannot be reconstructed) stands an emphatic counter-argument (viz., Mk 14.22–24 presents the authentic words of Jesus). The possibility that Jesus has given his expected death an atoning sense from his basic attitude of "pro-existence" cannot be contested. As converging arguments of probability show (cf. Schürmann, Hengel), the actuality is more likely than its opposite. Accordingly we can conclude that in the face of the non-acceptance

of salvation (with the consequence of judgment) Jesus learned that the salvation that is God's lordship was to come no longer just in his existence for the lost but through his death for sinners. . . . At the last supper he has expressed this in unfamiliar gestures and with rather indirect words (Isa 53 or 2 Macc 7, and elsewhere)." Hans Kessler, "Erlösung/Soteriologie," *Neues Handbuch theologischer Grundbegriffe*, vol. 1, ed. Peter Eicher (Munich: Kösel-Verlag, 1984), 244. See also Joachim Jeremias, *New Testament Theology* (London: SCM Press, 1971), 286–288.

39. See Jeremias, *New Testament Theology*, 287–288.

40. See Karl Lehmann, " 'Er wurde für uns gekreuzigt,' " *Theologische Quartalschrift* 162 (1982): 297–317.

41. Ibid., 305.

42. Ibid., 307.

43. Ibid., 312.

44. See Pannenberg, *Jesus—God and Man*, 278: "Luther agrees with the main line of the patristic doctrine of reconciliation in seeing the cross as an action of God in and through Jesus, not as an accomplishment of the man Jesus in relation to God. Thus the character of the cross as something that happened to Jesus is maintained. However, Luther goes beyond the patristic doctrine by emphasizing the penal character of Jesus' passion."

45. See John McKenzie, *Second Isaiah* (Garden City, NY: Doubleday, 1968), 132.

46. In Luther and Protestant theology generally the obedience and submission of the substitute, a human work, must not be allowed to enter into the essential constitution of redemption, which must be preserved as entirely the work of God. Hence it is called "passive" rather than "active" obedience, and in the case of the Servant, and of Christ himself, is regarded only as a necessary *condition* of redemption. See Pannenberg, *Jesus—God and Man*, 195, 278.

47. See Moltmann, *The Way of Jesus Christ*, 186.

48. Carroll Stuhlmueller, "Deutero-Isaiah and Trito-Isaiah," *The New Jerome Biblical Commentary*, 342a.

49. See Joseph Fitzmyer, "The Letter to the Romans," *The New Jerome Biblical Commentary*, 857b-858a.

50. See W. Arndt and F. Gingrich, eds., *A Greek-English Lexicon of the New Testament and Other Early Christian Literature* (from W. Bauer's *Wörterbuch*) (Chicago: University of Chicago Press, 1957), 419.

51. See C. K. Barrett, *A Commentary on the Second Epistle to the Corinthians* (New York: Harper & Row, 1973), 179.

52. See ibid., 180.

53. See Cullmann, *Christology of the New Testament*, 76.

54. Here I have used, but modified, Barrett's words (*Commentary*, 180), partly in order to exclude something he has said that is not quite correct: in saying that "he (Christ) came to stand in that relation with God, etc.," he fails to take account of the principal emphasis of the Pauline text, to which I am drawing attention, the initiative of God. I have also added the word "external."

55. See Barrett, *Commentary*, 177.

56. We should be careful not to drive a wedge between objective and subjective redemption as has sometimes been done. God's redemptive act in Christ is sacramentalized in the Church's ministry (of word and sacrament) and thus directed to me personally *in medio ecclesiae* (in the midst of the Church), calling me to ongoing conversion. But within the single process of redemption objective and subjective elements can and should be distinguished.

57. cf. Barrett, *Commentary*, 180.

58. 4 Maccabees 6.28 does mention punishment incurred, but it is human, not divine, punishment.

59. See Vawter, *This Man Jesus*, 78–79.

60. For the teaching of the Church see the Constitution *Benedictus Deus* of Pope Benedict XII, DS 1002, and point no. 7 of the Letter of the Sacred Congregation for the Doctrine of the Faith on Certain Questions concerning Eschatology, *Acta Apostolicae Sedis* 71 (1979): 939–943.

61. It is interesting to note that contemporary thinking on "temporal punishment due to sin" proceeds along similar lines. Cf. Gerhard Ludwig Müller, "Ablass," *Lexikon für Theologie und Kirche*, 3rd ed., vol. 1, (Freirburg, Germany: Herder, 1993–), cols. 54–55; and Peter Beer, "Trent's Temporal Punishment and Today's Renewal of Penance," *Theological Studies* 35, no. 3 (1974): 478.

62. The Kantian view, that vindictive punishment is an end in itself and not a means to an end, is neither demonstrated nor demonstrable.

63. In human society it is necessary for the sake of legal and moral order for the nature and extent of the effects of wrongdoing to be identified and the nature and amount of expiation necessary to overcome them calculated, all this in a juridical judgment. This is punishment. It is an exercise of society's coercive power. It would be vindictive punishment if included in this object were the causation of suffering in the wrongdoer, for whatever purpose, including good purposes, such as the reformation of the wrongdoer or the deterrence of the wrongdoer and others. With God, because of his omniscience and omnipotence, the effects of our wrong-doing (sin) cannot be *escaped*, but in his love and mercy he freely *forgives* our sins if we repent and are willing to expiate their effects. The expiation remains to be done either in this life or the next. If we do not repent, the effects of our sins (alienation from God and the community) simply take their course. In neither case is there question of punishment, let alone vindictive punishment, though one can understand how the Bible and the popular mind might see them as such, because of the necessity of expiation in the first instance and because of alienation in the second. Nor are they exercises of coercive power. Human retribution, if just, is retributive justice. God's action, because it is not juridical, is not retribution. Therefore it cannot properly be called retributive justice, though, again, one can understand why it often is so called. However, we can speak of the justice of God, not in the sense that he owes us justice (except in a relative sense, that is, if he has promised to act toward us in a certain way), but in the sense that he cannot be unjust. We know from revelation that vicarious expiation can be carried out before God by an innocent person substituting for the guilty (as in the case of Christ), not in the sense that God has to be placated by *someone*, but in the sense that with God the love and obedience of the substitute, realized in unavoidable suffering, can overcome the refusal to love and the disobedience of the guilty (though personal conversion and expi-ation remain necessary). This possibility is grounded not in God's justice alone, nor in his mercy alone, but in a combination of both. See also Karl Rahner, "Punishment of Sins," *Sacramentum Mundi*, 6: 92b–94b.

64. See Edward Schillebeeckx, *Jesus—An Experiment in Christology* (London: Collins, 1975), 135.

65. See James D. G. Dunn, *Christology in the Making* (London: SCM Press, 1980), 312, note 82.

66. See David Coffey, *Grace: The Gift of the Holy Spirit* (Sydney: Faith and Culture, 1979), 217–218.

67. See note 37.

68. Bauckham, *Moltmann*, 99.

69. In *The Way of Jesus Christ* (pp. 175–177) Moltmann attempts, not very successfully, to defend his theology of the cross against the criticism of Dorothée Sölle (in *Suffering* [London: Darton, Longman, & Todd, 1975], 22–28). Two points are to be made. In the first place, Sölle's criticism does not rest on a "misunderstanding," as Moltmann claims. Sölle distinguishes

quite clearly between the opinion of Popkes and that of Moltmann, and, in any case, where Moltmann quotes Popkes in *The Crucified God*, p. 241, this is precisely to make the latter's opinion his own. Second, the substance of Moltmann's defense against attributing the causation of suffering to the Father is, in his own words, that "in the forsakenness of the Son the Father also forsakes himself" (p. 176). But this assertion is self-contradictory. If it be allowed to acquit the Father of causing suffering, it robs the forsakenness of the Son of precisely the efficacy that Moltmann insists on attributing to it.

70. For an account of these problems see Gérard Rossé, *The Cry of Jesus on the Cross* (New York: Paulist Press, 1987), 39–45.

71. See Moltmann, *The Crucified God*, 146–147.

72. See Dennis Nineham, *Saint Mark*, The Pelican Gospel Commentaries (Harmondsworth, Middlesex: Penguin Books, 1963), 429. The confusion could only really arise if Elijah's name were in Hebrew, as in Matthew, rather than in Aramaic, as in Mark. In this case, as Nineham suggests, probably the original Hebrew would have been changed to Aramaic under the influence of the knowledge that the latter was Jesus' native tongue. The alternative seems to be to regard the whole incident of the confusion as the creation of the community. But then, what useful purpose would it serve? My point stands: an effort, even if a botched one, has been made to reproduce the *ipsissima verba Jesu*, and this in itself is an indication of historicity.

73. It is interesting to note that, while these are the only words of Jesus on the cross in the Gospel of Mark, this gospel does record (v. 37) a second, nonverbal cry, which occurred only a short time later, Jesus' death-cry, and that both cries are said to be "loud," which is surprising in the case of someone dying of asphyxiation.

74. Nineham, *Saint Mark*, 428.

75. Ibid. One does not, therefore, even have to consider Moltmann's "bizarre" (his word) formulation of the opinion presented earlier, viz., "that the dying Jesus prayed the whole of Psalm 22 on the cross" (*God—His and Hers*, 66). It was sufficient for him to utter just the opening words.

76. John Meier, *Matthew*, New Testament Message, 3 (Wilmington, DE: Michael Glazier, 1981), 349–350.

77. Dillistone, *The Christian Understanding of Atonement*, 366–367.

78. Karl Rahner, *On the Theology of Death*, Quaestiones Disputatae, 2 (Edinburgh: Nelson, 1961).

79. See ibid., 50.

80. See ibid., 42.

81. Ibid., 48–49.

82. Ibid., 70.

83. For Rahner's own summary of this soteriology, see his *Foundations of Christian Faith: An Introduction to the Idea of Christianity* (New York: Seabury Press, 1978), 283–284. It is developed in detail in various essays of *Theological Investigations*.

84. Sandra Schneiders, *New Wineskins—Re-imagining Religious Life Today* (New York: Paulist Press, 1986), 127–128.

85. Moltmann notes, in *The Trinity and the Kingdom of God*, 25–30, that Judaism, too, addressed this problem on the basis of the self-differentiation of God. But the authorities he cites, Abraham Heschel and Franz Rosenzweig, are by no means typical of Judaism. Nor is it clear that their attempts succeed in upholding the central tenet of the Jewish religion, ethical monotheism. Nor, again, should the alternative to such attempts be dubbed simply "philosophical monotheism," with its divine "apathy." Rather, it is the one and undivided fellow-suffering God of the Old Testament, understood with the aid of the philosophical concept of the unlimited dynamism of his being.

86. See, for example, Leonardo Boff's *Trinity and Society* (Maryknoll, NY: Orbis, 1988). See also my comment on this in chapter 1, text corresponding to note 37.

87. See Patrick Burns, "Communion, Councils, and Collegiality," *Papal Primacy and the Universal Church,* Lutherans and Catholics in Dialogue, 5, ed. Paul Empie and T. Austin Murphy (Minneapolis, MN: Augsburg, 1974), 170.

88. For example, he says that "authority and obedience are replaced by dialogue, consensus and harmony" (*The Trinity and the Kingdom,* 202), as though these two states of affairs were mutually exclusive.

89. See "Ministry," *Baptism, Eucharist and Ministry,* Faith and Order Paper No. 111 (Geneva: World Council of Churches, 1982), nos. 27 and 53b (26a and 32b).

90. See Dogmatic Constitution on the Church, *Lumen Gentium,* art. 22.

91. See O'Donnell, *Trinity and Temporality,* 113, 116.

92. Moltmann, *The Crucified God,* 27.

93. For Luther on this matter see Gerhard Ebeling, *Luther—An Introduction to His Thought* (London: Collins, 1970), 226–241.

94. Ibid., 229. I have changed the word "seek" in R. A. Wilson's translation to "seeking."

95. See, for example, his remarks on p. 27 of *The Crucified God,* such as the following: "This analogical principle of knowledge is one-sided if it is not supplemented by the dialectical principle of knowledge."

96. See David Coffey, "Natural Knowledge of God: Reflections on Romans 1:18–32," *Theological Studies* 31 (1970): 690.

97. Vatican II, Decree on the Church's Missionary Activity, *Ad gentes divinitus,* art. 7. See also *Lumen Gentium,* art. 16, and Karl Rahner's essay, "Anonymous Christians," *Theological Investigations,* vol. 6 (Baltimore: Helicon, 1969), 390–398, and subsequent essays on this topic in the same series.

98. Jörg Splett and Lourencino Bruno Puntel, "Analogy of Being," *Sacramentum Mundi,* 1:21a.

99. Quoted by O'Donnell in *Trinity and Temporality,* 115.

100. O'Donnell, *Trinity and Temporality,* 115.

Seven. Recent Theology: Jüngel, Mühlen, and von Balthasar

1. Eberhard Jüngel, *God as the Mystery of the World—On the Foundation of the Theology of the Crucified One in the Dispute between Theism and Atheism* (Grand Rapids, MI: Eerdmans, 1983, original German 1977). See also his *The Doctrine of the Trinity—God's Being is in Becoming* (Edinburgh: Scottish Academic Press, 1976, original German 1966). Rather than burden the text with references, suffice it to note that the material here presented comes from pages 343–376 of *God as the Mystery of the World,* but direct quotations will be acknowledged in the usual way.

2. Jüngel, *God as the Mystery of the World,* 375.

3. Ibid.

4. Ibid., 368.

5. Ibid., 373.

6. Heribert Mühlen, *Der Heilige Geist als Person—In der Trinität, bei der Inkarnation und im Gnadenbund: Ich—Du—Wir* (Münster: Verlag Aschendorff, 1963).

7. Heribert Mühlen, *Die Veränderlichkeit Gottes als Horizont einer zukünftigen Christologie—Auf dem Wege zu einer Kreuzestheologie in Auseinandersetzung mit der altkirchlichen Christologie* (Münster: Verlag Aschendorff, 1969).

8. For my initial critique of this position see my book *Grace: The Gift of the Holy Spirit* (Sydney: Faith and Culture, 1979), 33–37.

9. See Mühlen, *Der Heilige Geist als Person*, 157, 164, for these five appellations.

10. John Cowburn, *Love and the Person* (London: Geoffrey Chapman, 1967), 295.

11. Cowburn's point must therefore be seen as a corrective to my statement on p. 29 of *Grace* that, as love has no immanent term, the mutual love of the Father and the Son cannot be said to be "productive" of the Holy Spirit. When we speak, as here, of a single act common to two subjects (see later in this treatment), the question of whether it has an immanent term or not does not arise, as the question is meaningful only in the context of a single subject. But mutual love is productive, in the sense that it requires to be objectivized.

12. See Mühlen, *Die Veränderlichkeit Gottes*, 23–24. The rest of the material of this paragraph, including its concluding quotation, is from p. 24.

13. The material in this paragraph is from *Die Veränderlichkeit Gottes*, 26, except for the concluding quotation, which is from p. 25.

14. Mühlen, *Die Veränderlichkeit Gottes*, 25.

15. Ibid., 32. This is also the reference for the remaining quotations in this paragraph.

16. Ibid., 33.

17. Ibid., 33–34.

18. By this criticism I do not wish to cast doubt on the correspondence between the ontological categories of the immanent Trinity and the historical ones of the economic Trinity. So, for example, I would want to say that, where in the immanent Trinity the Son, having come forth from the Father, returns to him in the Holy Spirit, bond of the Father and the Son, in the economic Trinity Christ, having been sent into the world by the Father, returns to him via his life and death by his obedience and love, in the power of the Holy Spirit. The difference between this kind of statement and that of Mühlen is that, whereas this depends for its validity on the literal exactness of its component formulations, Mühlen's depends a) on formulations at the level of the immanent Trinity that must be judged as exaggerations by the standards of literal truth, and b) on formulations at the level of the economic Trinity that result from flawed exegesis.

19. See Mühlen, *Der Heilige Geist als Person*, 148.

20. See Coffey, *Grace*, 24–25.

21. See Mühlen, *Der Heilige Geist als Person*, 76.

22. I say "probably," because, while Mühlen sides with Penido (and St. Thomas) in opting for the essential divine love over the mutual love of Father and Son as productive of the Holy Spirit, this is not precisely the same question as the one here under discussion, this being concerned with the love *of the Father and the Son* (a question specifically raised, though not answered, in *Die Veränderlichkeit Gottes*) and asking about precisely its object.

23. See Coffey, *Grace*, 36–37.

24. See Mühlen, *Der Heilige Geist als Person*, 197–214.

25. Wolfhart Pannenberg, "Person," *Die Religion in Geschichte und Gegenwart*, 3rd ed., vol. 5, col. 234.

26. Hans Urs von Balthasar, *Herrlichkeit. Eine theologische Ästhetik*, 7 vols. (Einsiedeln: Johannes Verlag, 1961–1969); *Theodramatik*, 5 vols. (Einsiedeln: Johannes Verlag, 1973–1983); *Theologik*, 3 vols. (Einsiedeln: Johannes Verlag, 1983–1987).

27. Johannes Feiner and Magnus Löhrer, eds., "Das Christusereignis," *Mysterium Salutis—Grundriss heilsgeschichtlicher Dogmatik*, vol. 3, part 2 (Einsiedeln: Benziger Verlag, 1969), 133–326.

28. Hans Urs von Balthasar, *Mysterium Paschale*, trans. Aidan Nichols (Edinburgh: T. and T. Clark, 1990).

29. Martin Kehl and Werner Löser, eds., *The von Balthasar Reader* (New York: Crossroad, 1982).

30. Von Balthasar, *Theodramatik* 3, 302.

31. Ibid., 304.

32. Von Balthasar, *The von Balthasar Reader*, 180–181, (from *Pneuma und Institution* [Einsiedeln: Johannes Verlag, 1974], 223–226).

33. Von Balthasar, *Theo-Drama* 3, 187.

34. Von Balthasar, *Mysterium Paschale* (original), 225–226.

35. Von Balthasar, *Mysterium Paschale* (English), 140.

36. See ibid., 146–147, note 106.

37. See ibid., 53.

38. See *The von Balthasar Reader*, 153 (from *Pneuma und Institution*, 401–404, 407–409).

39. See *The von Balthasar Reader*, 148 (from *Der dreifache Kranz* [Einsiedeln: Johannes Verlag, 1977], 64–67).

40. Ibid., 148–149.

41. See ibid., 151 (from *Pneuma und Institution*, 401–404, 407–409).

42. For this distinction in von Balthasar see *Mysterium Paschale* (English), 143–144, note 70.

43. Ibid., 170.

44. Von Balthasar, *The von Balthasar Reader*, 149 (from *Der dreifache Kranz*, 64–67).

45. For a brief account of this influence in this particular matter see Medard Kehl, "Hans Urs von Balthasar: A Portrait," from the introduction to *The von Balthasar Reader*, 42–43 and 44–45.

46. Von Balthasar, *Mysterium Paschale* (English), 168.

47. See ibid., 169.

48. See ibid., 169–170.

49. See ibid., 170–172.

50. Ibid., 173.

51. See Ibid., 174.

52. Thus, on von Balthasar's soteriology Edward Oakes in *Pattern of Redemption: The Theology of Hans Urs von Balthasar* (New York: Continuum, 1994), 237, writes: "But above all, he (Christ) was 'punished' because it was the essential moment of his mission to take on the sins of the world, to be our representative, to assume in our stead what was rightly our destiny: meaning not just death as a natural termination to organic life but death as banishment from the presence of God (which is the real meaning of hell)."

53. See von Balthasar, *Mysterium Paschale* (English), 143–144, note 70.

54. See Gérard Rossé, *The Cry of Jesus on the Cross—A Biblical and Theological Study* (New York: Paulist Press, 1987), 78–83, 84.

55. Von Balthasar, *The von Balthasar Reader*, 149 (from *Der dreifache Kranz* [Einsiedeln, 1977], 64–67).

56. Von Balthasar, *Mysterium Paschale* (original), 276.

57. Ibid., 277.

58. See von Balthasar, *Theo-Drama* 3, 183–191 (section 2.B.2,c, "Trinitarian Inversion").

59. See David Coffey, *Grace: The Gift of the Holy Spirit* (Sydney: Faith and Culture, 1979), 108–110.

60. See von Balthasar, *Theo-Drama* 3, 184–185.

61. Ibid., 185. However, for all his insight into this matter, Kasper lacks a theology of the Trinity equal to the task of grounding it properly. Thus the further sentence from him quoted by von Balthasar on the same page, "The Spirit as the personal bond of the freedom of the love between Father and Son is the medium into which the Father freely and out of pure grace sends the Son and in which he finds in Jesus the human partner in whom and through whom the Son obediently answers the Father's mission in an historical way," while being correct as far as it goes, fails to explain how *the Son* comes to be incarnate, as von

Balthasar is quick to point out (p. 186). I submit that my trinitarian theology, through its model of return, satisfactorily addresses this point.

62. Ibid., 190.

63. See Gerard O'Hanlon, "Does God Change?—H.U. von Balthasar on the Immutability of God," *Irish Theological Quarterly* 53, no. 3 (1987): 161–183; and *The Immutability of God in the Theology of Hans Urs von Balthasar* (Cambridge: Cambridge University Press, 1990).

64. O'Hanlon, "Does God Change?" 167.

65. Ibid., 162–163.

66. On von Balthasar's pneumatology see John Sachs, "Deus Semper Major—Ad Majorem Dei Gloriam: The Pneumatology and Spirituality of Hans Urs von Balthasar," *Gregorianum* 74, no. 4 (1993): 631–657.

67. See von Balthasar, *Mysterium Paschale* (English), 176.

68. See ibid., 144 (note 70).

69. See Hans Michael Baumgartner, "Transcendental Philosophy," *Sacramentum Mundi*, 6: 284b.

70. J. N. D. Kelly, *Early Christian Creeds* (London: Longmans, Green, 1950), 379.

71. See ibid.

72. See von Balthasar, *Mysterium Paschale* (English), 156–160.

73. See William Dalton, "The First Epistle of Peter," *The New Jerome Biblical Commentary*, 907a, 908a.

74. See part 3 of my book *Grace: The Gift of the Holy Spirit* (Sydney: Faith and Culture, 1979), 91–144.

75. In his review of Ralph del Colle's *Christ and the Spirit* in *The Thomist* 59, no. 4 (1995): 656–659, Thomas Weinandy takes me to task for my claim that the order—creation, sanctification, union—of the Holy Spirit's activity in regard to the humanity of Christ is a logical order. He writes, "It is not possible for the Holy Spirit to sanctify the humanity of Jesus prior to the union, for the humanity never exists separate or apart from the Son. Even on the level of logical priority, it is through the grace of union that the Holy Spirit sanctifies the humanity" (p. 658). If we grant that a logical order exists among the three elements, what comes first must be creation, and what comes last, third, must be union. We cannot conceive a union of divinity and humanity apart from a humanity that already exists, and indeed exists as disposed for union. Sanctification is precisely this disposition, and hence assumes mid place between creation and union. Weinandy's scheme overlooks creation; but with it included we would have from creation to union an ascending order, which would then be reversed, as it would move back from union to sanctification. This indeed would not be logical. Weinandy's statement that the Holy Spirit can sanctify the humanity of Jesus only in consequence of the union reflects the Thomistic theology, which operates out of a descending scheme that depends on the Holy Spirit as proceeding from the Son (as well as from the Father). In contrast with this my proposal, in line with ascending synoptic theology, has in the case of Jesus, Son of God, the Holy Spirit as—in St. Luke's words—"the power of the Most High" (Lk 1.35), the Spirit of the Father bringing the Son into existence in the economy of salvation. (For the orthodoxy and logic of this see my earlier note on Weinandy, note 7 in chapter 3.) From all this it will be clear that logical priority is determined by the context in which the ordering is to be done. In the ascending theology of the return model, with which we are dealing here, the correct logical order, pace Weinandy, is as I have given it—creation, sanctification, union.

Select Bibliography

Arndt, W., F. Gingrich, and W. Bauer, eds. *A Greek-English Lexicon of the New Testament and Other Early Christian Literature*. Chicago: University of Chicago Press, 1957.

Badcock, Gary D. "The Anointing of Christ and the *Filioque* Doctrine." *Irish Theological Quarterly* 60, no. 4 (1994): 241–258.

Balthasar, Hans Urs von. *Herrlichkeit. Eine theologische Ästhetik*, 7 vols. Einsiedeln: Johannes Verlag, 1961–1969.

———. *Theodramatik*, 5 vols. Einsiedeln: Johannes Verlag, 1973–1983.

———. *Pneuma und Institution*. Einsiedeln: Johannes Verlag, 1974.

———. *Der dreifache Kranz*. Einsiedeln: Johannes Verlag, 1977.

———. *Theologik*, 5 vols. Einsiedeln: Johannes Verlag, 1983–1987.

———. *Mysterium Paschale*, trans. Aidan Nichols. Edinburgh: T. and T. Clark, 1990.

Baptism, Eucharist and Ministry, Faith and Order Paper 111. Geneva: World Council of Churches, 1982.

Barnes, Michel René. "De Régnon Reconsidered." *Augustinian Studies* 26, no. 2 (1995): 51–79.

Barth, Karl. *Church Dogmatics* 1, no. 2 (The Doctrine of the Word of God). Edinburgh: T. and T. Clark, 1956.

———. *Church Dogmatics* 2, no. 1 (The Doctrine of God). Edinburgh: T. and T. Clark, 1957.

Barrett, C. K. *A Commentary on the Second Epistle to the Corinthians*. New York: Harper & Row, 1973.

Baumgartner, Hans Michael. "Transcendental Philosophy." *Sacramentum Mundi*, 6:281b–285a.

Beccos, John. *Refutatio photiani libri de Spiritu Sancto*. Migne: PG 141:725–864.

Beer, Peter J. "Trent's Temporal Punishment and Today's Renewal of Penance." *Theological Studies* 35, no. 3 (1974): 467–481.

Benoit, Pierre. "Préexistence et Incarnation." *Revue Biblique* 77 (1970): 5–29.

Bessarion, John. *De Spiritus Sancti processione ad Alexium Lascarin Philanthropinum*, ed. Emmanuel Candal. Rome: Pontificium Institutum Orientalium Studiorum, 1961.

Billot, Louis. *De Deo uno et trino*, 5th ed. Prato: Giachetti, 1910.

Boff, Leonardo. *Trinity and Society*. Maryknoll, NY: Orbis, 1988.

Boismard, M.-E. *Le Prologue de Saint Jean*, Lectio divina, 11. Paris: Éditions du Cerf, 1953.

Bouillard, Henri. *The Knowledge of God*. New York: Herder and Herder, 1968.

Bourke, Myles. "The Epistle to the Hebrews." *The New Jerome Biblical Commentary*, 920a–

941b. Ed. R. Brown, J. Fitzmyer, and R. Murphy. Englewood Cliffs, NJ: Prentice Hall, 1990.

Bracken, Joseph. "The Holy Trinity as a Community of Divine Persons." *Heythrop Journal* 15 (1974): 166–182, 257–270.

———. *What Are They Saying About the Trinity?* New York: Paulist Press, 1979.

———. "Subsistent Relation: Mediating Concept for a New Synthesis?" *Journal of Religion* 64 (1984): 188–204.

———. *The Triune Symbol: Persons, Process, and Community.* Lanham, MD: University Press of America, 1985.

———. "Process Perspectives and Trinitarian Theology." *Word and Spirit* 8 (1986): 51–64.

———. *Society and Spirit: A Trinitarian Cosmology.* Selingsgrove, PA: Susquehanna University Press, 1991.

Bradshaw, Timothy. "Karl Barth and the Trinity: A Family Resemblance." *Scottish Journal of Theology* 39 (1986): 145–164.

Brown, Raymond. *The Gospel According to John (XIII–XXI).* Garden City, NY: Doubleday, 1970.

Bruce, F. F. *Commentary on the Epistle to the Hebrews.* London: Marshall, Morgan, & Scott, 1964.

Bultmann, Rudolf. *"pisteuo."* *Theological Dictionary of the New Testament*, 6:174–228. Ed. Gerhard Kittel. Grand Rapids, MI: Eerdmans, 1968.

Burns, Patrick. "Communion, Councils, and Collegiality." *Papal Primacy and the Universal Church*, 151–177. Ed. Paul Empie and T. Austin Murphy. Lutherans and Catholics in Dialogue, 5. Minneapolis, MI: Augsburg, 1974.

Carnley, Peter. *The Structure of Resurrection Belief.* Oxford: Clarendon Press, 1987.

Chapman, G. Clarke. "What God Can Help? Trinity and Pop Religions of Crisis." *Cross Currents* (1994): 316–331.

Chevalier, Irenée. *S. Augustin et la pense greque: Les relations trinitaires.* Fribourg, Switzerland: Collectanea Friburgensia, 1940.

Clarke, W. Norris. "Person, Being, and St. Thomas." *Communio* 19 (1992): 601–618.

———. *Person and Being.* Milwaukee: Marquette University Press, 1993. Marquette University Aquinas Lecture, 1993.

Coffey, David. "Natural Knowledge of God: Reflections on Romans 1:18–32." *Theological Studies* 31 (1970): 674–691.

———. *Grace: The Gift of the Holy Spirit*, Faith and Culture, 2. Sydney: Catholic Institute of Sydney, 1979.

———. "Death as a Question of Negative Theology." *Reflections on Faith and Culture*, 66–76. Ed. Neil Brown. Faith and Culture, 5. Sydney: Catholic Institute of Sydney, 1981.

———. "The Teaching of the Constantinopolitan Creed on the Holy Spirit." *Issues for the Australian Church*, 65–75. Ed. Neil Brown. Faith and Culture, 6. Sydney: Catholic Institute of Sydney, 1982.

———. "The Pre-existent and Incarnate Word." *Contemporary Questions*, 62–76. Ed. Margaret Press. Faith and Culture, 8. Sydney: Catholic Institute of Sydney, 1983.

———. "The 'Incarnation' of the Holy Spirit in Christ." *Theological Studies* 45 (1984): 466–480.

———. "A Proper Mission of the Holy Spirit." *Theological Studies* 47 (1986): 227–250.

———. "Christian Anthropology." *Bicentennial Reflections*, 130–141. Ed. Neil Brown and Margaret Press. Faith and Culture, 14. Sydney: Catholic Institute of Sydney, 1988.

———. "The Palamite Doctrine of God: A New Perspective." *St. Vladimir's Theological Quarterly* 32, no. 4 (1988): 329–358.

———. "The Holy Spirit as the Mutual Love of the Father and the Son." *Theological Studies* 51 (1990): 193–229.

————. "Review of Anthony Kelly's *The Trinity of Love*." *Pacifica* 4, no. 2 (1991): 229–232.

Congar, Yves. *I Believe in the Holy Spirit*, 3 vols. New York: Seabury Press, 1983.

Connor, Robert. "Relational Esse and the Person." *American Catholic Philosophical Quarterly* 65 (1991): 253–267. Annual ACPA Proceedings.

Cowburn, John. *Love and the Person*. London: Geoffrey Chapman, 1967.

Cullmann, Oscar. *The Christology of the New Testament*. New Testament Library. London: SCM Press, 1963.

Dalton, William. "The First Epistle of Peter." *The New Jerome Biblical Commentary*, 903a–908b. Ed. R. Brown, J. Fitzmyer, and R. Murphy. Englewood Cliffs, NJ: Prentice Hall, 1990.

Del Colle, Ralph. *Christ and the Spirit: Spirit Christology in Trinitarian Perspective*. New York: Oxford University Press, 1994.

Denzinger, H., and Schönmetzer, A., eds. *Enchiridion Symbolorum Definitionum et Declarationum de Rebus Fidei et Morum*. 34th ed. Barcelona, 1967.

Diekamp, Franciscus. *Theologiae Dogmaticae Manuale secundum Principia S. Thomae Aquinatis*, vol. 1. Paris: Desclee, 1949.

Donceel, J. F. *Philosophical Anthropology*. New York: Sheed and Ward, 1967.

Dunn, James D. G. *Jesus and the Spirit*. London: SCM Press, 1975.

————. *Christology in the Making*. London: SCM Press, 1980.

Ebeling, Gerhard. *Luther—An Introduction to His Thought*. London: Collins, 1970.

Empereur, James. "Paschal Mystery." *The New Dictionary of Theology*, 744a–747a. Ed. J. Komonchak, M. Collins, and D. Lane. Wilmington, DE: Michael Glazier, 1987.

Fatula, Mary Ann. "A Problematic Western Formula." *One in Christ* 17 (1981): 324–334.

Feiner, Johannes, and Magnus Löhrer, eds. "Das Christusereignis." *Mysterium Salutis—Grundriss heilsgeschichtlicher Dogmatik*, vol. 3, part 2. Einsiedeln: Benziger Verlag, 1969.

Fitzmyer, Joseph. "The Letter to the Romans." *The New Jerome Biblical Commentary*, 830a–868b. Ed. R. Brown, J. Fitzmyer, and R. Murphy. Englewood Cliffs, NJ: Prentice Hall, 1990.

Flannery, Austin P., ed. *The Documents of Vatican II*. New York: Pillar, 1975.

Ford, Lewis S. "Process Trinitarianism." *Journal of the American Academy of Religion* 43 (1975): 199–213.

Garrigues, Jean-Miguel. "A Roman Catholic View of the Position Now Reached in the Question of the Filioque." *Spirit of God, Spirit of Christ—Ecumenical Reflections on the Filioque Controversy*, 149–163. Ed. Lukas Vischer. Faith and Order Paper 103. London/Geneva: SPCK/World Council of Churches, 1981.

Gaybba, Brian. *The Spirit of Love*. London: Geoffrey Chapman, 1987.

Gilson, Etienne. *Being and Some Philosophers*. Toronto: Pontifical Institute of Mediaeval Studies, 1952.

Greshake, G., and G. Lohfink. *Nahewartung-Auferstehung—Unsterblichkeit*, 4th ed. Freiburg, Germany: Herder, 1982.

Grillmeier, Aloys. *Commentary on the Documents of Vatican Two*, vol. 1. Ed. H. Vorgrimler. London: Burns & Oates, 1967.

————. *Christ in Christian Tradition*, 1:129–131. 2nd ed. Atlanta: John Knox Press, 1975.

Haight, Roger. "The Point of Trinitarian Theology." *Toronto Journal of Theology* 4, no. 2 (1988): 191–204.

Hartshorne, Charles. *Aquinas to Whitehead: Seven Centuries of Metaphysics of Religion*. Milwaukee: Marquette University Publications, 1976.

————. *Omnipotence and Other Theological Mistakes*. Albany: State University of New York Press, 1984.

Hartshorne, Dorothy C. "Charles Hartshorne: Primary Bibliography." *Process Studies* 6, no. 1 (1976): 73–93.

————. "Charles Hartshorne: 1980 Bibliographical Addenda." *Process Studies* 11, no. 2 (1981): 108–150.

Hicks, John, ed. *The Myth of God Incarnate*, London: SCM Press, 1977.

Hill, William J. "Does God Know the Future? Aquinas and Some Moderns." *Theological Studies* 36 (1975): 3–18.

————. *The Three Personed God—The Trinity as a Mystery of Salvation*. Washington, DC: Catholic University of America Press, 1982.

Hunt, Anne. *The Trinity and the Paschal Mystery—A Development in Recent Catholic Theology*. Collegeville, MI: Liturgical Press, 1997.

Jeremias, Joachim. *New Testament Theology*. London: SCM Press, 1971.

Johnson, Elizabeth. *She Who Is—The Mystery of God in Feminist Theological Discourse*. New York: Crossroad, 1994.

Jugie, Martin. *Theologia Dogmatica Christianorum Orientalium ab Ecclesia Catholica Dissidentium*, vol. 2. Paris: Letouzey et Ané, 1933.

Jüngel, Eberhard. *The Doctrine of the Trinity—God's Being Is in Becoming*. Edinburgh: Scottish Academic Press, 1976.

————. *God as the Mystery of the World—On the Foundation of the Theology of the Crucified One in the Dispute between Theism and Atheism*. Grand Rapids, MI: Eerdmans, 1983.

Kasper, Walter. *Jesus the Christ*. London: Burns & Oates, 1976.

————. *The God of Jesus Christ*. New York: Crossroad, 1986.

Kehl, Martin, and Werner Löser, eds. *The von Balthasar Reader*. New York: Crossroad, 1982.

Kelly, Anthony. *The Trinity of Love—A Theology of the Christian God*. Wilmington, DE: Michael Glazier, 1989.

Kelly, J. N. D. *Early Christian Creeds*. London: Longmans, Green, 1950.

————. *Early Christian Doctrines*, 5th ed. London: Adam & Charles Black, 1977.

Kessler, Hans. "Erlösung/Soteriologie." *Neues Handbuch theologischer Grundbegriffe*, 1:241–254. Ed. Peter Eicher. Munich: Kösel-Verlag, 1984.

Kilmartin, Edward. "The Active Role of Christ and the Holy Spirit in the Sanctification of the Eucharistic Elements." *Theological Studies* 45 (1984): 225–253.

Koch, Robert. "Spirit." *Encyclopedia of Biblical Theology*, 3:869b–889b. Ed. J. B. Bauer. New York: Herder and Herder, 1970.

Krasevac, Edward. " 'Christology from Above' and 'Christology from Below.' " *The Thomist* 51 (1987): 299–306.

LaCugna, Catherine. *God for Us: The Trinity and Christian Life*. San Francisco: HarperSanFrancisco, 1991.

Lehmann, Karl. "Er wurde für uns gekreuzigt." *Theologische Quartalschrift* 162 (1982): 297–317.

Lonergan, Bernard. *Insight*. San Francisco: Harper & Row, 1958.

————. *De Deo Trino*, vol. 2. Rome: Pontificia Universitas Gregoriana, 1964.

————. *Method in Theology*. London: Darton, Longman, & Todd, 1972.

————. *Philosophy of God, and Theology*. London: Darton, Longman, & Todd, 1973.

Lossky, Vladimir. *The Mystical Theology of the Eastern Church*. London: James Clarke, 1957.

Luther, Martin. "Lectures on Galatians, 1535, Chapters 1–4." *Luther's Works*, 26:276–91. Ed. Jaroslav Pelikan. Saint Louis, MO: Concordia, 1963.

Macquarrie, John. "Review of Robert W. Jenson's *The Triune Identity*." *Scottish Journal of Theology* 36, no. 3 (1983): 388–390.

Maritain, Jacques. "The Immanent Dialectic of the First Act of Reason." *The Range of Reason*. London: Geoffrey Bles, 1953.

Martin, Francis. *The Feminist Question: Feminist Theology in the Light of Christian Tradition*. Grand Rapids, MI: Eerdmans, 1994.

McDermott, John. "The Christologies of Karl Rahner." *Gregorianum* 67 (1986): 87–123, 297–327.

McKenzie, John. *Second Isaiah*. Garden City, NY: Doubleday, 1968.

Meier, John. *Matthew*, New Testament Message, 3. Wilmington, DE: Michael Glazier, 1981.

Mellert, Robert B. *What Is Process Theology?* New York: Paulist Press, 1975.

Meyendorff, John. *A Study of Gregory Palamas*. London: Faith Press, 1964.

Miller, Casey, and Kate Smith. "Who's in Charge of the English Language?" *The Norton Reader*, 363–369. 8th ed. New York: Norton, 1992.

Moloney, Francis. *The Johannine Son of Man*. Rome: Libreria Ateneo Salesiano, 1976.

Molnar, Paul. "The Function of the Immanent Trinity in the Theology of Karl Barth: Implications for Today." *Scottish Journal of Theology* 42 (1989): 367–399.

Moltmann, Jürgen. *The Crucified God—The Cross of Christ as the Foundation and Criticism of Christian Theology*. New York: Harper & Row, 1974.

———. *The Church in the Power of the Spirit—A Contribution to Messianic Ecclesiology*. London: SCM Press, 1977.

———. *The Future of Creation*. Philadelphia: Fortress Press, 1979.

———. *The Trinity and the Kingdom of God—The Doctrine of God*. London: SCM Press, 1981.

———. *The Way of Jesus Christ—Christology in Messianic Dimensions*. San Francisco: HarperSanFrancisco, 1990.

———. "The Cross of Christ: The Pain of the Love of God." *God—His and Hers*, 63–76. Jürgen Moltmann and Elizabeth Moltmann-Wendel. New York: Crossroad, 1991.

———. *History and the Triune God: Contributions to Trinitarian Theology*. London: SCM Press, 1991.

Mühlen, Heribert. *Sein und Person nach Johannes Duns Scotus*. Werl/Westf.: Dietrich-Coelde-Verlag, 1954.

———. *Der Heilige Geist als Person—In der Trinität, bei der Inkarnation und im Gnadenbund: Ich—Du—Wir*. Münster: Verlag Aschendorff, 1963.

———. *Die Veränderlichkeit Gottes als Horizont einer zukünftigen Christologie—Auf dem Wege zu einer Kreuzestheologie in Auseinandersetzung mit der altkirchlichen Christologie*. Münster: Verlag Aschendorff, 1969.

Muller, Earl. " 'Person' in Christian Thought, East and West." *CTSA Proceedings* 46 (1991): 171–173. Report on the Seminar on Trinitarian Theology.

———. "The Science of Theology—A Review of Catherine LaCugna's *God For Us*." *Gregorianum* 75, no. 2 (1994): 311–341.

Müller, Gerhard Ludwig. "Ablass." *Lexikon für Theologie und Kirche*, 2nd ed., 1:51a–55a.

Murphy-O'Connor, Jerome. "Christological Anthropology in Phil.2.6–11." *Revue Biblique* 83 (1976): 25–50.

The New Jerusalem Bible. London: Darton, Longman, & Todd, 1985.

Nineham, Dennis. *Saint Mark*. The Pelican Gospel Commentaries. Harmondsworth, Middlesex: Penguin, 1963.

Oakes, Edward. *Pattern of Redemption: The Theology of Hans Urs von Balthasar*. New York: Continuum, 1994.

O'Collins, Gerald. *Interpreting Jesus*. London: Geoffrey Chapman, 1983.

O'Donnell, John. *Trinity and Temporality—The Christian Doctrine of God in the Light of Process Theology and the Theology of Hope*. Oxford: Oxford University Press, 1983.

O'Hanlon, Gerard. "Does God Change?—H. U. von Balthasar on the Immutability of God." *Irish Theological Quarterly* 53, no. 3 (1987): 161–183.

———. *The Immutability of God in the Theology of Hans Urs von Balthasar*. Cambridge: Cambridge University Press, 1990.

Pailin, David. "The Utterly Absolute and the Totally Related: Change in God." *New Blackfriars* 68, no. 805 (1987): 243–255.

Pannenberg, Wolfhart. "Person." *Die Religion in Geschichte und Gegenwart: Handworterbuch für Theolgie und Religionswissenschaft*, 5:230–235. 3rd ed. Tübigen: Mohr, 1957.

————. *Jesus—God and Man*. London: SCM Press, 1968.

————. *Systematische Theologie*, 1. Göttingen: Vandenhoeck & Ruprecht, 1988. ET as *Systematic Theology*, 1. Grand Rapids, MI: Eerdmans, 1991.

Rahner, Karl. *Geist in Welt*, Munich: Kösel-Verlag, 1957. ET as *Spirit in the World*. London: Sheed and Ward, 1968.

————. "Concerning the Relationship between Nature and Grace." *Theological Investigations*, 1:297–317. London: Darton, Longman, & Todd, 1961.

————. *On the Theology of Death*, Quaestiones Disputatae, 2. Edinburgh: Nelson, 1961.

————. "Theos in the New Testament." *Theological Investigations*, 1:79–148. London: Darton, Longman, & Todd, 1961.

————. "Über die Einheit von Nächsten-und Gottesliebe." *Schriften zur Theologie*, 6:288. Einsiedeln: Benziger Verlag, 1965. ET as "Reflections on the Unity of the Love of Neighbour and the Love of God." *Theological Investigations*, 6:231–249. London: Darton, Longman, & Todd, 1969.

————. "On the Theology of the Incarnation." *Theological Investigations*, 4:105–20. London: Darton, Longman, & Todd, 1966.

————. "Der dreifaltige Gott als transzendenter Urgrund der Heilsgeschichte." *Mysterium Salutis—Grundriss heilsgeschichtlicher Dogmatik*, 2:317–404. Einsiedeln: Benziger Verlag, 1967.

————. "Anonymous Christians." *Theological Investigations*, 6:390–398. London: Darton, Longman, & Todd, 1969.

————. "The Unity of Spirit and Matter in the Christian Understanding of Faith." *Theological Investigations*, 6:174–175. London: Darton, Longman, & Todd, 1969.

————. *The Trinity*. London: Burns & Oates, 1970.

————. *Foundations of Christian Faith*, 117–126. London: Darton, Longman, & Todd, 1978.

————. "Grace and Freedom." *Sacramentum Mundi*, 2:424a–427b.

————. "Person." *Sacramentum Mundi*, 4:415a–419b.

————. "Revelation: 'God's Self-Communication.' " *Sacramentum Mundi*, 5:353b–355b.

————. "Punishment of Sins." *Sacramentum Mundi*, 6:92b–94b.

————. "Selbstmitteilung Gottes." *Lexikon für Theologie und Kirche*, 1st ed., 9:627a.

Rahner, Karl, and Herbert Vorgrimler. "Person." *Dictionary of Theology*, 378–381. 2nd ed. New York: Herder and Herder, 1981.

Rahula, Walpula. *What the Buddha Taught*. 2nd ed. London: Gordon Fraser, 1967.

Régnon, Théodore de. *Études de théologie positive sur la Sainte Trinité*, 3 vols. (4 bound as 3). Paris: Retaux, 1898.

Richard of St. Victor. *De Trinitate*, books 3: 2, 3, 6, 11, 14, 15, 20; 4:15; and 6: 7. Migne: PL 196:916–919, 922–925, 927, 928, 939, 972.

Rossé, Gérard. *The Cry of Jesus on the Cross—A Biblical and Theological Study*. New York: Paulist Press, 1987.

Sachs, John. "Deus semper major-ad majorem dei glorium: The Pneumatology and Spirituality of Hans Urs von Balthasar." *Gregorianum* 74, no. 4 (1993): 631–657.

Sacred Congregation for the Doctrine of the Faith. "Certain Questions Concerning Eschatology." *Acta Apostolicae Sedis* 71 (1979): 939–943.

Scheeben, Matthias. *Die Mysterien des Christentums: Gesammelte Schriften*, vol. 2. Freiburg, Germany: Herder, 1958.

Schillebeeckx, Edward. *Jesus—An Experiment in Christology*. London: Collins, 1975.

————. *Christ: The Experience of Jesus as Lord.* New York: Seabury Press, 1980.

Schneiders, Sandra. *New Wineskins—Re-imagining Religious Life Today.* New York: Paulist Press, 1986.

Schweizer, Eduard. "*pneuma, pneumatikos.*" *Theological Dictionary of the New Testament,* 6:332–451. Ed. Gerhard Kittel. Grand Rapids, MI: Eerdmans, 1968.

Sia, Santiago. "A Changing God?" *Word and Spirit: A Monastic Review* 8 (1986): 13–30.

————. "The Doctrine of God's Immutability: Introducing the Modern Debate." *New Blackfriars* 68, no. 805 (1987): 220–232.

Sölle, Dorothée. *Suffering.* London: Darton, Longman, & Todd, 1975.

Splett, Jörg, and Lourencino Bruno Puntel. "Analogy of Being." *Sacramentum Mundi,* 1:21a–25b.

St. Anselm of Canterbury. *Cur Deus Homo,* books 1 and 2. Migne: PL 158:359–432.

————. *Monologium.* Migne: PL 158:141–224.

St. Augustine. *De trinitate.* Migne: PL 42:815–1098.

St. Basil of Caesaria. *On the Holy Spirit.* Migne: PG 32:67–218.

St. Gregory of Nyssa. *Catechetical Oration.* Migne: PG 45:9–106.

St. Gregory of Nazianzus. Oratio 29. Migne: PG 36:73–104.

Stuhlmueller, Carroll. "Deutero-Isaiah and Trito-Isaiah." *The New Jerome Biblical Commentary,* 329–348. Ed. R. Brown, J. Fitzmyer, and R. Murphy. Englewood Cliffs, NJ: Prentice Hall, 1990.

Tanner, Norman, P., ed. *Decrees of the Ecumenical Councils.* 2 vols. Washington, DC: Georgetown University Press, 1990.

TeSelle, Eugene. *Augustine the Theologian.* London: Burns & Oates, 1970.

Tyrrell, Francis M. *Man: Believer and Unbeliever.* New York: Alba House, 1974.

Vatican II. *Decree on the Church's Missionary Activity, Ad gentes divinitus.*

————. *Decree on Ecumenism, Unitatis redintegratio.*

————. *Dogmatic Constitution on the Church, Lumen Gentium.*

————. *Dogmatic Constitution on the Church, Dei Verbum.*

Vatican's Pontifical Council for Promoting Christian Unity. "The Greek and Latin Traditions Regarding the Procession of the Holy Spirit," *L'Osservatore Romano,* no. 38 (20 September 1995): 3, 6.

Vawter, Bruce. *This Man Jesus—An Essay Toward a New Testament Christology.* London: Geoffrey Chapman, 1973.

Vertin, Michael. "Is God in Process?" *Religion and Culture: Essays in Honor of Bernard Lonergan, S.J.,* 45–62. Ed. T. Fallon and P. Riley. Albany, NY: State University of New York Press, 1987.

Ware, Timothy. *The Orthodox Church.* Harmondsworth, Middlesex: Penguin (Pelican), 1963.

Weinandy, Thomas. *Does God Change? The Word's Becoming in the Incarnation.* Still River, MA: St. Bede's Publications, 1985.

————. "The Immanent and the Economic Trinity." *The Thomist* 57 (1993): 655–666.

————. "Review of Ralph Del Colle's Christ and the Spirit." *The Thomist* 59, no. 4 (1995): 356–359.

————. *The Father's Spirit of Sonship: Reconceiving the Trinity.* Edinburgh: T. and T. Clark, 1995.

Wetter, Friedrich. *Die Trinitatslehre des Johannes Duns Scotus.* Münster/Westf.: Aschendorffsche Verlagsbuchhandlung, 1967.

Whitehead, Alfred North. *Science and the Modern World.* Cambridge: Cambridge University Press, 1932.

————. *Process and Reality: An Essay in Cosmology.* Ed. David Ray Griffin and Donald W. Sherburne. New York: Free Press, 1978.

Williams, Rowan. "The Philosophical Structures of Palamism." *Eastern Churches Review* 9, nos. 1–2 (1977): 27–44.

Wood, Susan, Roger Haight, Mary Ann Donovan, and Barbara A. Finan. "Four Perspectives on Catherine LaCugna's *God for Us.*" *Horizons* 20, no. 1 (1993): 127–135. "Rejoinder" by LaCugna, pp. 135–142.

Wright, John H. "The Method of Process Theology: An Evaluation." *Communio* 6 (1979): 38–55.

Wuellner, Bernard. *Dictionary of Scholastic Philosophy*. Milwaukee: Bruce, 1956.

Zizioulas, John. "Human Capacity and Human Incapacity: A Theological Exploration of Personhood." *Scottish Journal of Theology* 28 (1975): 401–448.

———. *Being as Communion*. Crestwood, NY: St. Vladimir's Seminary Press, 1985.

Index

Printed in the United States
3326